비지니스 영어작문

기초와 실전

비지니스 영어작문

기초와 실전

조기석 지음

Business Management Writing

Basis and Application

HU:iNE

Preface

일상생활에서 영어작문이 필요한 상황이 있다. 영어로 email 쓰기, 일기 쓰기, 팩스 보내기, 이력서 쓰기, 지원서 쓰기, 자기소개서 쓰기 등은 일상생활에서 영어로 문서작업을 해야 하는 대표적인 상황이다. 비즈니스영어작문은 이러한 상황에서 영어로 문서작업을 하는 데 필요한 어휘, 문법, 숙어, 문서양식 등을 학습하고 실제 TASK를 통해서 영어로 문서를 작성하는 학습 과정을 제공한다. 상황별 영어작문을 추구하는 본 교재는 대학에서 영어를 전공하는 사람들뿐만 아니라 비즈니스에 종사하는 일반인들에게도 실질적인 도움을 줄 수 있다. 본 교재를 통해서 실제 생활에서 자주 사용하는 문서를 영어로 작성하는데 조금이나마 도움이 되길 바란다.

끝으로 본 교재가 나올 수 있도록 도움과 격려를 아끼지 않은 김지인 교수님, 김귀원 교수님, 이혜영 선생님, 최연미 선생님, 이민욱 선생님, 임진태 선생님, 이보름 선생님, 송인숙 원장님, 성순임 원장님, 최혜인 원장님, 이보람 선생님, 김서연 선생님, 박원길 선생님, 오미혜 선생님, 이진영 원장님, 김유리 선생님, 양호숙 원장님, 최솔민 선생님 그리고 한국외국어대학교 지식출판원 신선호 팀장님께 감사의 마음을 전하며 부족한 나를 사이버한국외국어대학교 영어학부로 인도하신 하나님께 이 저서를 바친다.

2015년 8월

저자 **조기석**

Contents

Business
Management
Writing
Basis and Application

Lesson 01

Asking favors

Lesson 01

Asking favors

Introduction

Lesson objectives

1. Learning the email format

2. Learning expressions for asking favors

(1) I would like to ask you a favor.

(2) Can you pick me up at the airport?

3. Learning abbreviated expressions in email

(1) ASAP

(2) P.S.

(3) RSVP

(4) BTW

(5) IMO

(6) ATM

(7) ETA

Warm up

The format of email

email을 작성하기 전에 email의 구조에 대해서 먼저 알아보겠습니다. email(보내는 email)은 다음과 같은 형식으로 되어있습니다.

① **To: :** *****@cufs.ac.kr ② **Cc: :** *****@cufs.ac.kr ③ **Bcc :** *****@cufs.ac.kr ④ **Subject:** Weekend Paln ⑤ **Attachments:**
⑥ **Dear James,**
⑦ **Body**
⑧ **Best wishes,**
⑨ **Soyoung Kim**

① **To :** 수신인

② **Cc :** 참조

- Cc는 Carbon Copy의 약자로서 참조를 의미합니다.
- 참조는 email을 받는 사람 외에 email을 참고로 받게 되는 사람이 있을 때 사용합니다.

③ **Bcc :** 숨은 참조

- Bcc는 Blind Carbon Copy의 약자로서 숨은 참조를 의미합니다.
- 숨은 참조는 email을 받는 사람에게 email을 참고로 받는 이가 누구인지 알리고 싶지 않을 때 사용합니다.

④ **Subject :** 제목

- 제목은 email의 내용을 잘 나타내고 또 email을 받는 사람이 email의 내용을 짐작할 수 있는 구체적인 문구로 작성합니다.

⑤ **Attachments :** 첨부파일

- 문서파일, 그림파일, 또는 음성파일을 첨부할 때 사용할 수 있습니다.

⑥ **Greeting :** 인사

• 인사는 격식체, 비격식체, 그리고 약식체가 있습니다. 업무적인 이유 등의 공식적인 email을 쓸 때는 격식체를 사용하고 비공식적인 email을 쓸 때는 비격식체를 사용합니다. 가까운 사이에는 약식체를 사용합니다.

구분	형식	비고
격식체	Dear Mr. + 수신인의 성:	남성
	Dear Mrs. + 수신인의 성:	기혼 여성
	Dear Miss + 수신인의 성:	미혼 여성
	Dear Ms. + 수신인의 성:	기혼 또는 미혼 여성
비격식체	Dear + 수신인의 이름,	–
약식체	Hi + 수신인의 이름,	–
격식체(상대방의 이름을 모르는 경우)	Dear Sir:	남성
	Dear Madam:	여성
	Dear Sir or Madam:	남성 또는 여성
	To whom it may concern:	남성 또는 여성

⑦ **Body :** 본문

• 본문은 email을 보내는 사람이 email을 받는 사람에게 말하려고 하는 메시지입니다.
• 본문은 간결하고 명료하게 작성하는 게 바람직합니다.

⑧ **Closing :** 끝인사

• 끝인사는 격식체, 비격식체, 그리고 약식체가 있습니다. 업무적인 이유 등의 공식적인 email을 쓸 때는 격식체를 사용하고 비공식적인 email을 쓸 때는 비격식체를 사용합니다. 가까운 사이에는 약식체를 사용합니다.

구분	격식체	비격식체	약식체
형식	Sincerely, Sincerely yours, Cordially, Cordially yours,	Regards, Best regards, Best wishes, With best wishes, Yours truly,	Best, Warmly, Love, Yours,

⑨ **Name :** 이름

• email의 마지막에 이메일을 보내는 사람의 이름을 입력합니다.

Warm up

Check up

1. email 구성의 각 부분에 대한 명칭을 우리말로 작성해 보세요.

- To [ ]
- Cc [ ]
- Bcc [ ]

2. email의 Greeting(인사)과 잘 어울리는 Closing(끝인사)을 작성해 보세요.

Dear Mr. Jackson ______________

Dear Lina, ______________

Hi Freddy, ______________

3. 다음 email에 적합한 제목을 본문에 있는 4개의 단어를 이용하여 하나의 문장으로 작성하세요.

Subject [ ]
From judy@*****.com
To john@*****.com

Dear Mr. Jackson:

We are doing our best, but we need some more time to finish the work. We will try to complete it by the end of this month. We are sorry for the delay.

Cordially yours,
Judy Brown

4. email에서 @는 무엇을 나타내는지 선택해 보세요.

① from ② with ③ at ④ for

Practice 1 Comprehension Check up

Subject A favor
From minjeong@*****.com
To sangmin@*****.com

Hi Sangmin,

I am so happy that classes are over for the second semester. I miss my family so much. I can't wait to see them. I would like to ask you a favor. Can you pick me up at Jeju airport this coming Saturday? I am arriving at 6:20 p.m. If you meet me at the Airport, I will treat you to a good dinner. Last time we met downtown in Jeju, you told me about the new Japanese restaurant. This is a good opportunity to try that restaurant. Let's go there for dinner. How does that sound? Let me know ASAP.

Best,
Minjeong

P.S. You can bring your brother.

1. Who wrote the email?
   ① Sangmin
   ② Minjeong

2. Who received the email?
   ① Sangmin
   ② Minjeong

3. What is the purpose of the email?
   ① To say hello
   ② To ask a favor
   ③ To invite a friend to a party

상민에게

2학기 수업이 끝나서 기뻐. 가족들이 매우 그리워. 지금 당장이라도 그들을 보고 싶어. 내가 너에게 부탁을 하나 하려고 하는데. 너 이번 주 토요일 제주 공항에 차로 나를 마중 나올 수 있니? 나는 오후 6시 20분에 도착할 예정이야. 네가 공항에 나를 마중 나오면 내가 너에게 근사한 저녁 살게. 지난번 우리가 제주 시내에서 만났을 때, 네가 나에게 새로 오픈한 일식 레스토랑에 대해서 얘기했었지. 이번이 그 레스토랑에서 식사해 볼 수 있는 좋은 기회야. 그곳에서 저녁식사 하자. 어때? 여부를 가능한 빨리 알려 줘.

안녕
민정

추신: 동생을 데리고 와도 좋아.

1. 이메일을 쓴 사람은 누구인가요?
   ① Sangmin
   ② Minjeong

2. 이메일을 받은 사람은 누구인가요?
   ① Sangmin
   ② Minjeong

3. 이메일을 쓴 목적은 무엇인가요?
   ① 안부 인사하려고
   ② 부탁하기 위해서
   ③ 친구를 파티에 초대하기 위해서

Practice 1 Lecture

01 I am so happy that classes are over for the second semester.

2학기 수업이 끝나서 매우 기뻐.

어 휘

① the second semester : 2학기

② be over : 끝나다

구 문

① [기본]

주어 + be + so happy + that + 주어 + 동사: ~해서 매우 기쁘다

예문1) John is so happy that his son is healthy.
(존은 자신의 아들이 건강해서 매우 기쁘다.)

예문2) They are so happy that the vacation has begun.
(그들은 방학이 시작되서 매우 기쁘다.)

② [응용]

주어 + be + so happy + to - 부정사: ~해서 매우 기쁘다

예문1) She was so happy to receive a birthday present.
(그녀는 생일선물을 받고 매우 기뻤다.)

예문2) They are so happy to have a new English teacher.
(그들은 새로운 영어 선생님을 맞이해서 매우 기쁘다.)

02 I miss my family so much.

가족들이 매우 그리워.

어 휘

① miss: 그리워하다

예문1) Her children have gone to Hawaii, so she misses them so much.
(그녀의 아이들은 하와이에 가고 없다. 그래서 그녀는 아이들이 매우 그립다.)

03 I can't wait to see them.

나는 그들을 지금 당장 보고 싶다.

관용표현 ① can't wait + to-부정사: 지금 당장 ~하고 싶다

예문1) I can't wait to eat the cake.
(나는 케이크를 지금 당장 먹고 싶다.)

예문2) I can't wait to go on vacation.
(나는 지금 당장 휴가를 가고 싶다.)

04 I would like to ask you a favor.

내가 너에게 부탁을 하나 하고 싶어.

관용표현 ① would like + to-부정사: ~하고 싶다

예문1) I would like to have a cup of coffee.
(나는 커피 한잔 마시고 싶다.)

② ask + 목적어 + a favor: ~에게 부탁을 하다

예문1) I asked him a difficult favor.
(나는 그에게 어려운 부탁을 했다.)

05 Can you pick me up at the Jeju Airport this coming Saturday?

너 이번 주 토요일 제주 공항에 차로 나를 마중 나올 수 있니?

관용표현 ① pick up: 차로 마중하다

예문1) I will pick you up at the airport.
(내가 차를 가지고 너를 공항에 마중 나갈게.)

어 휘 ① this coming Saturday: 이번 주 토요일

예문1) She will come back this coming Saturday.
(그녀는 이번 주 토요일 날 돌아올 것이다.)

06 I am arriving at 6:20 p.m.

나는 오후 6시 20분에 도착할 예정이야.

문 법 ① 현재진행형(be + V-ing) → 가까운 미래

예문1) She is getting married next week.
(그녀는 다음 주에 결혼할 예정이야.)

예문2) What are you doing tomorrow?
(너는 내일 무엇을 할 예정이니?)

07 If you meet me at the airport, I will treat you to a good dinner.

네가 공항에 나를 마중 나오면, 내가 너에게 근사한 저녁을 살게.

관용표현 ① meet + 목적어 + 장소: ~을/를 ~로 마중 나가다

예문1) I will meet you at the airport.
(내가 너를 공항으로 마중 나갈게.)

예문2) Thanks so much for meeting me at the railroad station.
(기차역으로 나를 마중 나와줘서 고마워.)

08 Last time we met downtown in Jeju, you told me about the new Japanese restaurant.

지난번 우리가 제주 시내에서 만났을 때, 네가 새로 오픈한 일식 레스토랑에 대해서 얘기했었지.

구 문 ① Last time + 주어 + 과거동사: 지난번 ~했을 때

예문1) Last time she visited me, I was ill in bed.
(지난번 그녀가 나를 찾아 왔을 때 나는 아파서 누워있었다.)

예문2) Last time I saw her, she was wearing her diamonds.
(지난번 내가 그녀를 보았을 때 그녀는 다이아몬드를 착용하고 있었다.)

09 This is a good opportunity to try that restaurant.

이번이 그 식당에서 식사해 볼 수 있는 좋은 기회야.

어 휘 ① try: 먹어보다, 시험 삼아 해보다

예문1) I want to try different kinds of food.
(나는 다른 종류의 음식을 먹어보고 싶어.)

구 문 ① This is a good opportunity + to-부정사: ~하기 좋은 기회다

예문1) This is a good opportunity to visit the museum.
(이번이 박물관에 가볼 수 있는 좋은 기회다.)

10 Let's go there for dinner.

저녁식사 하러 거기에 가자.

관용표현 ① Let's + 동사원형: ~하도록 하자

예문1) Let's go to the movies.
(영화를 보러 가자.)

예문2) Let's hurry.
(서두르자.)

11 How does that sound?

그거 어때?

구 문 ① sound + 형용사: ~처럼 들리다

예문1) That sounds great.
(그거 좋겠는데.)

12 Let me know ASAP.

가능한 빨리 여부를 알려 줘.

관용표현

① Let + 목적어 + know : ~에게 ~여부를 알려주다

예문1) I will let you know tomorrow.
(내가 너에게 내일 여부를 알려 줄게.)

② ASAP (as soon as possible) : 가능한 빨리

예문1) I have to write to her as soon as possible.
(나는 가능한 빨리 그녀에게 편지를 써야 해.)

13 P.S. You can bring your brother.

동생을 데리고 와도 좋아.

어 휘

① P.S. (post script) : 추신

② bring : 데리고 오다

Practice 1 Vocabulary & Expression

민정이 상민에게 보낸 email에 나왔던 어휘와 관용표현을 정리해 보았습니다.

구분	어휘 & 표현	의미
어휘	be over	끝나다
	miss	그리워하다
	the second semester	2학기
	treat	특별한 대접을 하다
	try	먹어보다, 시험 삼아 써보다
	ask + 목적어 + a favor	~에게 부탁을 하다
관용표현	ASAP(as soon as possible)	가능한 빨리
	can't wait + to-부정사	지금 당장 ~하고 싶다
	let + 목적어 + know	~에게 ~여부를 알려주다
	let's + 동사원형	~하도록 하자
	pick up	차로 마중하다
	would like + to-부정사	~하고 싶다

Practice 1 Task 1

보기에 있는 단어를 이용하여 문장을 완성해 보세요. 필요한 경우는 동사의 형태를 변형시켜 보세요.

be over	miss	treat	try	pick up

(1) I am so happy that classes (　　)(　　) for the second semester.

(2) I (　　)my family so much.

(3) Can you (　　) me (　　) at Jeju Airport this coming Saturday?

(4) If you meet me at the airport, I will (   ) you to a good dinner.

(5) This is good opportunity to (   ) that restaurant.

Practice 1 Task 2

빈칸에 해당하는 표현을 입력하여 문장을 완성하세요.

(1) 너에게 부탁을 하나 하고 싶어.

I would like to (   ) you (   )(   ).

(2) 거기에 저녁을 먹으러 가자.

(   )(   ) there for dinner.

(3) 가능한 빨리 알려줘.

Let me know (   ).

(4) 나는 그들을 지금 당장 보고 싶다.

I (   )(   ) to see them.

Practice 1 Task 3

제시되어 있는 단어를 배열하여 올바른 문장을 입력해 보세요. (첫 단어는 대문자로 시작하세요.)

(1) 당신이 돌아와서 매우 기쁩니다.

that	I	happy	so	am

(   )(   )(   )(   )(   ) you have come back.

(2) 지난번 내가 서울에 왔을 때, 나는 삼촌을 찾아 뵈었다.

to　　last　　came　　I　　time　　Seoul

(　　)(　　)(　　)(　　)(　　)(　　), I visited my uncle.

(3) 이번이 돈을 많이 벌 수 있는 좋은 기회다.

opportunity　　this　　good　　a　　is　　make　　to

(　　)(　　)(　　)(　　)(　　)(　　)(　　) a lot of money.

(4) 그거 좋겠는데.

sounds　　that　　great

(　　)(　　)(　　).

Coffee break

The Origins of the Names of the Days of the Week

A week has seven days. Each day of the week has its own name. The names of the seven days are Sunday, Monday, Tuesday, Wednesday, Thursday, Friday, and Saturday. The seven days are named after heavenly bodies and some of the gods in mythology. Sunday is the sun's day. Monday is the moon's day. Tuesday is named after Tiw, the war god in Norse mythology. Wednesday comes from Woden, chief of the Norse gods. Thursday is the day of Thor, the Norse god of thunder. Friday derives from Frig, goddess of marriage and wife of Woden.

요일명의 기원

일주일은 칠 일로 되어있다. 일주일을 구성하는 각 요일은 명칭을 가지고 있다. 일곱 요일들의 명칭은 일요일, 월요일, 화요일, 수요일, 목요일, 금요일, 그리고 토요일이다. 일곱 요일들은 천체와 신화에 등장하는 신의 이름을 따서 지어진 것이다. 일요일은 '태양의 날'에 해당한다. 월요일은 '달의 날'에 해당한다. 화요일인 '튜스데이'는 노르웨이 신화에 나오는 전쟁의 신 '티우'에서 유래되었다. 수요일인 '웬스데이'는 노르웨이 신화에 등장하는 최고 우두머리 신 '워든'에서 유래되었다. 목요일인 '서스데이'는 노르웨이 신화에 등장하는 천둥의 신 '소르'에서 왔다. 금요일인 '프라이데이'는 결혼의 여신이자 '워든'신의 아내인 '프리그'에서 유래되었다.

Quiz

Where does the name 'Saturday' come form?

① Saturn (토성) ② Uranus (천왕성) ③ Pluto (명왕성) ④ Neptune (해왕성)

정답 : ①

Practice 2 Comprehension Check up

Subject Re: A favor
To minjeong@*****.net

Hi Minjeong,

It has been a long time since I saw you last. It is so nice to hear from you again. You must be happy that your classes for the second semester are over. I will be glad to pick you up at Jeju Airport. Since you are arriving at 6:20 p.m., I will get to the airport 30 minutes before you arrive. I look forward to seeing you soon. Take care.

Best Regards,
Sangmin Park

1. Who wrote the email?
   ① Sangmin
   ② Minjeong

2. Who received the email?
   ① Sangmin
   ② Minjeong

3. What is the purpose of the email?
   ① Saying hello
   ② Doing favor
   ③ Inviting a friend to a party

4. What time will Sangmin Park arrive at Jeju Airport?
   ① At 6 pm
   ② At 5:50 pm
   ③ At 5:30 pm

민정에게

오랜만이다. 네 소식을 다시 들으니 매우 반갑다. 2학기 수업이 끝나서 기쁘겠구나. 내가 기꺼이 제주공항으로 너를 차로 마중 나갈게. 네가 오후 6시 20분에 도착하니까 나는 공항에 네가 도착하기 30분 전에 도착할게. 너를 빨리 볼 수 있기를 기대한다. 잘 지내.

안녕

박상민

1. 이메일을 쓴 사람은 누구인가요?
   ① Sangmin
   ② Minjeong

2. 이메일을 받은 사람은 누구인가요?
   ① Sangmin
   ② Minjeong

3. 이메일을 보낸 목적은 무엇입니까?
   ① 안부 인사하려고
   ② 부탁을 들어주기 위해서
   ③ 친구를 파티에 초대하기 위해서

4. 상민은 제주 공항에 몇 시쯤 도착하나요?
   ① 오후 6시
   ② 오후 5시 50분
   ③ 오후 5시 30분

Practice 2 Lecture

01

It has been a long time since I saw you last.

오랜만이다.

어 휘 ① since: ~이래로 ② last: 마지막으로

구 문 ① It has been + 기간 + since + 주어 + 과거동사: ~한 이래로 ~이 되다

예문1) It has been five years since she graduated from Harvard.
(그녀가 Harvard 대학을 졸업한 이래로 5년이 지났다.)

예문2) It has been two years since he left his hometown.
(그가 고향을 떠난 지 2년이 지났다.)

02

It is so nice to hear from you again.

네 소식을 다시 들으니 매우 반갑다.

어 휘 ① hear from: ~ 소식을 듣다

예문1) I haven't heard from him since he retired.
(그가 은퇴한 이래로 나는 그의 소식을 듣지 못했다.)

예문2) I heard from him last week.
(지난주에 그의 소식을 들었다.)

03

You must be happy that your classes for the second semester are over.

너는 2학기 수업이 끝나서 기쁘겠구나.

문 법 ① must + 동사원형: ~임에 틀림없다

예문1) You must feel tired after your long walk.
(너는 오랫동안 걸은 후 틀림없이 피곤할 거야.)

예문2) He must be the new English teacher.
(그는 새로운 영어선생님임에 틀림없다.)

04 **I will be glad to pick you up at Jeju Airport.**
내가 기꺼이 제주공항으로 너를 차로 마중 나갈게.

관용표현 ① 주어 + will + be + glad + to-부정사: 기꺼이 ~하려고 하다

예문1) I will be glad to help you repair the car.
(내가 기꺼이 네가 자동차 수리하는 것을 도와줄게.)

05 **Since you are arriving at 6:20 p.m, I will get to the airport 30 minutes before you arrive.**
네가 오후 6시 20분에 도착하니까, 나는 공항에 네가 도착하기 30분 전에 도착할게.

어 휘 ① get to: ~에 도착하다

예문1) He got to the station on time.
(그는 제시간에 역에 도착했다.)

문 법 ① 시간부사절에서 현재가 미래를 대신한다

예문1) I will finish the work before he comes back.
(나는 그가 돌아오기 전 일을 끝낼 것이다.)

06 **I look forward to seeing you soon.**
나는 너를 빨리 볼 수 있기를 기대한다.

어 휘

① look forward 동명사: ~하기를 몹시 바라다

예문1) Minho looks forward to seeing his family soon.
(민호는 자신의 가족을 빨리 보기를 몹시 바란다.)

예문2) I am looking forward to seeing you.
(저는 당신을 만나 뵙기를 고대하고 있습니다.)

07 Take care.

잘 지내.

관용표현

① take care: 잘 지내 (편지 마지막에 사용하는 인사)

예문1) John: It was nice running into you here in Namdaemun.
(남대문에서 너를 우연히 만나게 되어 반갑다.)
Mary: I Know! What a nice surprise! Would you like to have dinner with me?
(그렇지, 정말 뜻밖이야. 혹시 저녁 식사 같이 할래?)
John: Actually, I've got to catch my train.
(사실, 나는 곧 기차를 타야해.)
Mary: Okay, take care.
(그래, 잘지내.)

Practice 2 Vocabulary & Expression

상민이 민정에게 보낸 회신 이메일에 나왔던 어휘와 구문을 정리해 보겠습니다.

구분	어휘 & 표현	의미
어휘	since	~ 이래로
	last	마지막, 마지막으로
	hear from	소식을 듣다
	look forward + 동명사	기대하다
	get to	도착하다
관용표현	It has been + 기간 + since + 주어 + 과거동사	~한 이래로~기간이 흐르다
	It is so nice + to-부정사	~해서 매우 반갑다

Practice 2 Task 4

보기에 있는 단어를 이용하여 문장을 완성하세요.

be gald	get to	care	since	hear from

(1) It has been a long time (　　) I saw you last.

(2) It is so nice to (　　) you again.

(3) Since you are arriving at 6:20 p.m., I will (　　) the airport 30 minutes before you arrive.

(4) I will (　　) to pick up at Jeju Airport.

(5) Take (　　)

Practice 2 Task 5

제시되어 있는 단어를 배열하여 올바른 문장을 입력해 보시오.

(1) 그녀가 은퇴한 지 6년이 되었습니다.

it six been years retired she has since

( )

(2) 그의 소식을 다시 듣게 되어 매우 반가웠다.

was hear it him from nice so again to

( )

(3) 그녀는 승진해서 기쁘겠구나.

happy get must she to promotion a be

( )

(4) 내가 기꺼이 공항으로 너를 차로 마중 나갈게.

glad I be pick you at will up to the airport

( )

(5) 나는 그녀가 도착하기 20분 전 서울역에 도착할거야.

arrives she before will I twenty minutes get to Seoul Station

( )

(6) 나는 너를 빨리 볼 수 있기를 기대한다.

to I look forward seeing soon you

( )

Exercise Writing

미나가 친구 민수에게 보내는 email입니다. 영어로 작성해보세요.

민수에게

나는 지미가 내일 한국으로 돌아오게 되어 매우 기뻐.
나는 그가 매우 그리워.
나는 그를 지금 당장이라도 보고 싶어.
내가 너에게 부탁을 하나 하고 싶은데.
너 내일 공항에 차로 그를 마중 나갈 수 있어?
그의 예상도착 시각은 오후 4시야.
만약 네가 공항에 그를 마중 나가면 내가 너에게 영화를 보여줄게.
그거 어때?
여부를 가능한 빨리 알려줘.
안녕.

미나

Exercise You be the editor

다음 email을 읽고 틀린 부분을 찾아 고치세요. 틀린 곳이 5개가 있습니다.

Hi Mina,

It has been 6 months since I see you last.
It is so nice to hear you again. You must happy that your vacation has begun. I would like to see you this coming Friday. Last time we met downtown in Jeju, we went to the Japanese restaurant. I would like to treat you a good lunch there. How does that sound? Let me know APAS.

Best,
James

Wrap up
Summary

1. The format of email

Greeting
Body
Closing
Name

2. Expressions for asking favors

(1) I would like to ask you a favor.
(2) Can you pick me up at the airport?

3. Abbreviated expressions in emails

(1) ASAP = as soon as possible
(2) P.S. = post script
(3) RSVP = reply, if you please
(4) BTW = by the way
(5) IMO = in my opinion
(6) ATM = at the moment
(7) ETA = estimated time of arrival

Wrap up

Assignment I

오늘 학습한 주요 문형을 활용하여 영어문장을 작성하여 봅시다.

ask + 목적어 + a favor	~에게 부탁을 하다
can't wait + to-부정사	지금 당장 ~하고 싶다
hope to + 동사원형	~하기를 바란다
It has been + 기간 + since + 주어 + 과거동사	~한 이래로 ~기간이 흐르다
It is so nice + to-부정사	~해서 매우 반갑다
Let + 목적어 + know	~에게 ~여부를 알려주다
Let's + 동사원형	~하도록 하자
would like + to-부정사	~하고 싶다

Wram up

Assignment II

오늘 학습한 주요 문형을 활용하여 제시된 조건에 맞게 email을 작성해 봅시다.

[조건]

1. 메일내용
   가까운 사람에게 무언가를 부탁하는 내용

2. 사용문형
   - Hi,
   - I would like to ask you a favor.
   - Can you ~~~?
   - If you ~~~, I will treat ~~~.
   - ASAP

3. 문장 개수
   - 8~15문장 (인사, 끝인사, 이름 제외하고 8-15문장)

[과제]

To	
Cc	
Subject	

Answers

Lesson 1. Asking favors

Warm up

Check up

1) To : 수신인 (email을 받는 사람)
   Cc : 참조 (email을 참고로 받는 사람)
   Bcc: 숨은 참조 (수신인 모르게 email을 참고로 받는 사람)
2) Dear Mr. Jackson - Cordially yours,
   Dear Linda, - Best regards,
   Hi Freddy, - Warmly,
3) We need more time / We need more time.
4) ③

Practice 1 Comprehension Check up

1) ②
2) ①
3) ②

Practice 1 Task 1

1) I am so happy that classes are over for the second semester.
2) I miss my family so much.

3) Can you pick me up at Jeju airport this coming Saturday?
4) If you at the airport, I will treat you to a good dinner.
5) This is a good opportunity to try that restaurant.

Practice 1 Task 2

1) I would like to ask you a favor.
2) Let's go there for dinner.
3) Let me know ASAP.
4) I can't wait to see them.

Practice 1 Task 3

1) I am so happy that you have come back.
2) Last time I came to Seoul, I visited my uncle.
3) This is a good opportunity to make a lot of money.
4) That sounds great.

Practice 2 Comprehension Check up

1) ①
2) ②
3) ②
4) ②

Practice 2 Task 4

1) It has been a long time since I saw you last.
2) It is so nice to hear from you again.
3) Since you are arriving at 6:20 p.m, I will get to the airport 30 minutes before you arrive.
4) I will be glad to pick you up at the Jeju airport.
5) Take care.

Practice 2 Task 5

1) It has been six years since she retired.
2) It was so nice to hear from him again.
3) She must be happy to get a promotion.
4) I will be glad to pick you up at the airport.
5) I am arriving at Seoul Station twenty minutes before he arrives.
6) I look forward to seeing you soon.

Exercise Writing

Hi Minsoo,

I am so happy that Jimmy is coming back to Korea tomorrow. I miss him so much. I can't wait to see him. I would like to ask you a favor. Can you pick him up at the airport tomorrow? His ETA is 4 p.m. If you meet him at the airport, I will treat you to a movie. How does that sound? Let me know ASAP.

Best,
Mina

Exercise You be the editor

Hi Mina,

It has been 6 months since I saw (since + 주어 + 과거동사) you last. It is so nice to hear from (~소식을 듣다) you again. You must be (must + 동사원형) happy that your vacation has begun. I would like to see you this coming Friday. Last time we met downtown in Jeju, we went to the Japanese restaurant. I would like to treat you to (treat + 목적어 + to + 음식) a good lunch there. How does that sound? Let me know ASAP (as soon as possible).

Best,
James

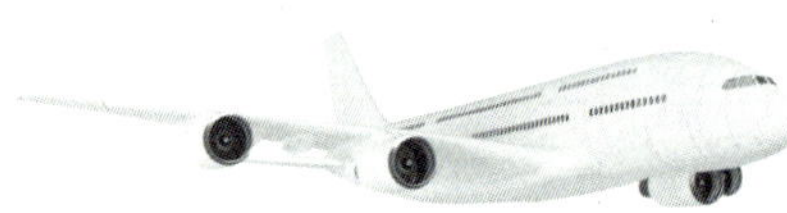

Business
Management
Writing
Basis and Application

Lesson 02

Birthday party

Lesson 02

Birthday party

Introduction

Lesson objectives

1. Learning the format of a diary
2. Learning the key expressions
   (1) Making sentences using *after* and *when*
   (2) Making sentences using *pleased*

Warm up

The format of a diary

[① Title]
[② Weather] [③ Day] [④ Date]
[⑤ Body]

① **제목:** 일기 전체의 내용을 나타내는 간결한 문구

② **날씨:** 형용사로 표현합니다.

(1) 맑은 날씨: clear, fine, sunny, beautiful, fair
(2) 흐린 날씨: cloudy, gray
(3) 비 오는 날씨: rainy, wet
(4) 눈이 내리는 날씨: snowy
(5) 바람 부는 날씨: windy, stormy
(6) 추운 날씨: cold, chilly
(7) 더운 날씨: hot, sultry
(8) 선선한 날씨: cool
(9) 따뜻한 날씨: warm
(10) 안개 낀 날씨: foggy, misty

③ **요일:** 첫 글자는 대문자로 시작합니다. 요일을 약자로 쓸 수도 있습니다.

월요일: Monday → Mon.
화요일: Tuesday → Tues.
수요일: Wednesday → Wed.
목요일: Thursday → Thurs.
금요일: Friday → Fri.
토요일: Saturday→ Sat.
일요일: Sunday → Sun.

④ **날짜**

월, 일, 연도 순서로 날짜를 기록합니다. 월의 첫 철자는 대문자로 시작하며 약자를 사용할 수도 있습니다.

월-일과 연도 사이에는 쉼표를 사용합니다. 날짜를 쓸 때는 기수 또는 서수로 쓸 수도 있습니다.

1월: January → Jan.
2월: February → Feb.
3월: March → Mar.
4월: April → Apr.
5월: May
6월: June → Jun.
7월: July → Jul.
8월: August → Aug.
9월: September → Sep.
10월: October → Oct.
11월: November → Nov.
12월: December → Dec.

[날짜를 읽을 때는 언제나 서수로 읽음]

• 한글: 2013년 3월 5일
• 영문: March 5th, 2013 또는 March 5, 2013 (영문읽기: March fifth two thousand thirteen)

⑤ **본문**

가장 중심이 되는 부분으로 하루 일과 중 가장 인상 깊었던 일을 중심으로 시간순서대로 간결하게 기록합니다.

Warm up

Check up

일기의 구조와 내용에 대한 다음 문제를 풀어보겠습니다.

1. 아래 제시된 항목을 순서대로 나열하세요.

2013 Cloudy March 15 Friday

( ), ( ), ( )( ),( )

2. 보기에 제시된 어휘를 활용하여 날씨에 대한 표현을 적어보세요.

보기	cloudy snowy fair misty chilly cool rainy windy scorching warm

① 맑은 날씨 [ ]

② 흐린 날씨 [ ]

③ 비오는 날씨 [ ]

④ 눈이 내리는 날씨 [ ]

⑤ 바람 부는 날씨 [ ]

⑥ 추운 날씨 [ ]

⑦ 더운 날씨 [ ]

⑧ 신선한 날씨 [ ]

⑨ 따뜻한 날씨 [ ]

⑩ 안개 낀 날씨 [ ]

3. 아래 제시된 날짜를 입력하세요.

① 2013년 3월 12일 화요일, 비 옴

( )

② 2013년 3월 28일 목요일, 추움

( )

③ 2013년 4월 1일 월요일, 따뜻함

( )

4. 일기 내용의 일부 문장입니다. 일어난 순서에 맞게 A, B, C, D에 들어갈 문장을 보기에서 골라 적어보세요.

A: ______________________________

B: ______________________________

First, I arranged the official documents and the books.
Second, I swept the floor with a broom.
Finally, I used the vacuum cleaner. Soon the office became tidy.

C: ______________________________

D: ______________________________

| 보기 |

- I was happy that my office was in order.
- So today I cleaned up my office.
- I decided to clean my office everyday.
- I had not cleaned my office for several days, and the office was untidy.

A ____.

B ____.

C ____.

D ____.

Practice 1 Comprehension Check up

A Visit to a Fire Station

Fine, Wednesday, March 5, 2013

Today we learned about fire in class. After the class was over, we went to a fire station. It was a very exciting trip. When we arrived at the fire station, there were 14 fire fighters there. They showed us fire trucks and fire suits. We tried wearing the fire suits. They were very heavy.

I think fire fighters are heroes. They help to save people's lives. They are brave people. I respect them very much. When I grow up, I want to be a brave fire fighter. The trip to the fire station was a good experience.

1. What did Jim learn about in class?

① Fire ② Water

③ Snow ④ Rain

2. Where did the class visit?

① Museum ② Fire station

③ Police station ④ City Hall

3. What did the class see at the fire station?

① Fire trucks

② Fire Suits

③ Fire trucks and fire suits

④ A fire

4. Why does Jim respect the fire fighters?

① They wear fire suits.

② They are kind.

③ They make a lot of money.

④ They help to save people's lives.

소방서 견학

2013년 3월 5일 수요일, 맑음

오늘은 수업시간에 화재에 대해서 배웠다. 수업이 끝난 후 소방서에 갔다. 매우 신나는 견학이였다. 우리가 소방서에 도착했을 때 14명의 소방대원 아저씨들이 있었다. 소방대원 아저씨들은 우리에게 소방차와 소방복을 보여주었다. 우리는 소방복을 착용해보았다. 소방복은 매우 무거웠다.

나는 소방대원 아저씨들이 영웅이라고 생각한다. 그들은 인명을 구하는 일을 거든다. 그들은 용감하다. 나는 그들을 존경한다. 내가 어른이 되면 용감한 소방대원이 되고 싶다. 소방서 견학은 좋은 경험이었다.

1. 짐은 수업시간에 무엇에 대해서 배웠습니까?
   ① 화재 ② 물
   ③ 눈 ④ 비

2. 반 학생들은 어디를 방문했나요?
   ① 박물관 ② 소방서
   ③ 경찰서 ④ 시청

3. 반 학생들은 소방서에서 무엇을 보았나요?
   ① 소방차
   ② 소방복
   ③ 소방차와 소방복
   ④ 화재

4. 짐은 왜 소방대원들을 존경하나요?
   ① 소방복을 착용하기 때문에
   ② 친절하기 때문에
   ③ 돈을 많이 벌기 때문에
   ④ 인명을 살리는 일을 하기 때문에

Practice 1 Lecture

01 A Visit to a Fire Station.
소방서 견학

어 휘

① visit: 방문, 견학

예문1) I think that you should pay a visit to the doctor.
(나는 네가 의사에게 가서 진찰을 받아야 한다고 생각해.)

② fire station : 소방서

예문1) We visited Youngsan fire station in Seoul to learn about fire safety.
(우리는 화재 안전을 배우기 위해 서울에 있는 용산소방서를 방문했다.)

02 Fine, Thursday, May 10, 2013.
2013년 5월 10일, 목요일, 날씨 맑음

어 휘

① fine: 날씨가 좋은

예문1) Maria : How is the weather outside?
(밖의 날씨가 어때요?)
Kerry : It is fine.
(날씨가 좋아요.)

03 Today we learned about a fire in class.
우리는 오늘 수업시간에 화재에 대해서 배웠다.

어 휘

① learn about : ~에 대해서 배우다

예문1) Today we learned about American history in class.
(오늘은 수업시간에 미국역사에 대해서 배웠다.)

② a fire : 화재

문 법 ① fire는 물리적 의미의 불일 때는 불가산명사이며 화재일 때는 가산명사입니다

예문1) Animals are afraid of fire.
(동물들은 불을 무서워한다.)

예문2) Yesterday there was a big fire in my town.
(어제 우리 마을에 큰 화재가 났다.)

04

After the class was over, we went to a fire station.

수업이 끝난 후 우리는 시내로 갔다.

어 휘 ① be over : 끝나다

② a fire station : 소방서

구 문 After 주어 + 동사, 주어 + 동사 : ~한 후에 ~하다

예문1) After I finish my work, I will leave.
(일을 끝낸 후에 떠날 것이다.)

예문2) After school was over, we went downtown.
(수업이 끝난 후 우리는 시내로 갔다.)

05

It was a very exciting trip.

그것은 매우 신나는 견학이었다.

어 휘 ① exciting: 신나는, 재미있는

예문1) The game was very exciting.
(그 경기는 매우 재미있었다.)

② trip : 여행, 견학

06

When we arrived at the fire station, there were 14 fire fighters there.

우리가 소방서에 도착했을 때, 14명의 소방대원 아저씨가 있었다.

어 휘

① fire station : 소방서

② fire fighter : 소방대원

구 문

When + 주어 + 동사, 주어 + 동사 : ~할 때 ~하다

예문1) When he comes, I will tell him the truth.
(그가 오면 나는 그에게 진실을 말할 것이다.)

예문2) When she goes out, she takes her puppy with her.
(그녀는 외출할 때 강아지를 데리고 간다.)

07

They showed us fire trucks and fire suits.

그들은 우리에게 소방차와 소방복을 보여주었다.

어 휘

① fire truck : 소방차

② fire suit : 소방복

구 문

① 주어 + show + 간접목적어 + 직접목적어 : ~에게 ~을 보여주다

예문1) I will show you the photographs from my vacation.
(휴가 가서 찍은 사진 보여 줄게.)

예문2) She showed me a book.
(그녀는 나에게 책을 보여주었다.)

08

We tried wearing the fire suits.

우리는 소방복을 착용해보았다.

어 휘

① try~V-ing : 시험 삼아 ~해보다

예문1) She tried smoking a cigarette.
(그녀는 담배를 피워 보았다.)

② wear : ~을 착용하다, 입다

예문1) He tried wearing sunglasses.
(그는 시험 삼아 선글라스를 착용해 보았다.)

09 They were very heavy.

그것들은 매우 무거웠다.

어 휘

① heavy : 무거운

예문1) The box is very heavy.
(그 상자는 매우 무겁다)

10 I think fire fighters are heroes.

나는 소방대원들이 영웅이라고 생각한다.

어 휘

① hero : 영웅

구 문

① 주어 + think + 주어 + 동사 : ~가 ~라고 생각한다

예문1) He thinks that she is a beauty.
(그는 그녀가 미인이라고 생각한다.)

예문2) She thinks that he is intelligent.
(그녀는 그가 똑똑하다고 생각한다.)

11 They help to save people's lives.

그들은 인명을 구하는 일을 거든다.

관용표현

① save one's life : 생명을 구하다

예문1) The brave man saved her life.
(그 용감한 남자는 그녀의 목숨을 구했다.)

구 문

① 주어 + help + (to) + 동사 : ~가 ~을 거들다, ~가 ~을 돕다

예문1) Go and help (to) repair the car.
(가서 자동차 수리를 거들어라.)

예문2) He helped (to) open the door.
(그가 문을 여는데 거들었다.)

12 **They are brave people.**

그들은 용감한 사람들이다.

어 휘 ① brave : 용감한

예문1) The soldiers were very brave.

(그 군인들은 매우 용감했다.)

13 **I respect them very much.**

나는 그들을 매우 존경한다.

어 휘 ① respect : ~를 존경하다

예문1) I respect my parents.

(나는 부모님을 존경한다.)

14 **When I grow up, I want to be a brave fire fighter.**

내가 어른이 되면 용감한 소방대원이 되고 싶다.

어 휘 ① grow up : 성인 되다

예문1) When you grow up, I will let you smoke.

(네가 성인이 되면 나는 네가 흡연하는 것을 허락할게.)

구 문 ① 주어 + want + to-부정사 : ~하기를 원한다

예문1) I want to be a singer.

(나는 가수가 되길 원한다.)

15 The trip to the fire station was a good experience.

소방서 견학은 좋은 경험이었다.

어 휘

① trip : 여행, 견학

② experience : 경험

문 법

① experience는 일반적인 경험일 때는 불가산명사이며 구체적인 특정 경험일 때는 가산명사로 사용됩니다.

예문1) Sue got a job because she had a lot of experience.
(그녀는 경험이 많아서 직업을 구했다.)

예문2) He had interesting experiences in Hawaii.
(그는 하와이에서 흥미 있는 경험을 했다.)

Practice 1 Vocabulary & Expression

Jim의 일기에 나왔던 어휘와 관용표현을 정리해 보겠습니다.

구분	어휘 & 표현	의미
어휘	learn about	~에 대해서 배우다
	a fire	화재
	be over	끝나다
	a fire station	소방서
	exciting	신나는, 재미있는
	trip	여행, 견학
	fire station	소방서
	fire fighter	소방대원
	fire truck	소방차
	fire suit	소방복
	try ~ing	시험 삼아 ~해보다
	wear	~을 착용하다, 입다
	heavy	무거운
	hero	영웅
	brave	용감한
	respect	~를 존경하다
	experience	경험
관용표현	save one's life	생명을 구하다

Practice 1 Task 1

보기에 있는 단어를 이용하여 문장을 완성하세요. 필요한 경우는 동사의 형태를 변형시키세요.

| 보기 |

brave	heroes	respect	trip	experience

(1) It was a very exciting (   ).

(2) I think fire fighters are (   ).

(3) They are (   ).

(4) I (   ) them very much.

(5) The trip to the fire station was a good (   ).

Practice 1 Task 2

빈칸에 해당하는 표현을 입력하여 문장을 완성하세요.

(1) 오늘은 수업시간에 화재에 대해서 배웠다.
Today we (   )(   ) fire in class.

(2) 우리는 소방복을 착용해보았다.
We (   )(   ) the fire suits.

(3) 수업이 끝난 후 소방서에 갔다.
After the class was over, we went to a (   )(   ).

(4) 그들은 인명을 구하는 일을 거든다.

They (　　)(　　)(　　) people's lives.

Practice 1 Task 3

제시되어 있는 단어를 배열하여 문장을 완성하시오.

(1) 회의가 끝난 후에 우리는 저녁 식사를 하기 위해 나갔다.

the meeting over was after , went out dinner for we

(　　)

(2) 비가 그쳤을 때 우리는 외출하였다.

it raining stopped , when went out we

(　　)

(3) 메리는 자신의 친구에게 선물을 보여주었다.

showed gift her Mary friend a

(　　)

(4) 나는 그가 틀렸다고 생각했다.

thought wrong was I he

(　　)

Coffee break

The Origins of Valentine's Day

February 14 is Valentine's Day when lovers confess their love by exchanging gifts and cards. It is not clear how Valentine's Day originated. However, there are theories that explain the origins of Valentine's Day.

The origins of Valentine's Day date back to the Roman empire. Claudius II, the Roman emperor at that time, prevented the marriage of young people in order to maintain the combat capability of the armed forces. However, despite the emperor's imperial order against marriage, the priest Valentinus married young men and women secretly. This was found out, and the emperor Claudius II executed the priest Valentinus. The ceremony in commemoration of the death of Valentinus took place in the middle of February, and this is how Valentine's Day started.

Another theory about the origins of Valentine's Day relates to Lupercalia in Roman times. In Lupercalia, which was a pagan festival at that time, young women put their names in a box, and men were matched with the women whose, names they drew from the box. Such activities seemed to the Pope to be unchristian and the Pope declared February 14, 494 St. Valentine's Day for men and women to express their love.

The third theory about the origins of Valentine's Day comes from the belief of some European people that birds begin to mate on February 14. In particular, people in France and the UK thought that birds first began to mate on February 14, and this is why they designated February 14 a day for young lovers to express their love.

밸런타인데이의 유래

매년 2얼14일은 밸런타인데이로서 연인들이 선물과 카드를 주고받으며 사랑을 고백하는 날입니다. 이러한 밸런타인데이의 유래는 어디에서 시작되었는지 명확하지 않습니다. 하지만 밸런타인데이의 유래를 설명해주는 설을 살펴보겠습니다.

밸런타인데이의 유래는 고대 로마시대로 거슬러 올라갑니다. 당시 로마의 황제였던 Claudius II는 군대의 전투력을 유지하기 위해 젊은이들의 결혼을 금지하였습니다.

그런데 사제 Valentinus는 황제의 금혼령에도 불구하고 젊은 남녀들을 몰래 결혼시켰다고 합니다. 이 사실이 발각되자 황제 Claudius II는 Valentinus를 사형시켰습니다. 이 Valentinus의 죽음을 추모하는 의식을 2월 중순에 가진 것에서 밸런타인데이가 유래되었다고 합니다.

밸런타인데이의 유래에 대한 또 두 번째 설은 고대 로마시대에 있었던 Lupercalia축제와 관련이 있습니다. 당시 이교도의 축제였던 Lupercalia 축제에서는 젊은 여성들이 상자에 자기이름을 넣고 젊은 남성들이 상자에서 이름표를 골라 젊은 남성과 여성이 맺어졌다고 합니다. 이러한 행사가 교황이 보기에 비기독교적 이여서 서기 498년 2월 14일을 St. Valentine's Day로 선포하여 연인들이 서로 사랑을 표현하는 날로 삼았다고 합니다.

밸런타인데이의 유래에 대한 세 번째 설은 새들이 2월 14일 짝짓기를 시작한다는 유럽 사람들의 믿음에서 유래되었습니다. 특히 프랑스와 영국에서는 사람들이 2월 14일 날 새들이 짝짓기를 처음 시작한다고 생각하였고 이러한 이유로 2월 14을 젊은 연인들이 사랑을 표현하는 날로 지정했다고 합니다.

Practice 2 Comprehension Check up

Mom's birthday

Clear, Wednesday, March 12, 2013

Today was mom's birthday. Dad came home early with a birthday cake. My sister Youngmee and I prepared a birthday party for mom. After lighting the candles on the cake, we all together sang a birthday song to celebrate mom's birthday. Mom blew out the candles. Dad gave mom a nice ring for her birthday. My sister and I together gave mom a pair of shoes. Mom was very pleased to receive the birthday presents. It was a great party.

1. How many people were at the party?

① Three ② Four
③ Five ④ Six

2. What did dad give mom for her birthday?

① A ring ② Shoes
③ Candles ④ A songbook

3. What did the writer of the diary and her sister give mom for her birthday?

① A ring
② Shoes
③ Candles
④ A songbook

4. Who blew out the candles on the cake?

① Dad
② Mom
③ Youngmee
④ The whole family

엄마의 생일

2013년 3월 12일 수요일, 맑음

오늘은 엄마의 생일이었다. 아빠는 생일케이크를 가지고 집에 일찍 들어오셨다. 영미언니와 나는 엄마를 위해서 생일파티를 준비했다. 케이크 위에 있는 초에 불을 붙인 후 우리는 엄마의 생일을 축하하기 위해서 모두 함께 생일 축하 노래를 불렀다. 엄마는 촛불을 불어 끄셨다. 아빠는 엄마에게 멋진 반지를 생일 선물로 주셨다. 언니와 나는 함께 엄마에게 신발을 드렸다. 엄마는 생일 선물을 받고 매우 기뻐하셨다. 멋진 파티였다.

1. 파티에는 몇 명이 참석했나요?
   ① 세 명
   ② 네 명
   ③ 다섯 명
   ④ 여섯 명

2. 아빠는 엄마에게 생일선물로 무엇을 주었나요?
   ① 반지
   ② 신발
   ③ 초
   ④ 찬송가집

3. 일기의 저자와 그녀의 언니는 엄마에게 생일선물로 무엇을 주었나요?
   ① 반지
   ② 신발
   ③ 초
   ④ 찬송가집

4. 케이크 위의 촛불을 누가 껐나요?
   ① 아빠
   ② 엄마
   ③ 영미
   ④ 가족 전체

Practice 2 Lecture

01 Mom's Birthday
엄마의 생일

어 휘 ① birthday : 생일

예문1) When is your birthday?
(네 생일이 언제니?)

02 Clear, Thuesday, May 22, 2013
2013년 5월 22일, 화요일, 날씨 맑음

어 휘 ① clear : 날씨가 좋은, 맑은

예문1) Maria: How is the weather there?
(그곳은 날씨가 어때요?)
Kerry: It is clear here.
(여긴 날씨가 좋아요.)

03 Today was mom's birthday.
오늘은 엄마의 생일이었다.

어 휘 ① birthday : 생일

구 문 Today is + 기념일 : 오늘은 ~날이다

예문1) Today is Valentine's Day.
(오늘은 밸런타인데이다.)

예문2) Today is Arbor Day.
(오늘은 식목일이다.)

04 Dad came home early today with a birthday cake.

아빠는 오늘 생일케이크를 가지고 일찍 집에 오셨다.

어 휘 ① birthday cake : 생일케이크

구 문 주어 + 동사 + with + 물건 : ~을 가지고 ~하다

예문1) He cut an apple in half with a knife.
(그는 칼로 사과를 이등분하였다.)

예문2) She opened the door with a key.
(그녀는 열쇠로 문을 열었다.)

05 My sister Youngmee and I prepared a birthday party for mom.

영미언니와 나는 엄마를 위해서 생일파티를 준비했다.

어 휘 ① prepare : ~을 준비하다

예문1) My mom is preparing a dinner.
(엄마는 저녁을 준비하고 계신다.)

06 After lighting the candles on the cake, we all together sang a birthday song to celebrate her birthday.

케이크 위에 있는 초에 불을 붙인 후, 우리는 모두 함께 엄마의 생일을 축하하기 위해서 생일 축하 노래를 불렀다.

어 휘

① light : 불을 붙이다 (cf. light–lit–lit)
② all together: 모두 함께
③ sing a birthday song: 생일축하 노래를 부르다
④ celebrate: ~을 축하하다

구 문 ① After + 동사-ing, 주어 + 동사 : ~한 후에 ~하다

예문1) After finishing the work, he went home.
(일을 끝마친 후에 그는 집으로 갔다.)

07 **Mom blew out the candles.**
엄마는 촛불을 불어 끄셨다.

어 휘 ① blow out : 불어서 끄다

예문1) She blew out the candle.
(그녀는 촛불을 불어 껐다.)

08 **My dad gave her a nice ring for her birthday.**
아빠는 엄마에게 멋진 반지를 생일 선물로 주셨다.

구 문 ① 주어 + give + 간접목적어 + 직접목적어 : ~에게 ~을 주다

예문1) She gave me a book for my birthday.
(그녀는 나에게 생일선물로 책을 주었다.)

09 **My sister and I together gave her a pair of shoes.**
언니와 나는 함께 엄마에게 신발을 드렸다.

어 휘 ① a pair of : 같은 종류의 것이 두 개로 이루어진 한 쌍

예문1) I bought a pair of gloves.
(나는 장갑 한 벌을 샀다.)

예문2) He has two pairs of shoes.
(그는 구두 2켤레를 가지고 있다.)

구 문 ① 주어 + give + 간접목적어 + 직접목적어 : ~에게 ~을 주다

예문1) She gave him a book for his birthday.
(그녀는 그에게 생일선물로 책을 주었다.)

10 My mom was very pleased to receive the birthday presents.

엄마는 선물을 받고 매우 기뻐하셨다.

어 휘 ① receive : ~을 받다

예문1) She received many wedding gifts.
(그녀는 많은 결혼 선물을 받았다.)

② presents : 선물

구 문 ① 주어 + be + very + pleased + to + 동사원형 : ~해서 매우 기쁘다

예문1) John was very pleased to get a job.
(존은 직장을 구해서 매우 기뻤다.)

11 It was a great party.

멋진 파티였다.

어 휘 ① great : 멋진, 굉장한, 유쾌한

예문1) That sounds great.
(그거 멋진데.)

예문2) We had a great time.
(우리는 유쾌한 시간을 보냈다.)

Practice 2 Vocabulary & Expressions

영미의 일기에서 나왔던 어휘와 구문을 정리해 보겠습니다.

구분	어휘 & 표현	의미
어휘	birthday	생일
	birthday cake	생일케이크
	prepare	~을 준비하다
	light	~을 불을 붙이다
	all together	모두 함께
	sing a birthday song	생일 축하 노래를 부르다
	celebrate	~을 축하하다
	blow out	불어서 끄다
	receive	~을 받다
	present	선물
관용표현	Today is + 기념일	오늘은 ~날이다
	주어 + 동사 + with + 물건	~을 가지고 ~하다
	After + 동사 -ing, 주어 + 동사	~한 후에 ~하다
	주어 + give + 간접목적어 + 직접목적어	~에게 ~을 주다
	주어 + be + very + pleased + to-부정사	~해서 매우 기쁘다

Practice 2 Task 4

보기에 있는 단어를 이용하여 문장을 완성하세요. 동사는 과거 시제가 되도록 하며 필요하면 형태를 바꾸어 문장을 완성하세요.

a pair of	birthday	give	blow out	prepare

(1) Today was mom's (   ).

(2) My sister Youngmee and I (　　　) a birthday party for mom.

(3) Mom (　　　)(　　　) the candles.

(4) Dad (　　　) her a nice ring for her birthday.

(5) My sister and I gave mom (　　　) shoes.

Practice 2 Task 5

보기에 있는 단어를 배열하여 올바른 문장을 입력해 보세요. 문장의 첫 단어의 첫 철자는 대문자로 간주하세요.

(1) 오늘은 화이트 데이였다.

was　　today　　White Day

(　　　　　　　　　　)

(2) 나의 남편은 선물을 가지고 집에 일찍 들어왔다.

early　　home　　came　　my　　husband　　a present　　with

(　　　　　　　　　　)

(3) 저녁식사를 한 후 남편은 나에게 초콜릿을 화이트 데이 선물로 건네주었다.

dinner　　having ,　　after　　gave　　chocolate　　my　　husband　　me,

(　　　　　　　　　　) for White Day.

(4) 나는 화이트 데이 선물을 받고 매우 기뻤다.

was　　I　　very　　pleased　　to　　receive　　a　　present

(　　　　　　　　　　) for White Day.

Exercise Writing

아빠 생신에 대한 일기를 영작해 보겠습니다.

아빠의 생일

2013년 3월 19일 화요일, 맑음

오늘은 아빠의 생일이였다.

아빠는 집에 일찍 들어오셨다.

민호 형과 나는 아빠를 위해서 생일파티를 준비했다.

케이크 위에 있는 초에 불을 붙인 후 우리는 아빠의 생일을 축하하기 위해서 모두 함께 생일 축하 노래를 불렀다.

아빠는 촛불을 불어 끄셨다.

엄마는 아빠에게 멋진 넥타이를 선물로 주셨다.

형과 나는 함께 아빠에게 지갑을 드렸다.

아빠는 생일선물을 받고 매우 기뻐하셨다.

멋진 파티였다.

Exercise You be the editor

다음 email을 읽고 틀린 부분을 찾아 고치세요. 박스문장에 틀린 곳이 5개가 있습니다.

Wedding Anniversary

Windy, Sunday, March 31, 2013

Today was our 5th wedding anniversary. I took my wife the movies. We saw the movie Troy. Brad Pitt is my wife's favorite actor. I was happy that my wife enjoyed the movie.

My wife is an able person. She was an English teacher, but she quit her job after she marries me. My wife likes my job as a fire fighter. She thinks that I am a hero because I help to save people's lives. My wife is proud of me, and I am proud of her.

After return home from the movies, my wife and I had a party for our wedding anniversary. My wife and I light the candles on the cake and then we blew it out. I gave my wife a long coat and she gave me a nice pair of dress shoes to celebrate our 5th wedding anniversary. Today was a special day for my wife and me.

Wrap up

Summary

1. The Format of Diary

[Title]
[Weather] [Day] [Date]
[Body]

2. Key expressions

(1) After the class was over, we went to a fire station.

(2) When we arrived at the fire station, there were 14 fire fighters there.

(3) My mom was very pleased to receive the birthday presents.

Wrap up

Assignment I

오늘 학습한 주요 문형을 활용할 수 있는 문장을 작성하세요.

문형	의미
Today is + 기념일	오늘은 ~날이다
주어 + 동사 + with + 물건	~을 가지고 ~하다
After + 동사-ing, 주어 + 동사/After 주어 + 동사, 주어 + 동사	~한 후에 ~하다
주어 + give/show + 간접목적어 + 직접목적어	~에게 ~을 주다, 보여주다
When + 주어 + 동사, 주어 + 동사	~할 때 ~하다
주어 + think + 주어 + 동사	~가 ~라고 생각한다
주어 + help + (to) + 동사	~가 ~을 거들다 ~가 ~을 돕다
주어 + be + very + pleased + to + 동사원형	~해서 매우 기쁘다

Answers

Lesson 2. Birthday party

Warm up

Check up

1) ① Cloudy, Friday, March 15, 2013
② Cloudy, Friday, March 15th, 2013

2) ① 맑은 날씨 - fair
② 흐린 날씨 - cloudy
③ 비오는 날씨 - rainy
④ 눈이 내리는 날씨 - snowy
⑤ 바람 부는 날씨 - windy
⑥ 추운 날씨 - chilly
⑦ 더운 날씨 - scorching
⑧ 신선한 날씨 - cool
⑨ 따뜻한 날씨 - warm
⑩ 안개 낀 날씨 - misty

3) ① 2013년 3월 12일 화요일, 비 옴

Rainy, Tuesday, March 12, 2013
Rainy, Tuesday, March 12th, 2013

② 2013년 3월 28일 목요일, 추움

Cold, Thursday, March 28, 2013
Cold, Thursday, March 28th, 2013
Chilly, Thursday, March 28, 2013
Chilly, Thursday, March 28th, 2013

③ 2013년 4월 1일 월요일, 따뜻함

Warm, Monday, April 1, 2013
Warm, Monday, April 1st, 2013

4) A: I had not cleaned my office for several days, and the office was dirty.
B: so today I cleaned up my office.
C: I was happy that my office was in order.
D: I decided to clean my office every day.

Practice 1 Comprehension Check up

1) ① Fire
2) ② Fire station
3) ③ Fire trucks and fire suits
4) ④ They help to save people's lives.

Practice 1 Task 1

1) It was a very exciting trip.
2) I think fire fighters are heroes.
3) They are brave.
4) I respect them very much.
5) The trip to the fire station was a good experience.

Practice 1 Task 2

1) Today we learned about fire in class.
2) We tried wearing the fire suits.
3) After the class was over, we went to a fire station.
4) They help to save people's lives.

Practice 1 Task 3

1) After the meeting was over, we went out for dinner.
2) When it stopped raining, we went out.
3) Mary showed her friend a gift.
4) I thought he was wrong.

Practice 2 Comprehension Check up

1) ② Four
2) ① A ring
3) ② Shoes
4) ② Mom

Practice 2 Task 4

1) Today was mom's birthday.
2) My sister Youngmee and I prepared a birthday party for mom.
3) Mom blew out the candles.
4) Dad gave her a nice ring for her birthday.
5) My sister and I gave mom a pair of shoes.

Practice 2 Task 5

1) Today was White Day.
2) My husband came home early with a present.
3) After having dinner, my husband gave me chocolate for White Day.
4) I was very pleased to receive a present for White Day.

Exercise Writing

Dad's birthday

Fair, Tuesday, March 19, 2013

Today was dad's birthday.
Dad came home early.
My brother Minho and I planned a birthday party for dad.
After lighting the candles on the cake, we all together sang a birthday song to celebrate dad's birthday.
Dad blew out the candles. Mom gave dad a nice tie for his birthday.
My brother and I together gave dad a wallet.
Dad was very pleased to receive the birthday presents.
It was a great party.

Exercise You be the editor

Wedding Anniversary

Windy, Sunday, March 31, 2013

Today was our 5th wedding anniversary. I took my wife to the movies (take A to B: A를 B에 데리고 가다). We saw the movie Troy. Brad Pitt is my wife's favorite actor. I was happy that my wife enjoyed the movie.

My wife is an able person. She was an English teacher, but she quit her job after she married me (주어 + 과거동사 + after + 주어 + 과거동사: ~한 후에 ~하였다). My wife likes my job as a fire fighter. She thinks that I am a hero because I help to save people's lives. My wife is proud of me, and I am proud of her.

After returning (After + 동사 +ing: ~한 후에) home from the movies, my wife and I had a party for our wedding anniversary. My wife and I lit (light의 과거형: lit) the candles on the cake and then we blew them out (the candles를 선행사로 하는 복수대명사 they). I gave my wife a long coat and she gave me a nice pair of dress shoes to celebrate our 5th wedding anniversary. Today was a special day for my wife and me.

Business
Management
Writing
Basis and Application

Lesson 03

Talking about my life

Lesson 03

Talking about my life

Introduction

Lesson objectives

1. Understanding Resume Structure
2. Writing a Resume for Job Application
3. To study key expressions
   (1) Responsibilities include planning and management
   (2) Fluent in English and Japanese
   (3) Scored 940 on the TOEIC
   (4) Proficient in Excel
   (5) Visited UCLA for an Exchange Program

Warm up

The format of resume

이력서를 작성하기 전에 이력서의 구조에 대해서 먼저 알아보겠습니다.

Personal Information

Name:

Date of Birth:

Address:

Contact Information:

Home)

Cell Phone)

E-mail)

Job Objectives

Work Experience		
Period	Company, Job Title, Job description	Location Department
Education		
Period	School Major:	Location Minor:
Special Skills		
Foreign Language	Fluent in + 외국어 Scored 점수 on the 공인시험	
Computer	Proficient in + 소프트웨어	
License and Certificate		
Date	면허 및 자격증	
Activities		
Period	Activities	

① Personal Information (개인정보)

- 위치 : 이력서의 맨 위
- 기재 항목 : 이름(name), 생년월일(date of birth), 주소(address), 연락처(contact information)
- 선택적 항목 : 필요에 따라서 결혼여부, 성별, 종교 등도 기재 가능

② Objective (희망직종)

- 지원자가 원하는 희망직종
- 희망직종을 선택할 수 있을 때 기재

③ Work Experience (경력)

- 기재 순서 : 가장 최근의 경력부터 과거로 거슬러 올라가면서 기재
- 기재 항목 : 기간(period), 직장명(the name of the company), 직장소재지(location), 직책(job title), 부서명(the name of the department), 업무(responsibilities)

1. 직책

직원: Associate	대리: Assistant Manager
과장: Manager	차장: Senior Manager
부장: General Manager	이사: Director
상무: Managing Director	전무: Executive Director
부사장: Vice President	사장: President

2. 부서명

마케팅부: Department of Marketing
홍보부: Department of Public Relations

회계부: Department of Accounting
연구개발부: Department of Research and Development
기획부: Department of Planning
인사부: Department of Human Resources
기술지원부: Department of Technical Support

3. 담당업무

판매: Sales
회계: Accounting
채용: Recruitment
기금조성: Fund Raising
재정: Finance
생산: Production
광고: Advertising
이벤트 기획: Planning of Events
홍보: Public Relations
인사관리: Personal Management
관리: Management

④ **Education** (학력)

• 기재 순서 : 가장 최근의 학력사항부터 과거로 거슬러 올라가며 기재
• 기재 항목 : 기간, 학교명, 소재지, 전공, 부전공

1. 전공1 – 어문학 전공

영어 영문학: English and English Literature
일어 일문학: Japanese and Japanese Literature
불어 불문학: French and French Literature
독어 독문학: German and German Literature
중어 중문학: Chinese and Chinese Literature

2. 전공 2 – 사회과학 전공

경제학: Economics
경영학: Business Administration
행정학: Public Administration
정치학: Political Science
법학: Law

3. 전공 3 – 사범계열

영어교육: English Education
불어교육: French Education
독어교육: German Education
한국어교육: Korean Education

4. 전공 4 – 자연과학

수학: Math
물리: Physics
생물: Biology
화학: Chemistry
자연과학: Natural Science

5. 전공 5 - 공학

건축공학: Architectural Engineering

컴퓨터공학: Computer Engineering

환경공학: Environmental Engineering

6. 대학원학위 1 - 석사

Master of Arts (M.A.): 문학석사

Master of Science (M.S.): 이학석사

Master of Business Administration (M.B.A.): 경영학석사

7. 대학원학위 2- 박사

Doctor of Philosophy (Ph.D.): 박사

Doctor of Law (J.D.): 법학박사

Doctor of Medicine (M.D.): 의학박사

⑤ Special Skills (특기)

• 내용 : 특별히 잘 할 수 있는 사항으로, 주로 외국어와 컴퓨터능력 등을 기재

⑥ License and Certificate (자격)

• 내용 : 소지하고 있는 면허나 자격증 등을 기재

1. 자격증1

운전면허증 1종 보통: Driver’ s License, Class 1

운전면허증 2종 보통: Driver’ s License, Class 2

정보처리기사 자격증 1급:

Data Processing Engineer Certification, Grade 1

정보처리기사 자격증 2급:

Data Processing Engineer Certification, Grade 2

2. 자격증 2

번역사 자격증 1급:

Translation Certification, Grade 1

번역사 자격증 2급:

Translation Certification, Grade 2

공인중개사 자격증: Real Estate Agent License

공인회계사 자격증: Public Accountant Certification

교사자격증 1급: Teacher’ s Certification, Grade 1

교사자격증 2급: Teacher’ s Certification, Grade 2

⑦ Activities (활동사항)

• 내용 : 활동사항을 적음, 주로 학창시절의 과외활동 등의 내용으로 작성

Warm up

Check up

이력서의 구조와 내용에 대한 다음 문제를 풀어보겠습니다.

1. 이력서에 경력을 작성하는 부분입니다. 각 위치에 알맞은 말을 보기에서 골라 적어보세요.

보기	Period Location Job description Department Job Title Company

Work Experience

______	______	______
	______	______
	______	

2. 이력서에 학력을 작성하는 부분입니다. 각 위치에 알맞은 항목을 넣으세요.

보기	School Minor Major Period Location

Education

______	______	______
	______	______
	______	

3. 다음은 이력서의 특기사항입니다. 빈칸에 적절한 전치사를 입력하세요.

Special Skills	
Foreign Language	① Fluent ( ) English
	② Scored 990 ( ) the TOEIC
Computer	③ Proficient ( ) MS Word

4. 학력이나 경력, 경험 등을 작성할 때 기재 순서를 보기의 내용을 바탕으로 작성해 보세요.

보기	• June 2011 - February 2012 • March 2012 - February 2013 • March 2009 - February 2010 • March 2010 - May 2011

1. ______________________________

2. ______________________________

3. ______________________________

4. ______________________________

Practice 1 Comprehension Check up

Personal Information

Name: Jaeyoung Park
Date of Birth: September 12, 1981
Address: 270 Imun-dong, Dongdaemun-gu, Seoul 130-791
Contact Information   Home) 02-2173-****
Cell Phone) 010-3910-****
email) park@*****.net

Job Objective

Department of Planning

Work Experience

March 2010 - February 2013   GS Construction, Suwon
Intern, Department of Planning
Responsibilities included planning and management

Education

March 2003 - February 2010   Soongsil University, Seoul
Major: Computer Engineering,
Minor: Business Administration
March 2000 - February 2003   Sejong High School, Seoul

Special Skills

Foreign Language   Fluent in English and Japanese
Scored 925 on the TOEIC
Scored 880 on the JPT
Computer   Proficient in Excel, MS Word, and Internet searching

License and Certificate

March 2008   Data Processing Engineer Certification, Grade 2
February 2004   Translation Certification, Grade 1

Activities

May 2005 - February 2006   President of English Club, Soongsil University
March 2004 - February 2005   Visited UCLA for an Exchange Program

1. How many foreign languages is the applicant good at?
① One
② Two
③ Three
④ Four

2. What is the applicant's score on the JPT?
① 800
② 855
③ 880
④ 885

3. How many software programs is the applicant good at?
① One
② Two
③ Three
④ Four

4. How many certificates does the applicant hold?
① One
② Two
③ Three
④ Four

5. What certificate did the applicant obtain most recently?
① Data Processing Engineer Certification, Grade 1
② Data Processing Engineer Certification, Grade 2
③ Translation Certification, Grade 1
④ Translation Certification, Grade 2

개인정보

이름 : 박재영
생년월일 : 1981년 9월 12일
주소 : 서울 동대문구 이문동 270번지 130-791
연락처 집) 02-2173-****
휴대전화) 010-3910-****
전자우편) park@*****.net

희망직종

기획부

경력

2010년 3월 ~ 2013년 2월	GS 건설근무	수원
	인턴	기획부
	기획 관리 업무 담당	

학력

2003년 3월 ~ 2010년 2월	숭실대학교졸업	서울
	전공: 컴퓨터공학	부전공: 경영학
2000년 3월 ~ 2003년 2월	세종고등학교 졸업	서울

특기

외국어	영어와 일본어에 능통
	토익 925점 취득
	일본어능력시험 880점 취득
컴퓨터	엑셀, 워드, 그리고 인터넷 검색에 능숙

자격증 및 면허

2008년 3월	정보처리기사 자격증 2급
2004년 2월	번역사 자격증 1급

활동사항

2005년 5월 ~ 2006년 2월	숭실대학교 영어동아리 회장
2004년 3월 ~ 2005년 2월	교환학생으로 어학연수로 UCLA 방문함

1. 지원자는 몇 개의 외국어를 잘 할 수 있습니까?

① 하나
② 둘
③ 셋
④ 넷

2. 지원자의 JPT 점수는?

① 800
② 855
③ 880
④ 885

3. 지원자는 몇 개의 소프트웨어를 잘 사용할 수 있습니까?

① 하나
② 둘
③ 셋
④ 넷

4. 지원자는 몇 개의 자격증을 가지고 있습니까?

① 하나
② 둘
③ 셋
④ 넷

5. 지원자는 가장 최근에 어떠한 자격증을 취득했습니까?

① 정보처리기사 1급
② 정보처리기사 2급
③ 번역사 자격증 1급
④ 번역사 자격증 2급

Practice 1 Lecture

01

Personal Information

Name: Jaeyoung Park

Date of Birth: September 12, 1981

Address: 270 Imun-dong, Dongdaemun-gu, Seoul 130-791

Contact Home) 02-2173-****

Cell Phone) 010-3910-****

email) park@******.net

개인정보

① Name: 이름 + 성

② Date of Birth: 월 + 일, 연도

③ Address: 번지 + 동, 구, 시 + 우편번호

④ Contact Information

Home) 02-2173-****

Cell Phone) 010-3910-****

email) park@*****.net

02

Job Objective

Department of Planning

희망직종

① 희망직종을 선택할 수 있는 경우는 근무하고 싶은 부서나 담당하고 싶은 업무를 기재 할 수 있습니다.

03 Work Experience

March 2010 ~ February 2013	GS Construction,	Suwon
	Intern,	Department of Planning
	Responsibilities included planning and management	

경력

① 경력을 기재할 때는 기간, 직장명, 소재지, 직책, 부서, 담당업무 순서로 기재합니다.
② 경력이 여러개일때는 가장 최근의 경력부터 과거로 거슬러 올라가면서 기재합니다.

구 문 ① Responsibilities include + 담당업무 : ~업무를 담당함

예문1) Responsibilities include planning and management.
(기획관리 담당)

예문2) Responsibilities include sales and advertising.
(판매와 광고업무 담당)

04 Education

March 2003 - February 2010	Soongsil University, Seoul
	Major: Computer Engineering,
	Minor: Business Administration
March 2000 - February 2003	Sejong High School, Seoul

학력

① 기간, 학교명, 소재지, 전공, 부전공 순서로 기재합니다.
② 학력은 가장 최근부터 과거로 거슬러 올라가며 기재합니다.

05 Special Skills

Foreign Language	Fluent in English and Japanese
	Scored 925 on the TOEIC
	Scored 880 on the JPT
Computer	Proficient in Excel, MS Word, and Internet searching

특기

① 공인된 외국어 시험에서 취득한 점수를 기재 할 수 있습니다
② 구체적인 소프트웨어의 명칭을 기재합니다.

어 휘

① fluent in : ~유창한

② proficient in : ~능숙한

06 Licenses and Certificates

March 2008 Data Processing Engineer Certification, Grade 2

February 2004 Translation Certification, grade 1

자격증 및 면허

① 면허 및 자격증은 가장 최근 것부터 기재합니다.

어 휘

① Data Processing Engineer Certification, Grade 2: 정보처리기사 자격증 2급

② Translation Certification, grade 1: 번역사 자격증 1급

③ 자격증 1급은 grade 1, 2급은 grade 2로 기재합니다.

07 Activities

May 2005 - February 2006	President of English Club, Soongsil University
March 2004 - February 2005	Visited UCLA for an Exchange Program

활동사항

① 과외활동을 가장 최근부터 과거로 거슬러 올라가며 기재합니다.

어 휘

① President : 회장

구 문

① Visited + 학교 + for an Exchange Program: 교환학생으로 ~를 방문함

예문1) Visited Harvard University for an Exchange Program

(교환학생으로 하버드대학교 방문함)

Practice 1 Vocabulary & Expression

구분	어휘 & 표현	의미
어휘	department	부서
	planning	기획
	management	관리
	position	직
	sales	판매
	advertisement	광고
	major	전공
	minor	부전공
	fluent in	~에 유창한
	scored	점수를 획득하다
	proficient in	~에 능숙한
	president	회장
관용표현	Responsibilities include ~	~업무를 담당하다
	Visit + 학교 + for an Exchange Program	교환학생으로 ~학교를 방문하다

Practice 1 Task 1

보기에 주어진 정보를 가지고 영문 이력서를 작성해 보세요.

(1) 보기에 주어진 정보를 가지고 영문 이력서의 Personal Information을 완성해보세요.

개인 정보

이름: 한수진

생년월일: 1980년 12월 5일

주소: 서울 서초구 양재동 332-1 157-220

연락처

집 전화번호 : 02-2174-****

휴대 전화번호 : 010-3910-****

전자우편 : hsj@*****.net

⇓

Personal Information

Name: Sujin Han

Date of Birth: ________________________________

Address: ____________________________________

Contact Information

Home) 02-2174-****

Cell Phone) 010-3910-****

email) hsj@*****.net

(2) 보기에 주어진 정보를 가지고 영문이력서의 Education을 완성해 보세요.

보기			
	2009년 3월 ~ 2013년 2월	사이버한국외국어대학교 졸업 영어 전공	서울 경영학 부전공
	2006년 3월 ~ 2009년 2월	서울외국어고등학교 졸업	서울

⇓

문제		
	_________ ~ _________	Cyber Hankuk University of Foreign Studies, Seoul Major:_________, Minor: ___________
	_________ ~ _________	________________________________, Seoul

Practice 1 Task 2

계속해서 보기에 주어진 정보를 가지고 영문 이력서를 작성해 보겠습니다.

(1) 보기에 주어진 정보를 가지고 영문 이력서의 Special Skills를 완성해 보세요.

보기		
	외국어	영어에 능통 TOEIC 880점 TEPS 900점
	컴퓨터	Adobe Photoshop과 Excel에 능숙

⇓

문제		
	Foreign Language	______________________ ______________________ ______________________
	Computer	______________________

(2) 보기에 주어진 정보를 가지고 영문 이력서의 License and Certificate를 완성해 보세요.

보기		
	2007년 7월	데이터처리기사 자격증 2급 취득
	2005년 4월	번역사 자격증 1급 취득

⇓

문제		
	__________ 2007	______________, Grade 2
	__________ 2005	______________, Grade 1

Practice 1 Task 3

제시되어 있는 단어를 배열하여 이력서에 들어갈 형태로 작문하세요. 첫 자는 대문자로 입력하세요.

(1) 기획과 관리업무 담당

include management responsibilities and planning

( )

(2) 영어와 일어에 능통함

in Japanese English and Fluent

( )

(3) 토익에서 925점 취득

925 on TOEIC the Scored

( )

(4) 엑셀과 인터넷 검색에 능숙함

in Internet searching Excel Proficient and

( )

(5) 교환학생으로 UCLA를 방문함

UCLA an Exchange Program for Visited

( )

Nicknames

In English-speaking countries, many people have nicknames. A nickname is an informal substitute for a person's proper name. There are many kinds of nicknames: some nicknames are shortened versions of a person's real name, some are based on physical characteristics of the person concerned, and some may be humorous allusions to a person's job. Nicknames are usually used by close friends or family, but occasionally might be used by work colleagues, particularly if the nickname refers to the person's job.

Shortened forms of proper names include *Rob, Bob or Bobby for Robert* (or *Bobbie* for the woman's name *Roberta*) and *Will* for *William.* Here are some more proper names with their usual shortened form: *David Dave, Joseph Joe* (also *Jo* for the female name *Josephine*), *Katherine Kate, Michael* - Mike, *Nicholas Nick* and *Phillip Phil.* As you can see, some short forms are similar to the proper name, just shorter; others are a little harder to recognize. Here are some names with their shortened forms which are a bit harder to recognize: *Edward Ted, Margaret Peggy* and *Richard Dick.*

Nicknames based on a person's physical characteristics can sometimes be offensive, and so are only usually used by close friends (or enemies!). *Tubs and chubby* could be used affectionately about a fat person, but *fatso* is definitely offensive! *Ginger* or *Carrot top* might be used to talk about someone with ginger colored hair.

Examples of nicknames that allude to a person's job include *Bones* (short for *Sawbones*) for a doctor and *Sparks* or *Sparkie* for an electrician.

Coffee break

별명

영어권 국가에서는 많은 사람들이 별명을 가지고 있다. 별명은 사람의 고유한 이름을 비공식적으로 대신한다. 별명에는 여러 가지 종류가 있다. 사람의 실제 이름을 축약해서 만든 별명도 있고 신체상의 특징에 근거해서 만들어진 별명도 있으며, 직업을 유머러스하게 말해주는 별명도 있다. 별명은 대개 가까운 친구나 가족들에 의해 불린다. 그러나 때로는 직장동료에 의해 사용되는 경우도 있다. 별명이 직업을 나타내는 경우는 특히 그렇다.

고유한 이름을 축약해서 별명을 만드는 경우에는 *Robert*의 축약형인 *Rob*, *Bob* 또는 *Bobby*와 (또는 여자이름 *Roberta*의 축약형인 *Bobbie*), *William*의 축약형인 *Will*이 있다. 이름과 이름의 축약형의 예를 들면 다음과 같다. *David*와 *Dave*, *Joseph*과 *Joe* (*Jo*는 또한 여자이름인 *Josephine*의 축약형이다), *Katherine*과 *Kate*, *Michael*과 *Mike*, *Nicholas*와 *Nick*, 그리고 *Phillip*과 *Phil*. 당신도 알다시피 몇몇 축약 형태는 원래 이름과 비슷하다. 단지 줄여졌을 뿐이다. 이름과 이름의 축약 형태의 관계를 인식하기 약간 어려운 경우도 있다. 그 예는 다음과 같다. *Edward*와 *Ted*, *Margaret*과 *Peggy*, 그리고 *Richard*와 *Dick*.

사람의 외모에 근거해서 만들어진 별명은 가끔 감정을 상하게 할 수 있다. 따라서 대부분 가까운 친구에 의해서 (또는 적에 의해서)만 사용된다. *Tubs*와 *chubby*는 뚱뚱한 사람의 애정어린 별명으로 사용될 수 있다. 그러나 fatso는 분명히 감정을 상하게 할 수 있다. *Ginger or Carrot top*은 빨간 머리를 가지고 있는 사람의 별명으로 사용될 수 있다.

사람의 직업을 나타내는 별명에는 의사를 나타내는 *Bones*(*Sawbones*의 축약형)와 전기기술자를 의미하는 *Sparks* 또는 *Sparkie*가 있다.

Practice 2 Comprehension Check up

'한상진'의 이력서를 읽고 질문에 답을 선택하세요.

Personal Information

Name: Sangjin Han

Gender: Male

Date of Birth: October 20, 1980

Marital Status: Married

Address: 57 Mukyo-dong, Jung-gu, Seoul 100-777

Contact Information

Home) 02-715-****

Mobile Phone) 010-5799-****

Email) han@*****.com

Job Objective

Management Position

Work Experience

March 2006 - February 2013	Hanjin Trade, Seoul Manager, Department of Marketing Responsibilities include sales and advertising
March 2004 - January 2006	Hana Enterprise, Incheon Assistant Manager, Department of Public Relations Responsibilities include advertising and fund raising

Education

March 2002 - February 2004	Graduate School of Kyunghee University, Seoul Major: Business Administration, Master of Business Administration
March 1998 - February 2002	University of Seoul, Seoul Major: English and English Literature

Special Skills	
Foreign Language	Fluent in English, Some French Scored 940 on the TOEIC Scored 900 on the TEPS
Computer	Proficient in Access, Excel, and Internet Searching
License and Certificate	
July 2007	Public Account Certification
April 2005	Real Estate Agent License
Activities	
September 2005 - Present	Member of Society of American Studies
March 2001 - February 2002	President of Student Association, University of Seoul
September 1999 - February 2000	Visited Stanford University for a Language Program

1. What kind of job does the applicant want?
   ① Secretary position
   ② Management position
   ③ Sales position
   ④ Production position

2. What was the applicant's job title when he worked for Hanjin Trade?
   ① Manager
   ② Assistant manager
   ③ Senior manager
   ④ General manager

3. What were the applicant's responsibilities when he worked for Hana Enterprise?
   ① Sales
   ② Accounting
   ③ Planning of events
   ④ Advertising and fundraising

4. What was the applicant's major at university?

① English and English Literature
② French and French Literature
③ Business Administration
④ Economics

5. When did the applicant obtain the public accountant certification?

① In 2005
② In 2006
③ In 2007
④ In 2008

6. How long did the applicant participate in the language program?

① About five months
② About ten months
③ About one year
④ About two years

개인정보

이름: 한상진
성별: 남성
생년월일: 1980년 10월 20일
결혼여부: 기혼
주소: 100-777 서울 중구 무교동 57번지
연락처 집) 02-715-****
휴대폰) 010-5799-****
전자우편) han@*****.com

희망직종

관리직

경력

2006년 3월 ~ 2013년 2월	한진 무역 근무	서울
	과장	마케팅부
	판매와 광고업무 담당	
2004년 3월 ~ 2006년 1월	하나 기업 근무	인천
	대리	홍보부
	광고와 기금모집 담당	

학력

2002년 3월 ~ 2004년 2월	경희대학교 대학원 졸업	서울
	전공: 경영	경영학석사
1998년 3월 ~ 2002년 2월	서울시립대학교	서울
	전공: 영어영문학	

특기

외국어	영어 능통 불어 약간
	토익 940점 취득
	텝스 900점 취득
컴퓨터	엑세스, 엑셀, 그리고 인터넷 검색에 능통

자격증 및 면허

2007년 6월 공인회계사자격증 취득
2005년 4월 공인중개사자격증 취득

활동사항

2005년 9월 ~ 현재	미국학 학회 회원	
2001년 3월 ~2002년 2월	총학생회 회장	서울시립대학교
1999년 9월 ~2000년 2월	어학연수로 스탠포드대학교 방문함	

1. 지원자는 어떤 직종을 원하나요?
   ① 비서직　② 관리직
   ③ 판매직　④ 생산직

2. 지원자가 한진 무역에서 근무했을 때 지원자의 직책은?
   ① 과장　② 대리
   ③ 차장　④ 부장

3. 지원자가 하나 기업에서 근무했을 때 지원자의 담당업무는?
   ① 판매　② 회계
   ③ 이벤트기획　④ 광고 및 기금모집

4. 지원자는 대학에서 무엇을 전공했나요?
   ① 영어영문학　② 불어 불문학
   ③ 경영학　④ 경제학

5. 지원자는 공인회계사 자격증을 언제 취득했나요?
   ① 2005년　② 2006년
   ③ 2007년　④ 2008년

6. 지원자가 어학연수에 참여한 기간은?
   ① 약 5개월　② 약 10개월
   ③ 약 1년　④ 약 2년

Practice 2 Lecture

01 Personal Information

Name: Sangjin Han

Gender: Male

Date of Birth: October 20, 1980

Marital Status: Married

Address: 57 Mukyo-dong, Jung-gu, Seoul 100-777

Mobile Home) 02-715-****

Cell Phone) 010-5799-****

Email) Han@*****.com

개인정보

① 개인정보에 이름, 생년월일, 주소, 연락처가 기재됩니다.

② 필요에 따라서 성별과 결혼여부를 기재할 수 있습니다.

③ 남성의 경우는 Male, 여성의 경우는 Female로 기재합니다.

④ 기혼인 경우는 Married, 미혼인 경우는 Single로 기재합니다.

02 Job Objective

Management position

희망직종

① Management position: 관리직

② 근무하고 싶은 부서나 담당하고 싶은 업무를 기재할 수 있습니다.

03

Work Experience

March 2006 - February 2013	Hanjin Trade, Seoul Manager, Department of Marketing Responsibilities include sales and advertising
April 2004 - January 2006	Hana Enterprise, Incheon Assistant Manager, Department of Public Relations Responsibilities include advertising and fund raising

경력

① 경력이 많은 경우는 가장 최근 경력부터 과거로 거슬러 올라가며 기재합니다.

어 휘

① Manager : 과장
② Department of Marketing : 마케팅 부
③ Sales and Advertising: 판매와 광고
④ Assistant Manager : 대리
⑤ Department of Public Relations : 홍보부
⑥ Advertising and Fund Raising: 광고와 기금조성

04

Education

March 2002 - February 2004	Graduate School of Kyunghee University, Seoul Major: Business Administration, Master of Business Administration
March 1998 - February 2002	University of Seoul, Seoul Major: English and English Literature

학력

① 대학원 학력을 기재하는 경우는 전공 외에 학위명을 함께 기재합니다.

어 휘

① Graduate School : 대학원
② Master of Business Administration : 경영학 석사
③ English and English Literature : 영어영문학

05 Special Skills

Foreign Language	Fluent in English, Some French
	Scored 940 on the TOEIC
	Scored 900 on the TEPS
Computer	Proficient in Excel and Adobe Photoshop

특기

① 특기에 외국어 능력과 컴퓨터 능력을 기재할 수 있습니다.

구 문 Some + 외국어: 외국어 보통

예문1) Fluent in English, Some Chinese (영어능통, 중국어 보통)

06 Licenses and Certificates

July 2007	Public Account Certification
April 2005	Real Estate Agent License

자격증 및 면허

① 취득한 자격증이나 면허를 기재합니다.

어 휘

① Public Account Certification : 공인회계사

② Real Estate Agent License: 공인중개사

07 Activities

September 2005 - Present	Member of Society of American Studies
March 2001 - February 2002	President of Student Association, University of Seoul
September 1999 - February 2000	Visited Stanford University for a Language Program

활동사항

① 과외 활동을 기재합니다.

어 휘	① Member : 회원 ② Society of American Studies : 미국학 학회 ③ President of Student Association : 총학생회장
구 문	Visited + 학교 + for a Language Program : 어학연수로 ~를 방문함

Practice 2 Vocabulary & Expression

한상진의 이력서에 나왔던 어휘와 구문을 정리해 보겠습니다.

구분	어휘 & 표현	의미
어휘	gender	성별
	male	남성
	martial status	결혼여부
	married	결혼한
	manager	과장
	assistant manager	대리
	public relations	홍보
	fund raising	기금모집
	graduate school	대학원
	master of business administration	경영학석사
	public accountant Certification	공인회계사
	real estate agent license	공인중개사
	member	회원
	student association	총학생회
관용표현	visited + 학교 + for a language program	어학연수로 ~를 방문하다

Practice 2 Task 4

보기에 주어진 정보를 가지고 영문 이력서를 작성해 보세요.

(1) 보기에 주어진 정보를 가지고 영문이력서의 Work Experience를 완성해보세요.

보기	2006년 3월 ~ 2013년 2월	한진무역 근무 과장 판매와 광고업무 담당	서울 마케팅부

⇓

문제	March 2006 ~ ________	________________ ________________ ________________

(2) 보기에 주어진 정보를 가지고 영문이력서의 Education을 완성해보세요.

보기	2002년 3월 ~ 2004년 2월	경희대학교 대학원 전공: 경영학	서울 경영학 석사

⇓

문제	________ ~ February 2004	________________of Kyunghee University, Seoul Major: ________________

(3) 보기에 주어진 정보를 가지고 영문이력서의 Activities를 완성해보세요.

보기		
	2005년 9월 ~현재	미국학 학회 회원
	2006년 6월 ~ 2007년 10월	서울시립대학교 총학생회회장
	2004년 3월 ~ 2005년 2월	어학연수로 스탠포드대학교 방문

⇓

문제		
	September 2005 ~ ________________	________________________________ ________________________________
	June 2006 ~ October 2007	________________________________ ________________________________
	March 2004 ~ Feburary 2005	________________________________ ________________________________

Practice 2 Task 5

제시되어 있는 단어를 배열하여 이력서에 들어가는 형태로 작문하세요. 첫 자는 대문자로 입력하세요.

(1) 영어에 능통, 불어는 조금

in Fluent French Some English ,

( )

(2) 미국학 학회 회원

Society of American Studies member of

( )

(3) 총학생회 회장

Student Association of President

( )

(4) 어학연수로 스탠포드대학교를 방문

for Language Program Stanford University Visited a

( )

Exercise Writing

경력과 학력 사항을 영작해 보겠습니다.

| 경력사항 |

2006년 8월 ~ 2013년 2월	하나기업	서울
	차장	연구개발부
	연구와 개발업무 담당	
2005년 3월 ~ 2006년 7월	삼성전자	서울
	대리	마케팅부
	회계와 재정업무 담당	

학력사항

2004년 3월 ~ 2007년 2월	서울시립대학교 대학원	서울
	전공: 경영학	경영학 석사
1999년 3월 ~ 2003년 2월	서울시립대학교	서울
	전공: 컴퓨터공학	부전공: 경영학

Work Expreience

_____ ~ _____ _____________ _______

_____________ _______

____

_____ ~ _____ _____________ _______

_____________ _______

____

Education

_____ ~ _____ _____________ _______

_____________ _______

_____ ~ _____ _____________ _______

_____________ _______

Exercise You be the editor

아래 이력서를 읽고 틀린 부분을 찾아 고치세요. 밑줄 친 부분을 올바르게 고치세요.

Personal Information

Name: Sangjin Han

Date of Birth: 1980, October 20

Address: 57 Mukyo-dong, Jung-gu, Seoul 100-777

Contact Home) 02-715-****
Cell Phone) 010-5799-****
Email) han@*****.com

Work Experience

March 2006 ~ February 2008	Hanjin Trade, Seoul Assistant Manager, Department of Marketing Responsible includes sales and advertising

Education

March 2002 ~ February 2006	Soongsil University, Seoul Minor: Business Administration, Major: Computer Engineering

Special Skills

Foreign Language	Fluent in English, Some French Scored 940 on the TOEIC Scored 900 on the TEPS
Computer	Proficient with Access, and Internet searching

License and Certificate

July 2007	Certified Public Account Certification
April 2005	Real Estate Agent License

Activities

June 2005 ~ February 2006	President of Student Association, Soongsil University
March 2003 ~ February 2004	Visiting Stanford University for a Language Program

Wrap up
Summary

1. Structure Resume

(1) Personal Information
(2) Job Objective
(3) Work Experience
(4) Education
(5) Special Skills
(6) Licenses and Certificates
(7) Activities

2. Key expressions

(1) Responsibilities include planning and management
(2) Fluent in English and Japanese
(3) Scored 940 on the TOEIC
(4) Proficient in Excel and Adobe Photoshop
(5) Visited UCLA for an Exchange Program

Wrap up

Assignment I

오늘 학습한 주요 문형을 이용하여 문장을 작성하세요.

Responsibilities include ~	~ 업무를 담당하다
Visited + 학교 + for an Exchange Program	교환학생으로 ~학교를 방문함
Visited + 학교 + for a Language Program	어학연수로 ~를 방문함

선택한 표현을 활용하여 '영문(한글)'의 형태로 문장을 입력하세요.

Wrap up

Assignment II

오늘 배운 이력서의 형식에 따라 자신의 이력서를 작성해 봅시다.

Personal Information

Name:

Date of Birth:

Address:

Contact Information

Home)

Mobile Phone)

Email)

Work Experience

Education

Special Skills

Licenses and Certificates

Activities

Answers

Lesson 3. Talking about my life

Warm up

Check up

1) Period — Company — Location
   Job Title — Department
   Job Description
2) Period — School — Location
   Major — Minor
3) ① Fluent in English
   ② Scored 990 on the TOEIC
   ③ Proficient in MS Word
4) • March 2012 ~ February 2013
   • June 2011 ~ February 2012
   • March 2010 ~ May 2011
   • March 2009 ~ February 2010

Practice 1 Comprehension Checkup

1) ② Two
2) ③ 880
3) ② Two
4) ② Two
5) ② Data Processing Engineer Certification, Grade 2

Practice 1 Task 1

1) Personal Information

Name : Sujin Han

Date of Birth : December 5, 1980

Address : 322-1 Yangjae-dong, Seocho-gu, Seoul 157-220

Contact : Home) 02-2174-****

Cell Phone) 010-3910-****

Email) hsj@*****.net

2) March 2009 ~ February 2013 Cyber University of Foreign Studies, Seoul

Major: English, Minor: Business Administration

March 2006 ~ February 2009 Seoul Foregin Language High School, Seoul

Practice 1 Task 2

1) Foreign Language	Fluent in English
	Scored 880 on the TOEIC
	Scored 900 on the TEPS
Computer	Proficient in Adobe Photoshop, and Excel
2) July 2007	Data Processing Engineer Certification, Grade 2
April 2005	Translation Certification, Grade 1

Practice 1 Task 3

1) Responsibilities include planning and management
2) Fluent in English and Japanese
3) Scored 925 on the TOEIC

4) Proficient in Excel and Internet searching
5) Visited UCLA for an Exchange Program

Practice 2 Comprehension Check up

1) ② Management position
2) ① Manager
3) ④ Advertising and fundraising
4) ① English and English Literature
5) ③ In 2007
6) ① About five months

Practice 2 Task 4

1) March 2006 ~ February 2013 Hanjin Trade, Seoul
Manager, Department of Marketing
Responsibilities include sales and advertising

2) March 2002 ~ February 2004 Graduate School of Kyunghee University, Seoul
Major: Business Administration, Master of Business Administration

3) September 2005 ~ Present Member of Society of American Studies
June 2006 ~ October 2007 President of Student Association, University of Seoul
March 2004 ~ February 2005 Visited Stanford University for a Language Program

Practice 2 Task 5

1) Fluent in English, some French
2) Member of Society of American Studies
3) President of Student Association
4) Visited Stanford University for a Language Program

Exercise Writing

Work Experience

August 2006 ~ February 2013	Hana Enterprise, Seoul Senior Manager, Department of Research and Development Responsibilities include research and production
March 2005 ~ July 2006	Samsung Electronics, Seoul Assistant Manager, Department of Marketing Responsibilities include accounting and finance

Education

March 2004 ~ February 2007	Graduate School of University of Seoul, Seoul Major: Business Administration, M.B.A.
March 1999 ~ February 2003	University of Seoul, Seoul Major: Computer Engineering, Minor: Business Administration

Exercise You be the editor

Personal Information

Name : Sangjin Han

Date of Birth : October 20, 1980

Address : 57 Mukyo-dong, Jung-gu, Seoul 100-777

Contact Home) 02-715-****

Cell Phone) 010-5799-****

email) han@*****.com

Work Experience

March 2006 ~ February 2008 Hanjin Trade, Seoul

Assistant Manager, Department of Marketing

Responsibilities(담당업무: Responsibilities) include sales and advertisement

Education

March 2002 ~ February 2006 Soongsil University, Seoul

Major: Computer Engineering,

Minor: Business Administration

(① 전공, ② 부전공)

Special Skills

Foreign Language Fluent in English, Some French

Scored 940 on the TOEIC

Scored 900 on the TEPS

Computer Proficient in (proficient in + 프로그램) Access, Excel, and Internet searching

License and Certificate

July 2007 Certificate of certified public account

April 2005 License of real estate agent

Activities

June 2005 ~ February 2006 President of Student Association, Soongsil University

March 2003 ~ February 2004 Visited (Visited + 학교) Stanford University for a Language Program

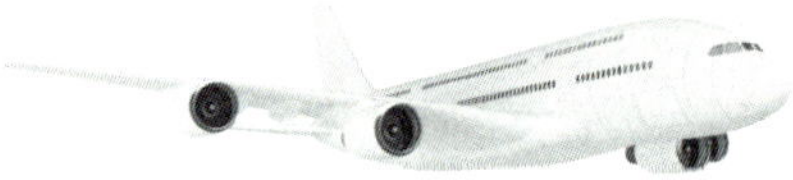

Business
Management
Writing
Basis and Application

Lesson 04

I am the youngest child in my family.

Lesson 04

I am the youngest child in my family.

Introduction

Lesson objectives

1. Writing a letter of self-introduction

• The format of a letter of self-introduction

(1) Personal History

(2) School Days

(3) Strengths and Weaknesses

(4) Career Objectives

2. Key expressions

(1) My family includes my parents, my elder brother, my elder sister, and me.

(2) After graduating from university, I entered graduate school.

(3) My optimistic character helps me to do my best.

(4) I will improve my Japanese until I achieve a score of 800 on the JPT.

Warm up

The format of a letter of self-introduction

자기소개서를 작성하기 전에 자기소개서의 구조에 대해서 알아보겠습니다.

Letter of Self-Introduction

Personal Information

Soojin Kim
281 Wolgye-dong, Nowon-gu, Seoul 139-050
Tel : 02-478-****
Cell Phone : 010-3268-****
E-mail : shn@*****.com

Personal History

School Days

Strengths and Weaknesses

Career Objectives

Personal Information (개인정보)

- 이름, 주소, 연락처를 기재
- 이름 : 이름 + 성
- 주소 : ① 번지, ② 동(-dong), ③ 구(-gu), ④ 시, ⑤ 우편번호
- 연락처 : ① 전화, ② 휴대전화, ③ Email

Personal History (성장과정)

- Family background: (1) 가족구성원, (2) 가족 내에서의 자신의 위치
- Unique aspects of childhood: (1) 성장과정 속에서의 자신의 특징

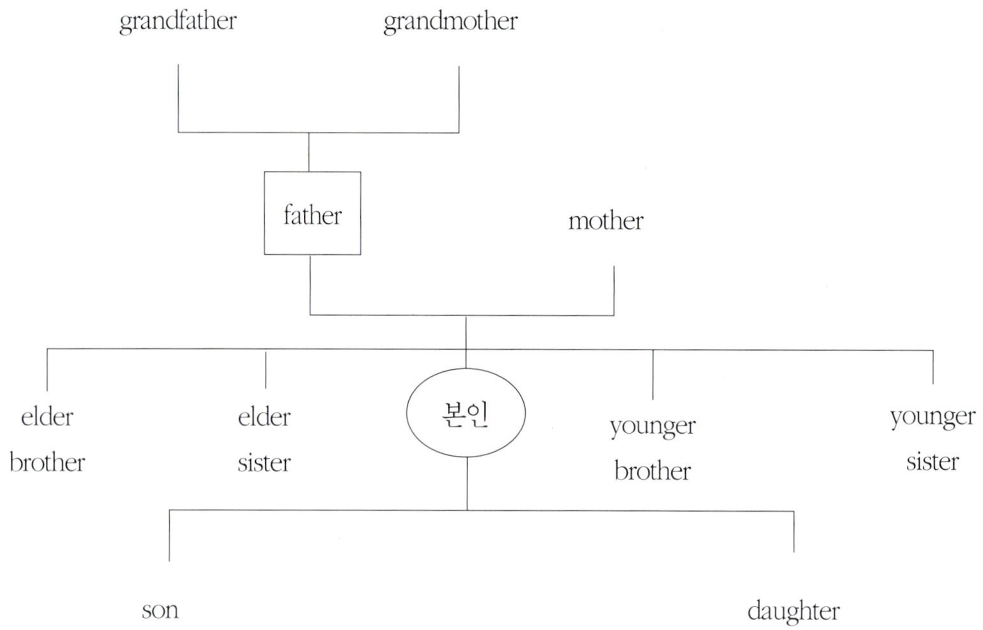

School Days (학창시절)

- High school life : 대표적으로 고등학교의 학창시절 기재
- College life : 주로 좋아했던 과목이나 관심분야에 대해 기재

(과목명)

English: 영어, Ethics: 윤리, Math: 수학, Korean History: 한국사
Korean: 국어, World History: 세계사, Biology: 생물, Geography: 지리
Chemistry: 화학, Music: 음악, Physics: 물리, Physical Education: 체육
Earth Science: 지구과학, Art: 미술, Social Studies: 사회

(전공별 1 – 어문학 전공)

영어영문학: English and English Literature
일어일문학: Japanese and Japanese Literature
불어불문학: French and French Literature
독어독문학: German and German Literature
중어중문학: Chinese and Chinese Literature

(전공별 2 – 사회과학 전공)

경제학: Economics
경영학: Business Administration
행정학: Public Administration
정치학: Political Science
법학: Law

(전공별 3 - 사범계열)

영어교육: English Education
불어교육: French Education
독어교육: German Education
한국어교육: Korean Education

(전공별 4 - 자연과학)

수학: Math
물리학: Physics
생물학: Biology
미생물학: Microbiology
화학: Chemistry

(전공별 5 - 공학)

건축공학: Architectural Engineering
컴퓨터공학: Computer Engineering
환경공학: Environmental Engineering

Strengths and Weaknesses (장점과 단점)

- 성격적인 측면 언급
- 단점을 기술할 경우는 단점을 극복하기 위해서 어떠한 노력을 했는지를 명시

(성격을 나타내는 표현들)

outgoing, extrovert(외향적인) ↔ introvert, reserved (내성적인)
active(적극적인) ↔ passive(소극적인)
optimistic(낙천적인) ↔ pessimistic(비관적인)
progressive(진취적인) ↔ conservative(보수적인)
good-natured(성격이 좋은) ↔ hard to please, picky(성격이 까다로운)
sociable(사교적인) ↔ nonsociable(비사교적인)
open-minded(포용력이 넓은) ↔ narrow-minded(포용력이 좁은)
realistic(현실적인) ↔ idealistic(이상적인)
positive(긍정적인) ↔ negative(부정적인)
caring(배려심이 있는) ↔ selfish(이기적인)
honest(정직한) ↔ dishonest(부정직한)
egocentric(자기중심적인) ↔ altruistic, selfless(이타적인)
cooperative(협력적인) ↔ noncooperative(비협력적인)

Career Objectives (발전계획 및 포부)

- 입사 후 자신의 발전을 위해서 어떠한 계획을 가지고 있는지를 명시

Warm up
Checkup

자기소개서의 구조와 내용에 대한 다음 문제를 풀어보겠습니다.

1. 보기에 제시된 개인정보에 관한 사항을 순서에 맞게 적어 보세요.

보기	① Email : jks2013@*****.net ② 233Yonghyun-dong, Nam-gu, Incheon, 402-753 ③ Park Minsoo ④ Tel : 032-887-**** ⑤ Cell Phone : 010-3358-****

A:________________________________

B:________________________________

C:________________________________

D:________________________________

E:________________________________

2. 다음 영문 자기소개서의 내용을 잘 읽고 각 내용에 해당하는 소제목을 넣으세요.

보기	Career Objectives Personal History Strengths and Weaknesses

A. [   ]

My family includes my parents, my younger brother, my younger sister, and me. I am the eldest son in my family. As the eldest son in the family, I was home-educated to be a responsible person.

B. [ ]

I try to have a good character. I always try to help people around me. On the other hand, I depend on others for making decisions. So I am trying to be an independent person.

C. [ ]

I will improve my English and Japanese until I become a fluent speaker of English and Japanese. I will work hard to develop more competitive products for the company.

Practice 1 Comprehension Check up

Personal History
My family includes my parents, my elder brother, my elder sister, and me. I am the youngest child in my family. I was home-educated to work well in a team environment. So since childhood I have been getting along with others.

School Days
In high school, biology and chemistry were my favorite subjects. I was more interested in biology than in chemistry. Because of my interest in biology, I majored in biology at university. After graduating from university I entered graduate school and majored in microbiology.

1. How many members are there in the applicant's family?
   ① Three
   ② Four
   ③ Five
   ④ Six

2. How many siblings does the applicant have?

① Two
② Three
③ Four
④ Five

3. What is the applicant's character like?

① Independent
② Realistic
③ Cooperative
④ Egocentric

4. What subjects did the applicant like in high school? (Choose two)

① Biology
② Chemistry
③ Biochemistry
④ Microbiology

5. What did the applicant study at university?

① Biology
② Microbiology
③ Chemistry
④ Biochemistry

6. What did the applicant study in graduate school?

① Biology
② Microbiology
③ Chemistry
④ Biochemistry

성장과정
나의 가족은 부모님, 형, 누나, 그리고 저입니다. 저는 집안에서 막내아들입니다. 저는 단체 환경에서 잘 일할 수 있도록 가정교육을 받았습니다. 그래서 어려서부터 다른 사람들과 잘 지내왔습니다.

학창시절
고등학교 때 생물학과 화학은 내가 좋아 했던 과목이었습니다. 화학보다는 생물에 더 관심이 있었습니다. 생물에 대한 관심 때문에 나는 대학에서 생물학을 전공했습니다. 대학 졸업 후 대학원에 진학해서 미생물학을 전공했습니다.

1. 지원자는 가족이 몇 명입니까?
① 세 명 ② 네 명 ③ 다섯 명 ④ 여섯 명

2. 지원자는 형제자매가 몇 명입니까?
① 두 명 ② 세 명 ③ 네 명 ④ 다섯 명

3. 지원자는 어떠한 성격입니까?
① 독립적인 ② 현실적인 ③ 협력적인 ④ 자기중심적인

4. 지원자는 고등학교 때 어떠한 과목을 좋아했습니까? (둘을 고르시오)
① 생물학 ② 화학 ③ 미생물학 ④ 생화학

5. 지원자는 대학에서 무엇을 공부했습니까?
① 생물학 ② 미생물학 ③ 화학 ④ 생화학

6. 지원자는 대학원에서 무엇을 공부했습니까?
① 생물학 ② 미생물학 ③ 화학 ④ 생화학

Practice 1 Lecture

자기소개서에 나왔던 문장에 대한 강의 입니다.

01 **My family includes my parents, my elder brother, my elder sister, and me.**

저의 가족은 저의 부모님, 형, 누나, 그리고 저입니다.

어 휘

① parents : 부모님

예문1) My parents are generous.
(나의 부모님은 관대하시다.)

② elder brother : 형, 오빠

예문1) He is my elder brother.
(그는 나의 형이다/그는 나의 오빠다.)

③ elder sister : 누나, 언니

예문1) She is my elder sister.
(그녀는 나의 누나다/그녀는 나의 언니다.)

구 문

① My family includes + 가족구성원 : 저의 가족은 ~로 되어있다

예문1) My family includes my father, my mother, and me.
(저의 가족은 아버지, 어머니, 그리고 저입니다.)

02 **I am the youngest child in my family.**

저는 집안에서 막내입니다.

어 휘

① the youngest child : 막내

예문1) He is the youngest child in his family.
(그는 자신의 집안에서 막내이다.)

03 I was home-educated to work well in a team environment.

저는 단체 환경에서 일을 잘 하도록 가정교육을 받았습니다.

어 휘 ① team environment : 단체 환경

예문1) She works well in a team environment.
(그녀는 단체 환경에서 일을 잘한다.)

구 문 ① 주어 + be + home-educated + to-부정사 : ~하도록 가정교육을 받다

예문1) She was home-educated to be an honest person.
(그녀는 정직한 사람이 되도록 가정교육을 받았습니다.)

04 So since childhood I have been getting along with others.

그래서 유년시절부터 저는 다른 사람들과 잘 지내왔습니다.

어 휘 ① so : 그래서

예문1) He was honest, so I lent him money.
(그는 정직했다. 그래서 나는 그에게 돈을 빌려줬다.)

② since : ~이래로, ~부터

③ childhood : 유년시절

④ get along with : ~와 잘 지내다

구 문 ① since + 과거 + 주어 + have + been + 동사-ing : ~이래로 ~해왔다

예문1) Since 2002 I have been studying English.
(2002년부터 나는 영어를 공부해왔다.)

05 In high school, biology and chemistry were my favorite subjects.

고등학교 때 생물과 화학은 제가 좋아하는 과목이었습니다.

어 휘 ① biology : 생물, 생물학

② chemistry : 화학

③ favorite : 좋아하는, 자기취향인

예문1) Tom Cruise is my favorite movie actor.
(톰크루즈는 내가 좋아하는 영화배우다.)

④ subject : 과목

예문1) Math is a difficult subject.
(수학은 어려운 과목이다.)

06 I was more interested in biology than in chemistry.

저는 화학보다는 생물에 더 관심이 있었습니다.

어 휘

① interested in : 관심 있는

예문1) She was very interested in music.
(그녀는 음악에 매우 관심이 있었다.)

구 문

① more A than B : B 보다 더 A하나

예문1) She was more interested in music than in art.
(그녀는 미술보다는 음악에 더 관심이 있었다.)

07 Because of my interest in biology, I majored in biology at university.

생물에 대한 관심 때문에 저는 대학에서 생물학을 전공했습니다.

어 휘

① because of : ~때문에

예문1) Because of the rain, I came back.
(비 때문에 나는 돌아왔다.)

② major in : ~을 전공하다

예문1) He majored in English Education at university.
(그는 대학에서 영어교육을 전공했다.)

08

After graduating from university, I entered graduate school and majored in microbiology.

대학을 졸업한 후 저는 대학원에 입학해서 미생물학을 전공했습니다.

어 휘

① enter : ~에 입학하다

예문1) She entered the university at the age of 19.
(그녀는 19세에 대학에 입학했습니다.)

② graduate school : 대학원

예문1) She attends graduate school.
(그녀는 대학원에 다닌다.)

③ microbiology : 미생물학

구 문

① after graduating from : ~를 졸업한 후

예문1) After graduating from high school, I entered the university.
(고등학교를 졸업 한 후 나는 대학에 입학했다.)

Practice 1 Vocabulary & Expression

이력서에 나왔던 어휘와 관용표현을 정리해 보겠습니다.

구분	어휘 & 표현	의미
어휘	elder brother	형, 오빠
	elder sister	언니, 누나
	the youngest child	막내
	cooperative	협력적인
	so	그래서
	childhood	유년시절
	team environment	단체 환경
	favorite	좋아하는
	subject	과목
	enter	입학하다
	major in	~을 진공하다
	minor in	~을 부전공하다
구문	My family includes + 가족구성원	저희 가족은 ~로 되어있다
	주어 + be + home-educated + to -부정사	~하도록 가정교육을 받다
	since + 과거시점 + 주어 + have + been + 동사-ing	~이래로 ~해왔다
	주어 + be + interested in ~	~에 관심이 있다
	After graduating from ~	~을 졸업한 후

Practice 1 Task 1

보기에 있는 단어를 이용하여 문장을 완성하세요. 필요한 경우 단어의 형태를 변형시켜 보세요.

보기	since include home-educate young

(1) My family ( ) my parents, my elder brother, my elder sister, and me.
(2) I am the ( ) child in my family.
(3) I was ( ) to work well in a team environment.
(4) So ( ) childhood I have been getting along with others.

Practice 1 Task 2

빈칸에 해당하는 표현을 입력하여 문장을 완성하세요.

(1) 고등학교 때 생물과 화학은 제가 좋아하는 과목이었습니다.
In high school, biology and chemistry were my ( )( ).

(2) 저는 화학보다는 생물에 더 관심이 있었습니다.
I was ( ) interested in biology ( ) in chemistry.

(3) 생물에 대한 관심 때문에 저는 대학에서 생물을 전공했습니다.
Because of my interest in biology I ( )( ) biology at university.

(4) 대학을 졸업한 후에 저는 대학원에 진학하여 미생물을 전공했습니다.
After ( )( ) the university, I ( ) graduate school and majored in microbiology.

Coffee break

Fox hunting

Fox hunting is one of the oldest and one of the most controversial sporting practices in the English-speaking world. For centuries, people in the countryside have considered foxes to be pests that attack their livestock and have hunted them in order to reduce their numbers. Traditionally, in the UK and other countries, foxes have been hunted by hunters on horseback, who wear special red jackets and black riding caps, and are accompanied by 'foxhounds', which are dogs specially bred and kept for this purpose. The hunt is led by the Master of foxhounds, and there is a great deal of tradition and ritual involved in fox hunting. Hunting foxes with hounds spread from England to other parts of the English speaking world, reaching America sometime around 1650.

The fox hounds have an excellent sense of smell, and it is this that enables them to pick up the scent of a fox. They are especially bred for the purpose of hunting. There are only very slight differences between English foxhounds and American foxhounds.

Supporters of fox hunting say that it is necessary to keep down the pest population and that it is not as cruel as shooting foxes because the foxes that are hunted in this way always have a chance of escaping. However, critics see it as extremely cruel. In particular, many critics are horrified by the idea of an exhausted and terrified fox being caught and torn to pieces by the fox hounds. Although hunting foxes with hounds originated in the UK, it was banned by the British government in 2004. Fox hunting is still legal in the United States, but it is no longer a very common practice.

Coffee break

여우사냥

여우사냥은 영어권세계에서 가장 오래되고 가장 논쟁의 여지가 많은 스포츠 활동 중의 하나다. 수세기 동안 시골에 사는 사람들은 여우를 가축을 공격하는 해로운 존재로 생각해왔으며 여우의 수를 줄이기 위해서 여우를 사냥해왔다. 전통적으로 영국과 영국 외의 다른 나라에서 여우는 말을 타고 사냥하는 사냥꾼에 의해서 사냥되어져 왔다. 이 사냥꾼들은 특별한 붉은 잠바와 검은 승마용 모자를 착용했으며 사냥목적으로 특별히 사육한 여우사냥개들을 데리고 사냥을 하였다. 사냥은 여우사냥개들의 주인이 주도한다. 여우사냥과 관련된 많은 전통과 의식이 있다. 사냥개를 이용하여 여우를 사냥하는 관행은 영국에서 영어권세계의 다른 지역으로 확산되었으며 1650년 무렵에는 미국에까지 확산되었다.

여우사냥개들은 후각이 아주 뛰어나며 이 후각 때문에 여우의 냄새를 감지할 수 있다. 이들은 특히 사냥의 목적을 위해서 사육되어진다. 영국여우사냥개와 미국여우사냥개는 단지 매우 근소한 차이만 있을 뿐이다.

여우사냥을 지지하는 사람들은 해를 끼치는 존재의 수를 줄일 필요가 있으며 여우를 사냥하는 것은 여우가 도망갈 수 있다는 점에서 여우를 사살하는 것보다 덜 잔인하다고 말한다. 하지만 비평가들은 여우사냥이 매우 잔인하다고 생각한다. 특히 많은 비평가들은 지치고 공포에 질린
여우가 사냥개들에게 잡혀 갈기갈기 물어뜯기는 것을 생각하면 경악을 금치 못한다. 비록 사냥개를 이용하여 여우를 사냥하는 것이 영국에서 시작되었지만 2004년에 영국정부에 의해서 금지되었다. 미국에서는 여우사냥이 여전히 합법적이다. 그러나 더 이상 매우 흔한 스포츠 활동은 아니다.

Practice 2 Comprehension Check up

자기소개서의 뒷부분을 읽고 질문에 답을 선택하세요.

Strengths and Weaknesses

I am an egocentric person. But I am also an outgoing and optimistic person. My optimistic character helps me to do my best in everything I do.

Career Objectives

I will improve my English until I achieve a score of 900 on the TOEIC. And I will improve my Japanese until I achieve a score of 880 on the JPT. In addition, I will work hard to make better products for the company.

1. What is the applicant's weak point?
   ① Being an egocentric person
   ② Being an outgoing person
   ③ Being an optimistic person
   ④ Doing his best in everything he does

2. What is the applicant's strong point?
   ① Being an egocentric person
   ② Being an outgoing and optimistic person
   ③ Being an egocentric and outgoing person
   ④ Helping others to do their best

3. How can the applicant overcome his weak point?
   ① By trying to be considerate of others
   ② By doing his best in everything he does
   ③ By trying to be more pessimistic
   ④ By trying to be more egocentric

4. What plan does the applicant have for his English?

① Achieve a better score on the TOEIC
② Achieve a better score on the JPT
③ Achieve a better score on the TOEIC and the JPT
④ Go abroad to study English

5. What plan does the applicant have for his Japanese?

① Achieve a better score on the TOEIC
② Achieve a better score on the JPT
③ Achieve a better score on the TOEIC and the JPT
④ Produce better products

6. What plan does the applicant have for the company?

① Achieve a better score on the TOEIC
② Achieve a better score on the JPT
③ Achieve a better score on the TOEIC and the JPT
④ Produce better products

장점과 단점

저는 자기중심적인 사람입니다. 그러나 저는 또한 외향적이고 적극적인 사람입니다. 저의 적극적인 성격은 제가 하는 모든 일에서 저의 최선을 다하도록 도와줍니다.

발전계획 및 포부

저는 토익에서 900점을 받을 때 까지 저의 영어실력을 향상시킬 것입니다. 그리고 저는 JPT에서 880점을 받을 때까지 저의 일본어실력을 향상시키겠습니다. 뿐만 아니라 저는 회사를 위해 더 좋은 제품을 만들기 위해서 열심히 일하겠습니다.

1. 지원자의 약점은 무엇입니까?
   ① 자기중심적인 사람이라는 것
   ② 외향적인 사람이라는 것
   ③ 낙천적인 사람이라는 것
   ④ 모든 일에 최선을 다하는 것

2. 지원자의 장점은 무엇입니까?
   ① 자기중심적인 사람이라는 것
   ② 외향적이고 낙천적인 사람이라는 것
   ③ 자기중심적이며 외향적인 사람이라는 것
   ④ 다른 사람이 최선을 다하도록 돕는 것

3. 지원자는 자신의 약점을 어떻게 극복할 수 있습니까?
   ① 다른 사람을 더 배려하도록 노력함으로써
   ② 모든 일에 최선을 다함으로써
   ③ 더 낙천적인 사람이 되도록 노력함으로써
   ④ 더 자기중심적인 사람이 되도록 노력함으로써

4. 지원자는 자신의 영어실력을 위해서 어떠한 계획을 가지고 있습니까?
   ① 토익에서 더 좋은 점수를 받기
   ② JPT에서 더 좋은 점수를 받기
   ③ 토익과 JPT에서 더 좋은 점수를 받기
   ④ 더 좋은 제품 생산하기

5. 지원자는 자신의 일본어실력을 위해서 어떠한 계획을 가지고 있습니까?
① 토익에서 더 좋은 점수를 받기
② JPT에서 더 좋은 점수를 받기
③ 토익과 JPT에서 더 좋은 점수를 받기
④ 일본어를 공부하기 위해서 해외로 가기

6. 지원자는 회사를 위해서 어떠한 계획을 가지고 있습니까?
① 토익에서 더 좋은 점수를 받기
② JPT에서 더 좋은 점수를 받기
③ 토익과 JPT에서 더 좋은 점수를 받기
④ 더 좋은 제품을 생산하기

Practice 2 Lecture

01

I am an egocentric person.

저는 자기중심적인 사람입니다.

어 휘

① egocentric : 자기중심적인

예문1) He is an egocentric person.
(그는 자기중심적인 사람이다.)

02

But I am also an outgoing and optimistic person.

그러나 저는 또한 외향적이고 낙천적인 사람입니다.

어 휘

① outgoing : 외향적인

예문1) Her son is an outgoing boy.
(그녀의 아들은 외향적인 소년이다.)

② optimistic : 낙천적인

예문1) He should be more optimistic to overcome his weaknesses.
(그는 자신의 약점을 극복하기 위해서 더 낙천적이어야 한다.)

03

My optimistic character helps me to do my best in everything I do.

저의 낙천적인 성격은 제가 하는 모든 일에 최선을 다하도록 도움을 줍니다.

어 휘

① character : 성격

예문1) My father has a good character.
(나의 아버지는 성격이 좋으시다.)

② do one's best : 최선을 다하다

예문1) He always does his best.

(그는 항상 최선을 다한다.)

구 문

① 주어 + help + 목석어 + to-부정사 :~가 ~하도록 돕다

예문1) We should help her to do her best even in a difficult situation.

(우리는 그녀가 어려운 상황에서도 최선을 다하도록 도와야 한다.)

04

I will improve my English until I achieve a score of 900 on the TOEIC.

저는 토익에서 900점을 받을 때까지 저의 영어실력을 향상시키겠습니다.

어 휘

① improve : 향상시키다

예문1) Money improves the quality of life.

(돈은 삶의 질을 향상시킨다.)

② until : ~까지

예문1) He will not start until she comes.

(그는 그녀가 올 때까지 출발하지 않을 것이다.)

③ achieve : 성취하다

예문1) She wants to achieve a score of 700 on the TEPS.

(그녀는 텝스 700점을 받고 싶어 한다.)

05

And I will improve my Japanese until I achieve a score of 880 on the JPT.

그리고 저는 JPT에서 880점을 받을 때까지 저의 일본어실력을 향상시키겠습니다.

어 휘

① JPT(Japaness Proficiency Test): 일본어 능력 시험

예문1) She achieved a score of 800 on the JPT.

(그녀는 일본어 능력 시험에서 800점을 받았다.)

06 **In addition, I will work hard to make better products for the company.**

뿐만 아니라 저는 회사를 위해 더 좋은 제품을 만들기 위해서 열심히 일하겠습니다.

어 휘

① In addition : 뿐만 아니라

예문1) I don't want to go out for a jog. In addition, I am too tired.

(나는 조깅하려 나가고 싶지 않다. 게다가 나는 너무 피곤하다.)

② products : 제품

예문1) The new product is better than the old one.

(새로운 제품이 이전 제품보다 더 좋다.)

Practice 2 Vocabulary & Expression

자기소개에 나왔던 어휘와 구문을 정리해 보겠습니다.

구분	어휘 & 표현	의미
어휘	egocentric	자기중심적인
	outgoing	외향적인
	ambitious	야심 있는
	character	성격
	improve	향상시키다.
	until	~까지
	achieve	성취하다.
	JPT	일본어 능력 시험
	In addition	뿐만 아니라
	products	제품
구문	주어 + help + 목적어 + to-부정사	~가 최선을 다하도록 돕다. 주어가 목적어가 ~하는데 도움을 주다.

Practice 2 Task 3

빈칸에 해당하는 표현을 입력하여 문장을 완성하세요.

(1) 저는 자기중심적인 사람입니다.

I am an (　　　　　　) person.

(2) 그러나 저는 또한 외형적이고 낙천적인 사람입니다.

But I am also an (　　　　　) and (　　　　　) person.

(3) 저의 낙천적인 성격은 제가 하는 모든 일에 최선을 다하도록 도움을 줍니다.

My optimistic (　　) (　　) me to do my (　　) in everything I do.

Practice 2 Task 4

제시되어 있는 단어를 배열하여 올바른 문장을 만들어 보세요.

(1) 저는 토익에서 900점을 받을 때 까지 저의 영어실력을 향상시키겠습니다.

improve will I my English until I achieve a
score of 900 on the TOEIC

( )

(2) 저는 JPT에서 800을 받을 때까지 저의 일본어 실력을 향상 시키겠습니다.

improve will I my Japaness until I achieve a
score of 800 on the JPT

( )

(3) 게다가 저는 회사를 위해서 더 좋은 소프트웨어를 만들기 위해서 열심히 일하겠습니다.

in addition to will produce I hard
work software better for the company

( )

Exercise Writing

자기소개서를 영작해 보겠습니다.

▎유년시절 (Personal History) ▎

저의 가족은 저의 아버지, 어머니, 그리고 저입니다. 저는 저의 집안에서 막내입니다.(or 저는 저의 집안에서 외동 아들/딸입니다.) 저는 협력적인 사람이 되도록 가정교육을 받았습니다. 그래서 저는 다른 사람을 도우려고 항상 노력합니다.

▎학창시절(School Days) ▎

고등학교 때 저는 영문학에 관심이 있었습니다. 영어와 불어는 제가 좋아하는 과목이었습니다.
저는 고등학교를 졸업한 후 고려대학교에 입학했습니다. 영문학을 전공했고 불문학을 부전공 했습니다.

▌장점과 단점(Strengths and Weaknesses)▐

저는 외향적이고 낙천적인 사람입니다. 저는 항상 모든일의 긍정적인 면을 보려고 노력합니다. 저의 낙천적인 성격은 제가 하는 모든 일에서 최선을 다하도록 도와줍니다.

▌발전계획 및 포부(Career Objectives)▐

토익에서 970점을 받을 때까지 영어를 향상시키겠습니다. 그리고 회사를 위해 더 경쟁력 있는 제품을 만들기 위해서 열심히 일하겠습니다.

Exercise You be the editor

다음 일기를 읽고 밑줄친 부분을 올바르게 고치세요.

Personal History
I am the youngest daughter in my family. My parents educated me to be an active and progressive person. So since childhood I <u>have been done</u> my best in everything I do.

School Days
In high school I <u>was interesting</u> in math. Math and Physics were my favorite subjects. <u>After graduated</u> from high school I entered Korea University. I majored in Math Education and minored in Computer Education.

Strengths and Weaknesses
I am an optimistic person. My optimistic character helps me <u>doing</u> my best. I always try looking at the bright side of things. On the other hand, I depend on others for making decisions. So I try to be an independent person.

Career Objectives
I will improve my English until I achieve a score of 950 with the TOEIC. And I will improve my Japanese until I achieve a score of 800 <u>at the JPT</u>. In addition, I will work hard to make more competitive products for the company.

Wrap up

Summary

1. The format of a letter of self-introduction

(1) Personal History
(2) School Days
(3) Strengths and Weaknesses
(4) Career Objectives

2. Key expressions

(1) My family includes my parents, my elder brother, my elder sister, and me.
(2) After graduating from university, I entered graduate school.
(3) My optimistic character helps me to do my best.
(4) I will improve my Japanese until I achieve a score of 800 on the JPT.

Wrap up

Assignment I

My family includes + 가족구성원	저의 가족은 ~로 되어있다.
주어 + be + home-educated + to + 동사	~하도록 가정교육을 받다.
since + 과거 + 주어 + have + been + 동사-ing	~이래로 ~해왔다.
주어 + be + one + of + 복수명사	~중에 하나다
주어 + be + interested in ~	~에 관심이 있다.
After graduating from ~	~을/를 졸업한 후
주어 + help + 목적어 + to do one's best	~가 최선을 다하도록 돕다.

Answers

Lesson 4. I am the youngest child in my family.

Warm up

Check up

1) A. Minsoo Park
   B. 233 Yonghyun-dong, Nam-gu, Incheon, 402-753
   C. Tel: 032-887-****
   D. Cell Phone: 010-3358-****
   E. Email: jks2013@*****.net
2) A. Personal History
   B. Strengths and Weaknesses
   C. Carrer Objectives

Practice 1 Comprehension Check up

1) ③ Five
2) ① Two
3) ③ Cooperative
4) ① Biology ② Chemistry
5) ① Biology
6) ② Microbiology

Practice 1 Task 1

1) My family includes my parents, my elder brother, my elder sister, and me.
2) I am the youngest daughter in my family.
3) I was home-educated to work well in a team environment.
4) So since childhood I have been getting along with others.

Practice 1 Task 2

1) In high school, biology and chemistry were my favorite subjects.
2) I was more interested in biology than in chemistry.
3) Because of my interest in biology I majored in biology at university.
4) After graduating from the university, I entered graduate school and majored in microbiology.

Practice 2 Comprehension Check up

1) ① Being an egocentric person
2) ② Being an outgoing and optimistic person
3) ① By trying to be considerate of others
4) ① achieve a better score on the TOEIC
5) ② Achieve a better score on the JPT
6) ④ Produce better products

Practice 2 Task 3

1) I am an egocentric person.
2) But I am also an outgoing and optimistic person.
3) My optimistic character helps me to do my best in everything I do.

Practice 2 Task 4

1) I will improve my English until I achieve a score of 900 on the TOEIC.
2) I will improve my Japanese until I achieve a score of 800 on the JPT.
3) In addition, I will work hard to produce better software for the company.

Exercise Writing

Personal History

My family includes my father, my mother, and me.
I am the youngest child in my family.
I was home-educated to be a cooperative person.
So I always try to help others.

School Days

In high school I was interested in English literature.
English and French were my favorite subjects.
After graduating from high school, I entered Korea University.
I majored in English literature and minored in French Literature.

Strengths and Weaknesses

I am an outgoing and optimistic person.

I always try to look at the bright side of things.

My optimistic character helps me to do my best in everything I do.

Career Objectives

I will improve my English until I achieve a score of 970 on the TOEIC.

And I will work hard to make more competitive products for the company.

Exercise You be the editor

Personal History

I am the youngest daughter in my family. My parents educated me to be an active and progressive person. So since childhood I have been doing (have been +동사-ing: 과거부터 지금까지 계속 ~하다) my best in everything I do.

School Days

In high school I was interested (be interested in: ~관심이 있다) in math. Math and Physics were my favorite subjects. After graduating (after graduating from: ~을/를 졸업 한 후) from high school I entered Korea University. I majored in Math Education and minored in Computer Education.

Strengths and Weaknesses

I am an optimistic person. My optimistic character helps me to do (help+목적어+to 부정사: ~가 ~하는 것을 돕다) my best. I always try **to look** (try to + 동사원형: ~하려고 노력하다) at the bright side of things. On the other hand, I depend on others for making decisions. So I try to be an independent person.

Career Objectives

I will improve my English until I achieve a score of 950 on the TOEIC. And I will improve my Japanese until I achieve a score of 800 on (on + the + 시험) the JPT. In addition, I will work hard to make more competitive products for the company.

Lesson 05

I am interested in the position of a secretary.

Lesson 05

I am interested in the position of a secretary.

Introduction

Lesson objectives

1. Writing a job application letter

2. Learning expressions for job applications
   (1) I am interested in the secretary position.
   (2) I am writing to apply for the account position at your company.
   (3) I would like to schedule an interview with you.
   (4) I look forward to discussing this position with you.

Warm up

The format of a job application letter

지원서를 작성하기 전에 지원서의 구조에 대해서 먼저 알아보겠습니다.

223 Yonghun-dong, Nam-gu
Incheon 402-751

March 27, 2013

Mr. Minsoo Kim
Manager, Department of Human Resources
New World Corporation
275 Yeoksam-dong, Gangnam-gu
Seoul 823-333

Dear Mr. Kim:

I am interested in the secretary position which was advertised in the Dong-a daily newspaper on March 12. I have enclosed my resume.
I hope that my application will be of interest to you. I would like to schedule an interview with you. I look forward to hearing from you soon.

Sincerely,

Haemin Park

Haemin Park

Enclosure

① 발신인주소

지원서를 보내는 사람의 주소를 입력합니다. 영문주소이므로 번지 + 동, 구, 시, 우편번호, 국가(국제우편인 경우)를 기재합니다.

② 날짜

지원서를 작성하는 날짜를 기재합니다. 날짜를 기재할 때는 월 + 일, 연도를 기재합니다.

③ 수신인주소

수신인 주소는 수신인, 직책, 부서, 회사, 번지 + 동, 구, 시, 우편번호, 그리고 국가 (국제우편인 경우)를 기재합니다.

수신인의 성별	수신인 기재
남성	Mr. + 이름 + 성
기혼 여성	Mrs. + 이름 + 성
미혼 여성	Miss + 이름 +성
기혼 또는 미혼 여성	Ms. + 이름 + 성

④ 인사

지원서의 인사는 격식체 인사를 사용합니다.

수신인의 성별	인사
남성	Dear Mr. + 성:
기혼 여성	Dear Mrs. + 성:
미혼 여성	Dear Miss + 성:
기혼 또는 미혼 여성	Dear Ms. + 성:

⑤ 본문

(1) 지원자가 관심을 가지고 있거나 지원하고 싶은 직무,
(2) 동봉한 서류,
(3) 자신의 업무능력 또는 경력 등을 기재할 수 있습니다.

⑥ 끝인사

지원서의 끝인사는 격식체를 사용합니다.
EX〉 Sincerely, Sincerely yours, Cordially, Cordially yours,

⑦ 서명

지원서를 쓰는 사람의 서명을 기재합니다.

⑧ 이름

지원서를 쓰는 사람의 이름을 기재합니다.

⑨ 동봉물

지원서와 함께 보내는 동봉물을 언급합니다. 동봉물에는 이력서, 추천서 등이 있습니다.

Warm up

Checkup

동봉물에 지원서의 구조와 내용에 대한 다음 문제를 풀어 보세요.

1. 보기에 주어진 각 항목을 이용하여 빈 칸을 채워보세요.

보기	Inside address Return address Name Signature Date

A.____________________

B.____________________

C.____________________

Greeting
Body
Closing

D.____________________

E.____________________

2. 다음 주어진 각 표현과 어울리는 지원서의 구성을 찾아 적어 보세요.

보기	Date Closing Signature Greeting

1) Dear Mr. Kim: ____________________

2) Sincerely, ____________________

3) Haemin Park ____________________

4) March 27, 2008 ____________________

3. 다음 지원서의 항목을 우리말 명칭으로 적어보세요.

1) Return address ____________________

2) Inside address ____________________

3) Enclosure ____________________

Practice 1 Comprehension Check up

다음 지원서를 읽고 질문에 대한 답을 선택한 후 확인 버튼을 클릭하세요.

52-4 Myongryoon-dong
Chongno-gu, Seoul 110-521

March 26, 2013

Mrs. Misoon Park
Assistant Manager, Department of Human Resources
Hanmi Corporation 155 Angug-dong, Chongno-ku
Seoul 110-240

Dear Mrs. Park:

I am interested in the secretary position at your company, and I would like to apply for that position. I am currently employed by New World Agency, but now I am seeking a new position. I believe that my experience and qualifications make me perfect for this job.

I am a quick typist and I am very familiar with all the software programs such as Word, Hangul and PowerPoint. Also, I am a neat and very well organized person. I feel sure that I will be able to cope with any secretarial duties at your company.

I am a reliable and trustworthy person. I am sure that you will not regret giving me this position. I am enclosing my resume with this letter.

I would like to discuss this position with you, so please feel free to contact me at any time.

Cordially yours,

Soyoung Kim

Soyoung Kim

Enclosure

1. What position does the writer apply for?
   ① The secretary position
   ② The accountant position
   ③ The management position
   ④ The clerk position

2. What company does the writer currently work for?
   ① Hanmi Corporation
   ② New World Agency
   ③ New World Corporation
   ④ New World Travel

3. Which of the following is not mentioned as the writer's strong point?
   ① Being a quick typist
   ② Being familiar with software programs
   ③ Being a neat and well organized person
   ④ Being a cooperative person

4. What has the writer enclosed with the letter?
   ① Resume
   ② Receipt
   ③ Photos
   ④ Check

5. What kind of the person does the writer say she is?

① Reliable and trustworthy person

② Quick person

③ Cooperative person

④ Strong-willed person

서울 종로구
명륜동 52-4번지 110-521

2013년 3월 26일

서울 종로구
안국동 155번지 110-240
한미 코퍼레이션
인사부 박미순 대리

박대리님께

저는 당신 회사의 비서직에 관심이 있습니다. 그 비서직에 지원하고 싶습니다. 저는 현재 뉴월드 에이전시에서 근무하고 있습니다. 하지만 새로운 자리를 찾고 있습니다. 저는 저의 경험과 자격 때문에 제가 이 직책에 아주 적합하다고 믿습니다.

저는 타자를 아주 빨리 치며 워드, 한글, 그리고 파워포인트와 같은 모든 소프트웨어를 잘 다룹니다. 또한 저는 단정하고 매우 조직화된 사람입니다. 저는 제가 당신 회사에서 어떠한 비서 직무도 처리할 수 있다고 확신합니다.

저는 믿을 수 있고 신뢰할 수 있는 사람입니다. 저는 당신이 저에게 이 일 자리를 주는 것을 후회하지 않을 것이라고 확신합니다. 저는 저의 이력서를 동봉합니다.

저는 이 자리에 대해서 당신과 논의하고 싶습니다. 그러므로 아무 때라도 저에게 자유롭게 연락하세요.

안녕히계세요.
김소영

동봉물

1. 편지를 쓰는 사람은 어떤 직무에 지원합니까?
   ① 비서직
   ② 회계직
   ③ 관리직
   ④ 사무직

2. 편지를 쓰는 사람은 현재 어느 회사에서 일하고 있습니까?

① 한미 코퍼레이션

② 뉴월드 에이전시

③ 뉴월드 코퍼레이션

3. 다음 중에서 편지를 쓰는 사람의 장점으로 언급되지 않은 것은?

① 타자를 빨리치는 것

② 소프트웨어를 잘 다루는 것

③ 단정하고 조직화 된 사람인 것

④ 협력적인 사람인 것

4. 편지를 쓰는 사람이 편지에 동봉한 것은?

① 이력서

② 영수증

③ 사진

④ 수표

5. 편지를 쓰는 사림은 자신이 어떠한 사람이라고 말하고 있습니까?

① 믿을 수 있고 신뢰할 수 있는 사람

② 민첩한 사람

③ 협력적인 사람

④ 의지가 강한 사람

Practice 1 Lecture

01

Dear Mr. Park

박 선생님께

구 문

① Dear + title + 성: ~선생님께

예문 1) Dear Mrs. Kim (김선생님께)

예문 2) Dear Miss Lee (이선생님께)

02

I am interested in the secretary position at your company, and I would like to apply for that position.

저는 당신 회사의 비서 직에 관심이 있으며 그 비서 직에 지원하고 싶습니다.

어 휘

① interested in: ~에 관심이 있는

예문1) She is interested in Russian literature.
(그녀는 러시아 문학에 관심이 있다.)

② secretary position: 비서 직

③ company: 회사

④ apply for: ~에 지원하다

예문1) He is applying for jobs.
(그는 구직 중이다.)

구 문

① would like to: ~하고 싶다

예문1) I would like to ask you a question.
(나는 너에게 질문을 하고 싶다.)

03 **I am currently employed by New World Agency, but now I am seeking a new position.**

저는 현재 뉴월드 에이전시에서 근무하고 있습니다. 하지만 지금은 새로운 일자를 구하고 있습니다.

어 휘

① currently: 현재

② seek: ~을 구하다, 찾다

예문1) You should seek advice from your lawyer.

(당신은 당신의 변호사로부터 자문을 구해야 합니다.)

구 문

① be employed by: ~에서 근무하다

예문1) He is currently employed by First Bank.

(그는 현재 제일 은행에서 근무하고 있다)

04 **I believe that my experience and qualifications make me perfect for this job.**

저는 저의 경험과 자격 때문에 제가 이 직책에 아주 적합하다고 믿습니다.

어 휘

① experience: 경험

② qualifications: 자격

예문1) She has every qualification for success.

(그녀는 성공하는데 필요한 모든 자질을 가지고 있다.)

③ perfect: 완벽한

구 문

① 주어 + make + 목적어 + 형용사: ~을 ~하게 만들다

예문1) Her remark made me angry.

(그녀의 말은 나를 화나게 했다.)

05 **I am a quick typist and I am very familiar with all the software programs such as Word, Hangul and PowerPoint.**

저는 타자를 빨리 치며 워드, 한글, 그리고 파워포인트와 같은 모든 소프트웨어를 잘 다룹니다.

어 휘

① quick typist: 타자를 빨리 치는 사람

예문1) She is a quick typist.
(그녀는 타자를 빨리 칩니다.)

② familiar with: ~을 잘 다루다, ~을 잘 알다

예문1) Are you familiar with the rules of football?
(당신은 축구의 규칙을 잘 알고 있습니까?)

06 **Also, I am a neat and very well organized person.**

또한 저는 단정하고 매우 조직화된 사람입니다.

어 휘

① neat: 단정한, 말쑥한, 깔끔한

예문1) His room is always neat.
(그의 방은 언제나 깔끔하다.)

② organized: 조직화 된, 정돈된

예문1) Her office is quiet and organized.
(그녀의 사무실은 조용하고 정돈되어 있다.)

07 **I feel sure that I will be able to cope with any secretarial duties at your company.**

저는 제가 당신 회사에서 어떠한 비서 직무도 처리할 수 있다고 확신합니다.

어 휘

① be able to: ~ 할 수 있는

② cope with: ~을 처리하다, 대처하다

예문1) He is coping with difficulties.
(그는 어려운 일을 처리하고 있습니다.)

③ secretarial: 비서의

④ duties: 직무, 임무

구 문 ① feel sure that: ~을 확신하다

예문1) I feel sure that he is telling the truth.
(나는 그가 진실을 말하고 있다는 것을 확신합니다.)

08 I am a reliable and trustworthy person.

저는 믿을 수 있고 신뢰할 수 있는 사람입니다.

어 휘 ① reliable: 믿을 수 있는, 의지할 수 있는

② trustworthy: 신뢰할 수 있는

09 I am sure that you will not regret giving me this position.

저는 당신이 저에게 이 일 자리를 주는 것을 후회하지 않을 것이라고 확신합니다.

어 휘 ① regret: ~을 후회하다

예문1) He regretted selling the house.
(그는 집을 판 것을 후회했다.)

② resume: 이력서

구 문 ① be sure that: ~을 확신하다

예문1) Are you sure that this is the right bus?
(너는 이 버스가 옳은 버스라고 확신합니까?)

10 I am enclosing my resume with this letter.

저는 저의 이력서를 동봉합니다.

어 휘 ① enclose A with B: A를 B에 동봉하다

예문1) He enclosed a check with letter.
(그는 수표를 편지에 동봉했습니다.)

11 I would like to discuss this position with you, so please feel free to contact me at any time.

저는 이 자리에 대해서 당신과 논의하고 싶습니다. 그러므로 아무 때라도 저에게 자유롭게 연락하세요.

어 휘 ① discuss: ~을 논의하다

예문1) They discussed their plans for their summer vacation.
(그들은 그들의 여름방학계획을 논의 했습니다.)

② contact: 연락하다

예문1) It is difficult to contact him.
(그에게 연락하기가 힘들다.)

구 문 ① feel free + to-부정사: 자유롭게 ~하다

예문1) Please feel free to ask questions.
(자유롭게 질문하세요.)

Practice 1 Task 1

보기에 있는 단어를 이용하여 문장을 완성하세요. 필요한 경우는 동사의 형태를 변형시키세요.

보기	make me　interested in　apply for　seek　employed by

(1) I am (　　　　)(　　　　) the secretary position at your company.

(2) I would like to (　　　)(　　　　) that position.

(3) I am currently (　　　)(　　　　) New World Agency.

(4) I am (　　　　) a new position.

(5) I believe that my experience and qualifications (　　　　)(　　) perfect for this job.

Practice 1 Task 2

빈 칸에 들어갈 표현을 입력하여 문장을 완성하세요.

(1) 저는 타이핑를 빨리 칩니다.
I am a (　　　　) (　　　　).

(2) 저는 한글, 워드 그리고 파워포인트와 같은 모든 소프트웨어를 매우 잘 다룹니다.
I am very (　　　　) (　　　　　) all the software programs such as Word, Hangeul, and PowerPoint.

(3) 저는 단정하고 매우 조직화 된 사람입니다.

I am a neat and very well ( ) ( ).

(4) 저는 제가 당신 회사에서 어떠한 비서 직무도 처리할 수 있다고 확신합니다.

I feel sure that I will be able to ( ) ( ) any secretarial duties at your company.

Practice 1 Task 3

주어진 영어 단어를 이용하여 주어진 문장을 영어로 완성하세요. 첫 단어는 대문자로 사용하세요.

(1) 저는 믿을 수 있고 신뢰할 수 있는 사람입니다.

and am a trustworthy person I reliable

( )

(2) 저는 당신이 저에게 이 일자리를 주는 것을 후회하지 않을 것이라고 확신합니다.

Sure I am will regret not this position me giving that you

( )

(3) 저는 저의 이력서를 동봉합니다.

enclosing am I resume my with this letter

( )

(4) 저는 이 자리에 대해서 당신과 논의하고 싶습니다.

like I to discuss would this you with position

( )

(5) 아무 때라도 저에게 자유롭게 연락하세요.

free feel me to contact at please time any

( )

Practice 2 Comprehension Checkup

다음 지원서를 읽고 질문에 대한 답을 선택한 후 확인 버튼을 클릭하세요.

78-4 Wolgye-dong
Nowon-gu, Seoul 139-054

February 15, 2013

Mr. Sangsoo Park
General Manager, Department of Human Resources
Hanjin Publication
336 Imun-dong, Dongdaemun-gu
Seoul 130-080

Dear Mr. Park:

I am writing to apply for the accountant position which was advertised on your website. I have enclosed my resume with a photo and two reference letters from my previous employers.

I am an accountant with ten years of experience. I am a punctual and reliable worker.

My reference letters will show that my previous employers have been satisfied with my work.

I hope that my application will be of interest to you. I would like to schedule an interview with you. I look forward to discussing this position with you.

Sincerely,

Jaemin Kim

Jaemin Kim

Enclosure

1. Who is the letter addressed to?
① Sangsoo Park
② Jaemin Kim
③ Sangsoo Park's previous employer
④ Jaemin Kim's previous employer

2. What is the job title of the recipient of the letter?
① Assistant Manager
② Manager
③ General Manager
④ Senior Manager

3. What position does the writer apply for?
① The position of a secretary
② The position of an accountant
③ The position of a driver
④ The position of a clerk

4. What kind of person does the writer say he is?
① An honest person
② A cooperative person
③ A punctual and reliable person
④ An industrious person

5. What has the writer enclosed with the letter?
① Resume
② Reference letters
③ Resume and check
④ Resume and reference letters

525-389 서울 노원구
월계동 78-4 번지

2013년 2월 15일

135-78 서울 동대문구
이문동 336번지
한진 출판사
인사부 박상수 부장

박선생님께

저는 당신 회사의 홈페이지에 광고된 회계 직에 지원하기 위해서 편지를 씁니다. 사진이 있는 이력서와 이전 고용주로부터의 두통의 추천서를 동봉했습니다.

저는 10년의 경험이 있는 회계원입니다. 저는 시간을 잘 엄수하고 믿을 만한 사람입니다. 저의 추천서는 저의 이전 고용주가 저의 일에 만족했다는 것을 보여줄 것입니다.

저는 저의 지원이 당신에게 관심의 대상이 되길 바랍니다. 저는 당신과 면담을 약속하고 싶습니다. 저는 이 일자리에 대해서 당신과 논의하길 고대합니다.

안녕히 계십시오.

김재민

동봉물

1. 편지에 누구에게 발송되었습니까?
   ① 박상수
   ② 김재민
   ③ 박상수의 이전 고용주
   ④ 김재민의 이전 고용주

2. 편지 수신인의 직책은 무엇입니까?
   ① 대리
   ② 과장
   ③ 부장
   ④ 차장

3. 편지를 쓰는 사람은 어떤 직무에 지원합니까?
① 비서직
② 회계직
③ 기사직
④ 사무직

4. 편지를 쓰는 사람은 자신이 어떠한 사람이라고 말하고 있습니까?
① 정직한 사람
② 협력적인 사람
③ 시간을 잘 엄수하고 믿을 만한 사람
④ 근면한 사람

5. 편지를 쓰는 사람은 편지에 무엇을 동봉하였습니까?
① 이력서
② 추천서
③ 이력서와 수표
④ 이력서와 추천서

Practice 2 Lecture

01

I am writing to apply for the accountant position which was advertised on your website.

저는 당신 회사의 홈페이지에 광고된 회계 직에 지원하기 위해서 편지를 씁니다.

어 휘

① write: 편지를 쓰다

예문1) She writes me a letter every day.

(그녀는 매일 나에게 편지를 쓴다.)

② accountant: 회계원

③ advertise: 광고하다

예문1) The position of a secretary was advertised in the newspaper.

(그 비서 직은 신문에 광고되었다.)

④ website: 홈페이지

02

I have enclosed my resume with a photo and two reference letters from my previous employers.

저는 사진이 있는 이력서와 이전 고용주로부터의 두통의 추천서를 동봉했습니다.

어 휘

① enclose: 동봉하다

② photo: 사진

③ reference letter: 추천서

예문1) They should submit my resume and reference letters to the manager of human resources.

(나는 나의 이력서와 추천서를 인사부과장에게 제출해야 한다.)

④ previous: 이전의

예문1) I have a previous engagement.

⑤ employer: 고용주

03 I am an accountant with ten years of experience.

저는 10년의 경험이 있는 회계원입니다.

어 휘

① accountant : 회계원

예문1) His elder sister is an accountant.

(그녀의 누나는 회계원이다.)

② experience : 경험

예문1) He has no experience in teaching Chinese.

(그는 중국어를 가르친 경험이 없다.)

04 I am a punctual and reliable worker.

저는 시간을 잘 엄수하고 믿을만한 사람입니다.

어 휘

① punctual : 시간을 엄수하는

예문1) She is always punctual in answering letters.

(그녀는 언제나 편지에 답장하는데 시간을 엄수한다.)

② reliable : 믿을만한

예문1) He is forgetful of things. He is not reliable.

(그는 건망증이 있어서 믿을 수 없다.)

05 My reference letters will show that my previous employers have been satisfied with my work.

저의 추천서는 저의 이전 고용주가 저의 일에 만족했다는 것을 보여줄 것입니다.

어 휘

① reference letters : 추천서

예문1) Applicants should submit their reference letters.

(지원자들은 자신의 추천서를 제출해야 한다.)

② show : ~을 보여주다, 말해주다

예문1) His face showed that he was upset.

(그의 얼굴은 그가 화났다는 것을 보여주었다.)

③ satisfied with : ~만족하다

예문1) My parents were not satisfied with my examination results.

(나의 부모님은 나의 시험결과에 만족하지 않았다.)

06 I hope that my application will be of interest to you.

저는 저의 지원서가 당신에게 관심의 대상이 되길 바랍니다.

어 휘 ① hope : ~을 바라다, 희망하다

예문1) I hope that he will succeed in his business.

(나는 그가 사업에 성공하길 바란다.)

② application : 지원서

예문1) I will send you my application right away.

(서의 지원서를 지금 바로 보내드리겠습니다.)

관용표현 ① be of interest : 흥미 있는

예문1) Since you are interested in politics, this book will be of interest.

(당신이 정치에 관심이 있으므로 이 책은 흥미가 있을 것입니다.)

07 I would like to schedule an interview with you.

저는 당신과 면접을 약속하고 싶습니다.

어 휘 ① schedule : ~을 예정하다, 계획하다

예문1) We scheduled a meeting for December 3.

(우리는 12월 3일에 모임을 갖도록 계획했다.)

② interview : 면접, 면담

예문1) We will have an interview with the boss tomorrow.

(우리는 내일 사장님과 면접을 볼 것이다.)

08 I look forward to discussing this position with you.

저는 이 일자리에 대해서 당신과 논의하길 고대하고 있습니다.

어 휘

① position : 일자리

예문1) He lost his position.

(그는 실직했다.)

관용표현

① look forward to + 동사 + ing : ~을 고대하다

예문1) I look forward to seeing you soon.

(나는 너를 곧 볼 수 있기를 고대한다.)

Practice 2 Task 4

보기에 있는 단어를 이용하여 문장을 완성하세요. 필요한 경우 동사의 형태를 변형시키세요.

보기	write advertise enclose

(1) I am (   ) to apply for the accountant position which was (   ) on your website.

(2) I have (   ) my resume with a photo and two recommendation letters from my previous employers.

Practice 2 Task 5

빈 칸에 적절한 단어를 입력하여 문장을 완성하세요.

(1) 저는 10년의 경험이 있는 회계원입니다.
I am an (   ) (   ) ten years of experience.

(2) 저는 시간을 잘 엄수하고 믿을만한 사람입니다.
I am a (   ) and (   ) worker.

(3) 저의 추천서는 저의 이전 고용주가 저의 일에 만족했다는 것을 보여 줄 것입니다.
My (   ) (   ) will show that my previous employers have been (   ) with my work.

Practice 2 Task 6

보기에 주어진 영어 단어를 이용하여 주어진 문장을 영어로 완성하세요. 첫 단어는 대문자로 시작하세요.

(1) 저는 저의 지원서가 당신의 관심의 대상이 되길 바랍니다.

보기	hope that I application my be interest you of will to

______________________________.

(2) 저는 당신과 면담을 약속하고 싶습니다.

보기	like to schedule I would an interview with you

______________________________.

(3) 저는 이 일자리에 대해서 당신과 논의하길 고대합니다.

보기	look forward to I position this discussing with you

______________________________.

Exercise Writing

다음 글을 읽은 후 그를 바탕으로 자기소개서를 영작해 보시오.

저는 당신 회사의 비서직에 지원하기 위해서 편지를 씁니다.
저는 저의 이력서와 이전 고용주로부터의 두 통의 추천서를 동봉했습니다.
저는 6년의 경험이 있는 비서입니다.
저는 시간을 잘 엄수하고 믿을 만한 사람입니다.
저는 저의 지원이 당신에게 관심의 대상이 되길 바랍니다.
저는 당신과 면접을 약속하고 싶습니다.

Exercise You be the editor

다음 지원서를 읽고 밑줄친 부분을 올바르게 고치세요.

I am writing to apply for the clerk position which was <u>advertising</u> on your website. I have enclosed my resume and two reference letters from my previous <u>employees</u>.

I believe that I am a perfect candidate for this position. I am a reliable and trustworthy person. I am sure that you will be satisfied <u>in</u> my work. I would like to discuss this position with you, so please feel <u>freely</u> to contact me at any time.

Wrap up

Summary

1. The format of a job application letter

	[Return Address]
[Date]	
[Inside Address]	
[Greeting]	
[Body]	
[Closing]	
[Signature]	
[Name]	
[Enclosure]	

2. Key expressions

(1) I am interested in the secretary position.

(2) I am writing to apply for the accountant position at your company.

(3) I would like to schedule an interview with you.

(4) I look forward to discussing this position with you.

Wrap up

Assignment I

would like to	~하고 싶다.
be employed by	~에서 근무하다.
주어 + make + 목적어 + 형용사	~을 ~하게 만들다.
feel sure that / be sure that	을 확신하다.
feel free to + 동사원형	자유롭게 ~하다.
be of interest	흥미 있는
look forward to + 동사 + ing	~을 고대하다.

Wrap up

Assignment II

오늘 학습한 주요내용과 제시된 조건에 맞게 지원서를 작성해 봅시다. 영어(한글) 형태로 작성한 후 〔제출하기〕버튼을 클릭하면 〔과제방〉주관식 과제〕에 등록됩니다.

조건	과제
1. 사용문형 Interested in Advertised Apply for Enclosed Look forward to 2. 문장 개수 5~10문장(본문만 작성함)	

Answers

Lesson 5. I am interested in the position of a secretary.

Warm up

Check up

1)

A. Return Address

B. Date

C. Inside address

D. Signature

E. Name

2) Dear Mr.Kim – Greeting

Sincerely, - Closing

Haemin Park – Signature

March 27, 2008 - Date

3) (1) return address 발신인 주소 / 보낸 사람 주소

(2) inside address 수신인 주소 / 받는 사람 주소

(3) enclosure 동봉물

Practice 1 Comprehension Check up

1) ① The secretary position
2) ② New world Agency
3) ④ Being a cooperative person
4) ① Resume
5) ① Reliable and trustworthy person

Practice 1 Task 1

1) interested in
2) apply for
3) employed by
4) seeking
5) make me

Practice 1 Task 2

1) quick, typist
2) familiar, with
3) organized, person
4) cope with

Practice 1 Task 3

1) I am a reliable and trustworthy person.
2) I am sure that you will not regret giving me this position.
3) I am enclosing my resume with this letter.
4) I would like to discuss this position with you.
5) Please feel free to contact me at any time.

Practice 2 Comprehension Check up

1) ① Sangsoo Park
2) ③ General Manager
3) ② The position of an accountant
4) ③ A punctual and reliable person
5) ④ Resume and reference letters

Practice 2 Task 4

1) I am writing to apply for the position of an accountant which was advertised on your website.
2) I have enclosed my resume with a photo and two recommendation letters from my previous employers.

Practice 2 Task 5

1) accountant, with
2) punctual, reliable
3) reference, letters, satisfied

Practice 2 Task 6

1) I hope that my application will be of interest to you.
2) I would like to schedule an interview with you.
3) I look forward to discussing this position with you.

Exercise Writing

I am writing to apply for the secretary position at your company.
I have enclosed my resume and two reference letters from my previous employers.
I am a secretary with six years of experience. I am a punctual and reliable person.
I hope that my application will be of interest to you.
I would like to schedule an interview with you.

Exercise You be the editor

I am writing to apply for the position of a clerk which was advertised (be + advertised: 광고된) on your website. I have enclosed my resume and two reference letters from my previous employers (employers: 고용주).

I believe that I am a perfect candidate for this position. I am a reliable and trustworthy person. I am sure that you will be satisfied with (be satisfied with: ~에 만족하다) my work. I would like to discuss this position with you, so please feel free (feel free + to + 동사: 자유롭게 ~하다) **to contact** me at any time.

Lesson 06

Your account balance of $400 is three months overdue.

Lesson 06

Your account balance of $400 is three months overdue.

Introduction

Lesson objectives

1. Faxing a message

2. Learning the key expressions for faxing a message
   (1) Your account balance of $400 is three months overdue.
   (2) We will have to take appropriate action.
   (3) We look forward to your prompt response.
   (4) This is to confirm that all arrangements have been made for your trip.

Warm up

The format of a fax

FAX	
① **Date:**	April 1, 2013
② **To:**	Keechol Park Mirae Electronics
③ **From:**	Minyoung Kim World Tour
④ **Subject:**	Delivery of wrong products
⑤ **Reference:**	Purchase order 03-5345-9
⑥ **Number of pages:**	This page only

⑦ **Message:**	The wrong products were mailed. We are returning them. Please send new products ASAP. I look forward to your prompt action.

① 날짜 : 팩스를 보내는 날짜를 기재합니다. 날짜를 기재할 때는 월, 일, 연도 순서로 기재합니다. 일과 연도 사이에는 쉼표(,)가 들어갑니다.

Example

[1] 2013년 4월 15일 → April 15, 2013
[2] 2013년 5월 20일 → May 20, 2013
[3] 2013년 7월 6일 → July 6, 2013

② 수신인 : 팩스를 받는 사람의 이름과 소속회사를 기재합니다. 이름을 기재 할 때는 이름, 성의 순서로 기재합니다.

Example

[1]	박재민	Jaemin Park
	제일은행	The First Bank
[2]	김소진	Sojin Kim
	한미건설	Hanmi Construction
[3]	이민수	Minsoo Lee
	삼성전자	Samsung Electronics

③ 발신인 : 발신인의 이름과 소속회사를 기재합니다.

Example

[1]	김철민	Cheolmin Kim
		New World Corporation
[2]	조재진	Jaejin Cho
		Nubi Tour
[3]	강수연	Sooyeon Kang
		Hanjin Software

④ 제목: 팩스의 내용을 예측 할 수 있는 제목을 기재합니다. 제목을 기재할 때는 완전한 문장으로 기재하기보다는 간결한 문구로 기재합니다.

ex〉 ① The wrong products were delivered. → Delivery of wrong products
② Your rent is overdue. → Overdue rent
③ I would like to make a reservation at the hotel.
→ Reservation at the hotel / Hotel reservation

⑤ **참고 :** 팩스로 보내는 메시지 외에 참고사항이 될 수 있는 정보를 기재할 수 있습니다. 참고로 기재되는 내용에는 계좌번호, 구입주문서, 항공편번호, 항공여행 날짜 등이 있습니다.

① 계좌번호: Account number
ex〉 우리은행 계좌번호: 092-21-0463-558 →
Woori Bank account number: 092-21-0463-558
② 구입주문서: Purchase order
ex〉 구입주문서 03-5565-8 → Purchase order 03-5565-8 (P.O. 03-5565-8)
③ 항공편 번호: Flight number
ex〉 항공편 번호: 뉴욕행 25편 → Flight number: Flight 25 to New York
④ 항공여행 날짜: Date of Flight
ex〉 항공여행 날짜: 2013년 8월 19일 → Date of Flight: August 19, 2013

⑥ **페이지 :** 팩스의 총 페이지 수를 명시합니다. 팩스의 페이지에 따라서 다음과 같은 표현을 사용할 수 있습니다.

① 1 페이지: This page only
② 2 페이지: This page + 1
③ 3 페이지: This page + 2
④ 4 페이지: This page + 3
⑤ 5 페이지: This page + 4

⑦ **메시지 :** 메시지는 팩스로 상대방에게 전달하고자 하는 내용입니다. 메시지는 완전한 문장으로 작성합니다. 메시지의 내용이 많은 경우는 문단을 나눌 수 있습니다. 편지나 전자우편에서 사용하는 인사(greeting), 끝인사(closing), 서명(signature), 이름(name) 등을 팩스메시지에서는 사용하지 않습니다.

Warm up

Check up

1. 보기에 주어진 각 항목들을 보고 각 항목에 맞는 말을 적어보세요.

보기	Misdelivery of headphones This page only P.O. 04-2289-46 March 30, 2013

Date:	A:( )
To:	Mincheol Kim Woosung Construction
From:	Soojin Min The Frist Bank
Subject:	B:( )
Reference:	C:( )
Number of Pages:	D:( )
Message:	Today we received only 3 headphones. Yesterday we ordered 30 headphones, so please send the remaining headphones ASAP. I look forward to your prompt action.

A: ______________________

B: ______________________

C: ______________________

D: ______________________

2. 다음에 주어진 각 표현을 보고 각 항목에 맞는 말을 적어보세요.

보기	Date　Number of pages　Subject　Reference

1) Order Cancellation ______

2) Hana Bank Account number: 082-22-0537-998 ______

3) This page + 2 ______

4) July 12, 2013 ______

3. 다음 보기 중 팩스의 메시지에 적합한 제목을 고르세요.

보기	Mistake in hotel reservation　Confirmation of hotel reservation Cancellation of hotel reservation

Fax

Date: June 17, 2009
To: Michael Brown
Nex Tour Hotel
From: Andrew Johnson
New Tech Corporation
Subject: [A]
Reference: American Express credit card number:
8902-8790-3907-4577
Number of pages: This page only

Message: I would like to confirm my reservation at your hotel. I am arriving on June 20, and leaving on June 23. I will stay at your hotel for three nights.

Please guarantee my reservation with my American Express credit card. I am looking forward to your prompt action.

A ______

Practice 1 Comprehension Check up

다음 팩스를 읽고 질문에 대한 답을 선택한 후 확인 버튼을 클릭하세요.

FAX

Date:	April 12, 2013
To:	Minsoo Kim Hana Enterprise
From:	Hyewon Park World Travel
Subject:	Overdue account balance
Reference:	Foreign Exchange Bank account number: 100-65-4357-557
Pages:	This page only
Message:	Your account balance of $400 is three months overdue. As you know, full settlement of your account was due on January 5, 2013. However, we have not received even partial payment of the overdue amount. Furthermore, you have not responded to any of our earlier communications. This is our third reminder. If possible, make full payment by the end of this week. If we do not receive full payment of the overdue amount by April 30, we will have to take appropriate action. Please call us to confirm your intention. We look forward to your prompt response.

1. Who sent the fax?

① Minsoo Kim
② Hyewon Park
③ Minsoo Kim's secretary
④ Hyewon Park's secretary

2. Who was the fax addressed to?

① Minsoo Kim
② Hyewon Park
③ Minsoo Kim's secretary
④ Hyewon Park's secretary

3. What is the purpose of the fax?

① To ask for the full payment of the overdue amount
② To ask for the partial payment of the overdue amount
③ To borrow some money from the client
④ To lend some money to the client

4. How much money does Hyewon Park have to receive from Minsoo Kim?

① $ 300
② $ 400
③ $ 500
④ $ 600

FAX

날짜: 2013년 4월 12일

수신: 김민수
하나기업

발신: 박혜원
세계여행사

제목: 연체계좌잔액
참고: 외한은행 계좌번호: 100-65-4357-557
페이지: 총 1페이지

내용: 당신의 계좌잔액 400 달러가 3개월 연체되었습니다. 당신도 알다시피 계좌 총 결산이 2013년 1월 5일이었습니다. 하지만 우리는 심지어 연체금액의 일부분도 납부 받지 못했습니다. 더욱이 당신은 이전의 우리의 어떠한 연락에도 응답하지 않았습니다. 이것은 우리의 세 번째 독촉장입니다. 가능하다면 이번 주말까지 완불해주세요.
우리가 연체금액을 4월 30일까지 완납 받지 않는다면 우리는 적절한 조치를 취하게 될 것입니다. 우리에게 전화해서 당신의 의도를 확실히 알려주세요.
당신의 신속한 응답을 고대하겠습니다.

1. 누가 팩스를 보냈습니까?
   ① 김민수
   ② 박혜원
   ③ 김민수의 비서
   ④ 박혜원의 비서

2. 팩스는 누구에게 보내졌습니까?
   ① 김민수
   ② 박혜원
   ③ 김민수의 비서
   ④ 박혜원의 비서

3. 팩스의 목적은 무엇입니까?

① 연체된 금액의 완불을 요구하기 위해서

② 연체된 금액의 일부 지불을 요구하기 위해서

③ 고객에게 돈을 빌리기 위해서

④ 고객에게 돈을 빌려주기 위해서

4. 박혜원은 김민수로부터 얼마의 돈을 받아야 하나요?

① 300달러

② 400달러

③ 500달러

④ 600달러

Practice 1 Lecture

01 **Your account balance of $400 is three months overdue.**

당신의 계좌잔액 400 달러가 3개월 연체되었습니다.

어 휘 ① account balance : 계좌잔액

예문1) If you want to check your account balance, press 3.
(당신의 계좌잔액을 확인하려면 3번을 누르세요.)

② overdue : 지불기한이 넘은

예문1) The rent has been overdue for more than three months.
(집세가 3개월 이상 밀렸습니다.)

예문2) Your insurance payment is two months overdue.
(당신의 보험료가 두 달 밀렸습니다.)

02 **As you know, full settlement of your account was due on January 5, 2013.**

당신도 알다시피 계좌 총 결산이 2013년 1월 5일이었습니다.

어 휘 ① settlement : 결산, 청산

예문1) He has to make a settlement of his debt.
(그는 그의 빚을 청산해야 한다.)

예문2) She has to make a settlement of her medical bill.
(그녀는 의료비 청구서를 결산해야 한다.)

② due : 지급기일이 된

예문1) The rent is due today.
(집세는 오늘이 지급기일이다.)

관용표현 ① As you know : 당신도 알다시피

03 **However, we have not received even partial payment of the overdue amount.**
하지만 심지어 연체금액의 일부분도 납부 받지 못했습니다.

어 휘

① however : 하지만

예문1) It was raining hard. However, he did not stop working.
(비가 많이 오고 있었다. 하지만 그는 일을 멈추지 않았다.)

② receive : 받다

예문1) Judy received a letter from her friend.
(주디는 그녀의 친구에게 편지를 받았다.)

③ partial : 부분적인

④ payment : 지불금액

예문1) We will stop delivery until we receive full payment.
(우리는 금액을 완납 받을 때까지 배달을 중지하겠다.)

⑤ amount : 금액, 액수

04 **Furthermore, you have not responded to any of our earlier communications.**
더욱이 당신은 이전의 우리의 어떠한 연락에도 응답하지 않았습니다.

어 휘

① furthermore : 더욱이

예문1) The house is too small, and furthermore, it's too far from pubic transportation.
(그 집은 너무 작다. 그리고 더욱이 대중교통으로부터 멀리 떨어져있다.)

② respond to : ~에 응답하다

예문1) She still has not responded to my letter.
(그녀는 아직 나의 편지에 응답하지 않았다.)

③ communications : 연락 (편지, 이메일, 팩스)

05 This is our third reminder.

이것은 우리의 세 번째 독촉장입니다.

어 휘

① reminder : 독촉장

예문1) He hadn't paid the bill, so the owner of the store sent him a reminder.
(그는 청구서를 지불하지 않았다. 그래서 가게 주인이 그에게 독촉장을 보냈다.)

06 If possible, make full payment by the end of this week.

가능하다면, 이번 주말까지 완불해주세요.

구 문

① if possible : 가능하다면

예문1) If possible, send me the fax by 5 pm.
(가능하면 오후 5시까지 나에게 팩스를 보내주세요.)

관용표현

① make payment : 지불하다

예문1) He made full payment.
(그는 완불했다.)

예문2) She made partial payment.
(그녀는 일부만 지불했다.)

07 If we do not receive full payment of the overdue amount by April 30, we will have to take appropriate action.

우리가 연체대금을 4월 30일까지 완납 받지 않을 시에는 그에 적절한 조치를 취하게 될 것입니다.

어 휘

① full payment : 완납금액

② appropriate : 적절한

예문1) His dark clothes were not appropriate for a party.
(그의 어두운 옷은 파티에 적합하지 않았다.)

관용표현 ① take action : 조치를 취하다

예문1) We have to take action before it is too late.
(우리는 너무 늦기 전에 조치를 취해야 한다.)

구 문 ① If + 주어 + 조동사 + not + 본동사, 주어 + 동사: ~하지 않으면, ~ 하다

예문1) If it doesn't rain tomorrow, I will go fishing.
(내일 비가 오지 않는다면 나는 낚시하러 갈 것이다.)

08 Please call us to confirm your intention.

우리에게 전화해서 당신의 의도를 확실히 알려주세요.

어 휘 ① call : 전화하다

② confirm : 확인하다

예문1) Jim confirmed his hotel reservation.
(짐은 그의 호텔 예약을 확인했다.)

③ intention : 의도

09 We look forward to your prompt response.

고객님의 신속한 응답을 고대하겠습니다.

어 휘 ① prompt : 신속한, 빠른

예문1) He is prompt in action.
(그는 동작이 빠르다.)

② response : 응답, 대답

예문1) He made no response.
(그는 아무런 대답이 없었다.)

관용표현 ① look forward to : ~을 고대하다

예문1) I am looking forward to going on a date with her.
(나는 그녀와의 데이트를 고대한다.)

Practice 1 Task 1

보기에 있는 단어를 이용하여 문장을 완성하세요. 필요한 경우는 동사의 형태를 변형시키세요.

보기	settlement account balance due receive overdue

(1) Your (　　　　　) of $400 is three months (　　　　　　).

(2) As you know, full (　　　　　　) of your account was (　　　　　) on January 5, 2013.

(3) We have not (　　　　) even partial payment of the overdue amount.

Practice 1 Task 2

빈 칸에 들어갈 적절한 단어를 입력하여 문장을 완성하세요.

(1) 더욱이 당신은 이전의 우리의 어떠한 연락에도 응답하지 않았습니다.
Furthermore, you have not (　　　　) to any of our earlier (　　　　).

(2) 이것은 우리의 세 번째 독촉장입니다.
This is our (　　　　)(　　　　).

(3) 가능하다면 이번 주 말까지 완불해주세요.
If possible, (　　　　) full (　　　　) by the end of this week.

Practice 1 Task 3

제시되어 있는 단어를 배열하여 올바른 문장을 만들어 보세요.

(1) 우리가 연체금액을 4월 30일까지 완납 받지 않으면 우리는 적절한 조치를 취하게 될 것입니다.

action　have to　we　take　will　appropriate

If we do not receive full payment of the overdue amount by April 30,

(　　　　　　　　　　　　　　　　　　　　)

(2) 우리에게 전화해서 당신의 의도를 확실히 알려주세요.

please　to confirm　call　us　your　intention

(　　　　　　　　　　　　　　　　　　　　)

(3) 우리는 당신의 신속한 응답을 고대하겠습니다.

we　are　prompt　response　forward　looking　to　your

(　　　　　　　　　　　　　　　　　　　　)

Coffee break

Canals in Korea

There is a lot of talk in Korea at the moment about building a massive cross country canal linking Seoul and Busan. The plan itself is controversial; some claim that it will be an engineering marvel that will attract visitors from overseas as well as cutting transportation costs, while critics say that it makes no economic sense and will spoil the environment.

Whatever view you take of this plan, canals have played an important role in economic development throughout human history. Canals are artificial channels for water and come in two types: irrigation canals, which help to irrigate crops; and waterways, which are used for transport- which is what most people think of when they hear the word 'canal'. The earliest canals date from around 4000 B.C. in what is now modern-day Iraq. The longest canal ever constructed was the Grand Canal of China, which is more than 1500 years old.

Canals became great engines of economic progress in medieval Europe and helped to fuel Britain's industrial revolution. Other famous canals include the Suez Canal and the Panama Canal. Canals need to be flat, but sometimes two parts of a canal will be at different levels. In this case, the canal builders need to construct a 'lock' which is a kind of chamber within which the water level can be raised or lowered. Some stretches of canal require a number of small locks in quick succession, which slows down transportation.

Although there are now many alternative forms of transportation, many canals are still in use. These include the Suez Canal, the Panama Canal and Britain's Manchester Ship Canal.

Coffee break

한국의 운하

현재 한국에서는 한국을 관통하여 서울과 부산을 잇는 대운하를 건설하는데 많은 논의가 있다. 대운하 건설 계획에 대한 찬반이 엇갈리고 있다. 찬성론자는 대운하 건설이 교통수송비용을 절감시키고 해외 방문자를 유치시켜 주어 기적의 토목공사가 될 것이라고 예상하지만, 반대론자들은 운하건설이 경제적으로 이치에 맞지도 않고 환경을 파괴할 것이라고 비판한다.
대운하 건설에 어떤 입장을 취하든, 운하는 인류사에서 경제발달에 중요한 역할을 해왔다. 운하는 인공 수로이며 2가지 종류가 있다. 농작물에 물을 공급하는 관개용 운하, 사람들이 보통 '운하'라는 단어를 듣고 떠올리는 운송을 위한 수운용 운하가 있다. 최초의 운하는 기원전 4000년으로 거슬러 올라가는데 현재 이라크가 있는 곳에 있었다. 건설된 운하 중 가장 긴 것은 중국의 대운하이며, 이는 건설된 지 1500년도 더 되었다.
운하는 중세 유럽에서 경제 성장의 큰 동력이 되었고, 영국 산업혁명을 일으키는데도 도움이 되었다. 수에즈 운하와 파나마 운하가 대표적인 운하이다.
운하는 수평해야 하는데, 한 운하의 두 부분이 서로 다른 수위에 있을 때가 있다. 이런 경우에는 '갑문'이 세워져야 하는데, 갑문은 그 안에서 수위가 올라가거나 낮아질 수 있는 수위 차를 조절하는 일종의 방이다. 운하의 작은 수로들은 작은 갑문들이 연달아 필요한데 이것이 운송의 속도를 낮추게 한다.
현대에는 다양한 종류의 운송 수단이 있지만, 여전히 많은 운하가 이용되고 있다. 수에즈 운하, 파나마운하, 영국 맨체스터 운하가 여기에 해당된다.

Practice 2 Comprehension Check up

FAX	
Date:	January 2, 2013
To:	Soojin Kim LG Construction
From:	Hyemin Lee The First Tour
Subject:	Flight Arrangement
Reference:	Flight number: Flight 45 to Los Angeles, Flight 25 to New York
Number of Pages:	This page only
Message:	This is to confirm that all arrangements have been made for your trip. Your flight will leave JFK airport on February 3 at 9:20 am, arriving at Los Angeles airport at 7:50 pm. Your return flight will leave Los Angeles airport on February 6 at 8:10 am, arriving at JFK at 6:40 pm. You will be met at the airport by one of our drivers who will drive you to your hotel. Unfortunately, the Hilton is fully booked, so we have booked you into the Paradiso. Let me know if you have any further questions. We look forward to doing business with you in the future. Enjoy your trip.

1. Who was the fax addressed to?
   ① Soojin Kim
   ② Hyemin Lee
   ③ Soojin Kim's secretary
   ④ Hyemin Lee's secretary

2. What company does the sender of the fax work for?

① LG Construction
② The First Tour
③ Airline company
④ The First Bank

3. What is the purpose of the fax?

① To confirm a flight schedule
② To book an air ticket
③ To cancel a flight schedule
④ To purchase an air ticket

4. When is Soojin Kim scheduled to arrive at Los Angeles airport?

① 9:20 am
② 7:50 pm
③ 6:40 am
④ 8:10 am

5. Where is Soojin Kim scheduled to stay in Los Angeles?

① JFK hotel
② Hilton hotel
③ Paradiso hotel
④ Paradise hotel

FAX	
날짜:	2013년 1월 2일
수신:	김수진 LG 건설
발신:	이혜민 제일 여행사
제목:	항공여행 준비
참고:	항공편 번호: 로스앤젤레스 행 45편, 뉴욕 행 25편
페이지:	총 1페이지
내용:	이 메시지는 당신의 여행을 위한 모든 준비가 완료되었음을 확인 드리기 위함입니다. 당신의 항공편은 2월 3일 오전 9시 20분에 JFK 공항을 떠나 오후 7시 50분에 로스앤젤레스 공항에 도착할 예정입니다. 당신의 돌아오는 비행은 2월 6일 오전 8시 10분에 로스앤젤레스 공항을 떠나 오후 6시 40분에 JFK 공항에 도착할 예정입니다. 당신은 당신을 호텔까지 차로 태워 줄 마중 나온 운전기사를 공항에서 만나게 될 것입니다. 안타깝게도 Hilton 호텔의 예약이 다 찬 상태여서 우리는 당신이 Paradiso 호텔에 투숙하도록 예약했습니다. 더 문의할 사항이 있으면 알려주십시오. 우리는 미래에도 당신과 함께 일할 수 있기를 고대합니다. 즐거운 여행되십시오.

1. 팩스는 누구에게 보내졌습니까?
   ① 김수진
   ② 이혜민
   ③ 김수진의 비서
   ④ 이혜민의 비서

2. 팩스를 보내는 사람은 어느 회사에서 근무하고 있습니까?
   ① LG 건설
   ② 제일 여행사
   ③ 항공회사
   ④ 제일은행

3. 팩스의 목적이 무엇입니까?

① 비행편을 확인하기 위해서
② 비행기표를 예약하기 위해서
③ 비행편을 취소하기 위해서
④ 비행기 표를 구입하기 위해서

4. 김수진은 로스앤젤레스 공항에 언제 도착하기로 되어있나요?

① 오후 9시 20분
② 오후 7시 50분
③ 오전 6시 40분
④ 오전 8시 10분

5. 김수진은 뉴욕의 어디에서 투숙하기로 되어있나요?

① JFK 호텔
② Hilton 호텔
③ Paradiso 호텔
④ Paradise 호텔

Practice 2 Lecture

01 **This is to confirm that all arrangements have been made for your trip.**

이 메시지는 당신의 여행을 위한 모든 준비가 완료되었음을 확인 드리기 위함입니다.

어 휘 ① confirm : ~을 확인하다

예문1) He confirmed that the meeting would be on July 10.
(그는 모임이 7월 10일에 있을 거라는 것을 확인했다.)

예문2) I would like to confirm my hotel reservation.
(나는 나의 호텔 예약을 확인하고 싶다.)

② arrangements : 준비, 채비

예문1) Please make arrangements for the product to be delivered right away.
(그 제품이 즉시 배달될 수 있도록 준비해주세요.)

02 **Your flight will leave JFK airport on February 3 at 9:20 am, arriving at Los Angeles airport at 7:50 pm.**

당신의 항공편은 2월 3일 오전 9시 20분에 JFK 공항을 떠나 오후 7시 50분에 로스 앤젤레스 공항에 도착할 예정입니다.

어 휘 ① flight : 항공편

예문1) There are two flights to New York.
(뉴욕으로 가는 두 항공편이 있다.)

② leave : 떠나다

③ arrive : 도착하다

문 법 ① 주어 + 동사, and 주어 + 동사 → 주어 + 동사, 동사+ing

예문1) The train leaves Seoul at 5 am, and it arrives in Masan at 8 am.
(기차는 오전 5시에 서울을 떠나서 오전 8시에 마산에 도착한다.)

→ The train leaves Seoul at 5 am, arriving in Masan at 8 am.

03

Your return flight will leave Los Angeles airport on February 6 at 8:10 am, arriving at JFK at 6:40 pm.

당신의 돌아오는 비행은 2월 6일 오전 8시 10분에 로스앤젤레스 공항을 떠나 오후 6시 40분에 JFK 공항에 도착할 예정입니다.

어 휘

① return : 귀가, 귀국
② airport : 공항

문 법

① 주어 + 동사, and 주어 + 동사 → 주어 + 동사, 동사+ing

예문1) John started doing his homework in the morning, and he finished it in the evening.
(존은 오전에 숙제를 시작해서 저녁에 끝냈다.)
→ John started doing his homework in the morning, finishing it in the evening.

04

You will be met at the airport by one of our drivers who will drive you to your hotel.

당신은 당신을 호텔까지 차로 태워 줄 마중 나온 운전기사를 공항에서 만나게 될 것입니다.

어 휘

① drive A to B : A를 B까지 태워주다

예문1) She drove him to the airport.
(그녀는 그를 공항까지 차로 데려다 주었다.)

구 문

be + met + at + 장소 + by + 사람 : 마중 나온 ~를 만나다

예문1) I was met by my brother at the airport.
(나는 공항에서 마중 나온 형을 만났다.)

05 Unfortunately, the Hilton is fully booked, so we have booked you into the Paradiso.

안타깝게도 Hilton 호텔의 예약이 다 찬 상태여서 우리는 당신이 Paradiso 호텔에 투숙하도록 예약했습니다.

어 휘

① unfortunately : 안타깝게도, 불행하게도

② fully booked : 예약이 다 찬

예문1) The seats for the theater are fully booked.
(극장의 좌석이 모두 예약됐다.)

관용표현

① book A into the hotel : A가 호텔에 투숙하도록 예약하다

예문1) I booked all the guests into the hotel.
(나는 모든 손님들을 호텔에 예약시켜드렸다.)

06 Let me know if you have any further questions.

더 문의할 사항이 있으면 알려주십시오.

어 휘

① further : 이상의, 한층 더한

예문1) I have further questions.
(나는 문의 사항이 더 있다.)

관용표현

① Let me know : 제게 알려 주세요

예문1) John: When will you leave Seoul?
Mary: It is not decided yet.
John: Let me know ASAP

07 We look forward to doing business with you in the future.

우리는 미래에도 당신과 함께 일할 수 있기를 고대합니다.

관용표현 ① look forward to : ~을 고대하다

예문1) He is looking forward to returning hometown.
(그는 고향에 돌아가는 것을 고대한다.)

08

Enjoy your trip!

즐거운 여행되십시오.

어 휘 ① enjoy : 즐기다

② trip : 여행

예문1) Enjoy yourself at the party.
(즐거운 파티 되세요!)

Practice 2 Task 4

보기에 있는 단어를 이용하여 문장을 안성하세요.

보기	leave confirm arrive make return meet drive

(1) This is to (　　　　) that all arrangements have been (　　　　) for your trip.

(2) Your flight will (　　　　) JFK airport on Feburary 3 at 9:20 am., (　　　　) at Los Angeles airport at 7:50 pm.

(3) Your (　　　　) flight will leave Los Angeles airport on Feburary 6 at 8:10 am., arriving at JFK at 6:40 pm.

(4) You will be (　　　　) at the airport by one of our drivers who will (　　　　) you to your hotel.

Practice 2 Task 5

제시되어 있는 단어와 구문을 활용하여 올바른 문장을 만들어 보세요.

(1) 안타깝게도 Hilton 호텔 예약이 다 찬 상태여서 우리는 당신이 Paradise호텔에 투숙하도록 예약했습니다.

so　you　into　have　booked　the Paradise　we

Unfortunately, the Hilton is fully booked, (　　　　　　　　)

(2) 더 문의할 사항이 있으면 알려주십시오.

have　futher　if　you　questions

Let me know (　　　　　　　　)

(3) 우리는 미래에도 당신과 함께 일할 수 있기를 고대합니다.

to doing with you in future the business

We look forward (   )

(4) 즐거운 여행하십시오.

trip enjoy your

(   )

Exercise Writing

당신의 계좌잔액 300 달러가 4달째 밀렸습니다. 이것은 우리의 세 번째 독촉장입니다. 가능하다면 이번 주 말까지 완불해주세요. 만약 우리가 5월 20일까지 연체금액을 완납 받지 않으면 우리는 적절한 조치를 취하게 될 것입니다. 당신의 신속한 응답을 고대합니다.	

Exercise You be the editor

다음 FAX를 읽고 틀린 부분을 찾아 고치세요. 4개의 틀린 문장이 있습니다.

This is to confirm that all arrangements have now been made for your trip. Your flight will leave Incheon airport on April 6 at 2:20 pm, arrived at Jeju airport at 3:20 pm.

Your return flight will leave Jeju airport on April 9 at 8 : 20 am, arriving at Incheon airport at 9 : 20 am.

You will met at the airport by one of our drivers who will drive you to your hotel. Unfortunately, the Hilton is fully booking, so we have booked you with the Paradiso.

Let me know if you have any further questions. Enjoy your trip.

Wrap up

Summary

1. The format of a fax

(1) Date: (2) To: (3) From: (4) Subject: (5) Reference: (6) Number of pages: (7) Message:

2. The key expressions for sending a fax

(1) Your account balance of $400 is three months overdue.

(2) We will have to take appropriate action.

(3) We look forward to your prompt response.

(4) This is to confirm that all arrangements have been made for your trip.

Wrap up

Assignment I

오늘 학습한 주요 문형을 활용할 수 있도록 문장을 작성하세요.

if possible	가능하다면
If + 주어 + 조동사 + not + 본동사, 주어 + 동사	~하지 않으면 ~ 하다.
주어 + be + met + by	마중 나온 ~를 만나다.

Answers

Lesson 6. Your account balance of $400 is three months overdue.

Warm up

Check up

1.
   A. March 30, 2013
   B. Misdelivery of headphones
   C. P.O. 04-2289-46
   D. This page only
2.
   1) Subject
   2) Reference
   3) Number of Pages
   4) Date
3. Confirmation of hotel reservation

Practice 1 Comprehension Check up

1) ② Hyewon Park
2) ① Minsoo Kim
3) ① To ask for the full payment of the overdue amount
4) ② $ 400

Practice 1 Task 1

1) Your account balance of $400 is three months overdue.
2) As you know, full settlement of your account was due on January 5, 2013.
3) We have not received even partial payment of the overdue amount.

Practice 1 Task 2

1) Furthermore, you have not responded to any of our earlier communications.
2) This is our third reminder.
3) If possible, make full payment by the end of this week.

Practice 1 Task 3

1) If we do not receive full payment of the overdue amount by April 30, we will have to take appropriate action.
2) Please call us to confirm your intention.
3) We are looking forward to your prompt response.

Practice 2 Comprehension Check up

1) ① Soojin Kim
2) ② The First Tour
3) ① To confirm a flight schedule
4) ② 7:50 pm
5) ③ Paradiso Hotel

Practice 2 Task 4

1) This is to confirm that all arrangements have been made for your trip.
2) Your flight will leave JFK airport on February 3 at 9:20 am., arriving at Los Angeles airport at 7:50 pm.
3) Your return flight will leave Los Angeles airport on February 6 at 8:10 am., arriving at JFK at 6:40 pm.
4) You will be met at the airport by one of our drivers who will drive you to your hotel.

Practice 2 Task 5

1) Unfortunately, the Hilton is fully booked, so we have booked you into the Paradise.
2) Let me know if you have further questions.
3) We look forward to doing business with you in the future.
4) Enjoy your trip.

Exercise Writing

Your account balance of $300 is 4 months overdue. This is our third reminder. If possible, make full payment by the end of this week.
If we do not receive full payment of the overdue amount by May 20, we will have to take appropriate action. We look forward to your prompt response.

Exercise You be the editor

This is to confirm that all arrangements have now been made for your trip. Your flight will leave Incheon airport on April 6 at 2:20 pm, arriving (주어 + 동사, 동사+ing: 사건의 연속성) at Jeju airport at 3:20 pm.

Your return flight will leave Jeju airport on April 9 at 8 am, arriving at Incheon airport at 9 am.

You will be met (be met by: 마중 나온 ~를 만나다) at the airport by one of our drivers who will drive you to your hotel. Unfortunately, the Hilton is fully booked (fully booked: 예약이 다 찬), so we have booked you into (book A into the hotel: A가 호텔에 투숙하도록 예약하다) the Paradiso.

Let me know if you have any further questions. Enjoy your trip.

Lesson 07

We are delighted to invite you to our wedding anniversary.

Lesson 07

We are delighted to invite you to our wedding anniversary.

Introduction

Lesson objectives

1. Writing an invitation card
2. Learning key expressions for writing an invitation card
   (1) We are honored to invite you and your wife to Jina Park's wedding.
   (2) A party will be held to celebrate Mr. Dongho Choi's sixtieth birthday.
   (3) Please RSVP to Minseok Park at minseok@*****.com.
   (4) Please find directions on the enclosed map.

Warm up

The format of an invitation card

① **Title:** A Beautiful Moment in Time

② **Guest:** We are delighted to invite you and your family to the wedding anniversary of the lovely Mr. and Mrs. Kim.

③ **Event:** As you may be aware, the Kims are celebrating 40 beautiful years of marriage.

④ **Host:** The party will be hosted by the loving children of the honored couple.

⑤ **Date and Place:** The affair will be on the evening of March 23, 2013 at the home of Billy Kim. The night will begin at 5 pm.

⑥ **General Information:** The party is casual and there will be food and drinks. We hope that you can share this special and fun evening with our family.

⑦ **RSVP:** Please RSVP to Billy Kim at Billykim@*****.com

⑧ **Directions:** Directions will be sent through email after RSVP.

① **Title:** 제목

- 초대장에 제목을 기입합니다. 제목은 행사의 내용을 간접적으로 말해주는 은유적인 표현을 주로 사용합니다. "Title"을 쓸 필요는 없습니다.

② **Guest:** 초대손님

- 누구를 초대하는지 기재합니다. "Guest"를 쓸 필요는 없습니다.

③ **Event:** 행사

- 어떤 행사인지를 언급합니다. 행사에는 생일파티, 결혼식, 결혼기념일 등 여러 가지가 있습니다.

④ **Host:** 주최

- 행사를 누가 주최하는지 기재합니다.

⑤ **Date and Place:** 날짜와 장소

- 행사가 열리는 날짜와 장소를 기재합니다.

⑥ **General Information:** 안내

- 행사에 대한 부수적인 정보를 기재합니다. 예를 들어 행사장에 정장을 입고가야 되면 정장착용을 요청하는 내용과 가족동반가능성 여부는 General Information에 들어갑니다.

⑦ **RSVP:** 회답

- 초대 수락 여부를 알려 줄 수 있는 연락처를 기재합니다. email 주소나 전화번호가 연락처가 될 수 있습니다.

⑧ **Directions:** 교통편 안내

- 행사장으로 오는 교통편을 안내합니다.

Warm up

Check up

초대장의 구조와 내용에 대한 문제를 풀어보겠습니다.

1. 보기에 주어진 각 항목을 이용하여 각 항목에 알맞은 표현을 적어 보세요.

보 기	Event　Guest　Host　General　Information　RSVP Directions　Date and Palce

1st Candle on the Cake

A [ ] We are happy to invite you and your wife to John's birthday party.
B [ ] We are celebrating John's first birthday
C [ ] The party will be hosted by Mr. and Mrs. Smith.
D [ ] The event will take place on the evening of May, 2013 at the home of Mr. and Mrs. Smith. The night will begin at 6 pm.
E [ ] The party is informal and food and drinks will be offered. We hope to share this occasion with you.
F [ ] Please RSVP to Bill Smith at billsmith@*****.com
G [ ] Directions will be sent to you by email after RSVP.

2. 다음에 주어진 각 표현의 해당 구성 요소를 연결해보세요.

보기	제목　초대손님　행사　주최　날짜와 장소 교통편안내　회답　안내

1) It is time to celebrate an amazing moment. [ ]

2) We would like you to RSVP by June 3, 2013. [ ]

3) The directions will be emailed to you after confirmation of RSVP. [ ]

4) Please bring your friends and family to enjoy the evening. We are hoping for as many people to come as possible. [ ]

5) The party will be hosted by Mr. and Mrs. Jackson. [ ]

6) The birthday party will be held on June 22, 2009 at Mr. Choi's eldest son's home. The party will begin at 7 pm. [ ]

7) You and your family are invited to Mr. Choi's birthday party. [ ]

8) A party will be held to celebrate Mr. Choi's birthday. [ ]

3. RSVP는 원래 불어의 Repondez s'il vous plait 의 첫 글자를 이용해서 만들어진 표현으로서 영어에서 자주 사용되고 있습니다. 영어에서는 RSVP는 어떤 의미로 사용될까요?

① Please reply.
② Please be quiet.
③ Please be seated.
④ Please call back.

Practice 1 Comprehension Check up

다음 초대장을 읽고 질문에 대한 답을 선택한 후 확인 버튼을 클릭하세요.

It is Time to Celebrate a Beautiful Moment in Life

Mr. Dongho Choi is inviting you and your family to his birthday party.

Event

A party will be held to celebrate Mr. Dongho Choi's sixtieth birthday.

Host

The party will be hosted by the eldest daughter of Mr. Dongho Choi.

Date and Place

The occasion will be on the evening of June 23, 2013 at the home of Misoon Choi.

The celebration will begin at 6 pm.

General Information

This will be a momentous event because Mr. Dongho Choi is having his sixtieth birthday. Please bring your friends and family to enjoy the evening. We are hoping for as many people as possible to come to the party.

RSVP

We would like you to RSVP by May 20, 2013.

Please call us at 010-555-****.

Directions

Please find directions on the enclosed map.

1. What is the invitation about?

① Invitation to a birthday party

② Invitation to a wedding ceremony

③ Invitation to a graduation ceremony

④ Invitation to a charity

2. Who is hosting the event?

① Mr. Dongho Choi
② Mr. Dongho Choi's wife
③ Mr. Dongho Choi's son
④ Mr. Dongho Choi's daughter

3. Why is the event special?

① Because it is his 60th birthday.
② Because it is his 60th wedding anniversary.
③ Because it is at night.
④ Because many people are expected to attend the party.

4. When is the event?

① The evening of June 23, 2013
② The evening of May 20, 2013
③ The morning of May 20, 2013
④ To be announced later

5. How can guests reply to this invitation?

① By sending an email
② By sending a fax
③ By calling 010-555-****
④ By sending a text message

인생의 아름다운 순간을 축하할 때입니다.

최동호님께서 자신의 생일파티에 당신과 당신의 가족을 초대합니다.

행사
최동호님의 60번째 생일을 축하하기 위해서 파티가 열립니다.

주최
파티는 최동호님의 장녀께서 주최합니다.

날짜와 장소
행사는 2013년 6월 23일 저녁 최미순님의 댁에서 열립니다. 축하행사는 저녁 6시에 시작합니다.

안내사항
최동호님께서 60번째 생일을 맞이하시기 때문에 이 행사는 중요한 행사가 될 것입니다. 당신의 친구와 가족을 동반하셔서 즐거운 저녁시간을 보내세요. 우리는 가능한 많은 사람들이 파티에 올 수 있기를 바랍니다.

회답
2013년 5월 20일까지 회답을 부탁 드립니다.
010-555-****로 우리에게 전화주세요.

행사장 교통안내
행사장 교통안내는 동봉된 지도에 나와 있습니다.

1. 초대는 무엇에 관한 것인가요?
   ① 생일 파티에 초대
   ② 결혼식에 초대
   ③ 졸업식에 초대
   ④ 자선 바자회에 초대

2. 누가 행사를 주관하나요?
   ① 최동호 선생님
   ② 최동호 선생님의 부인
   ③ 최동호 선생님의 아들
   ④ 최동호 선생님의 딸

3. 행사가 특별한 이유는 무엇입니까?

① 60번째 생일이기 때문에
② 60번째 결혼 기념이기 때문에
③ 행사를 밤에 하기 때문에
④ 많은 사람들이 파티에 참석하기로 되어있기 때문에

4. 행사는 언제인가요?

① 2013년 6월 23일 저녁
② 2013년 5월 20일 저녁
③ 2013년 5월 20일 아침
④ 추후에 공지될 예정

5. 손님들은 이 초대에 어떻게 답장 할 수 있습니까?

① 전자우편을 보낸다
② 팩스를 보낸다
③ 010-555-****로 전화한다
④ 편지를 보낸다

Practice 1 Lecture

01

Title

It is time to celebrate a beautiful moment in life.

(인생의 아름다운 순간을 축하할 때입니다.)

어 휘

① celebrate: 축하하다, 기념하다

예문1) We celebrated the New Year with a party.

(우리는 새해를 파티를 하며 축하했다.)

② beautiful: 아름다운

③ moment: 순간

예문1) I recognized him the moment I saw him.

(나는 그를 보는 순간 그를 알아보았다.)

구 문

예문1) It is time + to-부정사: ~할 때다.

It is time to prepare for the final exam.

(기말시험을 준비할 때다.)

02

Guest

Mr. Dongho Choi is inviting you and your family to his birthday party.

(최동호님께서 자신의 생일파티에 당신과 당신의 가족을 초대합니다.)

어 휘

① invite A to B: A를 B에 초대하다

예문1) Mina invited her friends to her son's birthday party.

(미나는 그녀의 친구들을 자신의 아들 생일잔치에 초대했다.)

② birthday: 생일

예문1) When is your birthday?

(너의 생일이 언제냐?)

03

Event

A party will be held to celebrate Mr. Dongho Choi's sixtieth birthday.

(최동호님의 60번째 생일을 축하하기 위해서 파티가 열립니다.)

어 휘

① hold: ~을 개최하다, ~을 열다

예문1) We will hold a meeting tomorrow.
(우리는 내일 회의를 개최한다.)

예문2) A party was held to celebrate her birthday.
(그녀의 생일을 축하하기 위해서 파티가 열렸다.)

② sixtieth: 60번째의

예문1) Today is my grandparents' sixtieth wedding anniversary.
(오늘은 조부모님의 60번째 결혼기념일이다.)

04

Host

The party will be hosted by the eldest daughter of Mr. Dongho Choi.

(파티는 최동호님의 장녀께서 주최합니다.)

어 휘

① host: ~을 주최하다

예문1) China hosted the last Olympics.
(중국은 지난번 올림픽을 주최했다.)

예문2) The next meeting will be hosted by Mr. Johnson.
(다음 모임은 존슨 씨에 의해서 주최될 것이다.)

② eldest: 제일 연상의, 장남 또는 장녀의

예문1) She has three sons, and her eldest son has just started school.
(그녀는 세 명의 아들이 있으며, 큰 애가 이제 막 학교에 입학했다.)

05

Date and Place

The occasion will be on the evening of June 23, 2013 at the home of Misoon Choi.

(행사는 2013년 6월 23일 저녁 최미순님의 댁에서 열립니다.)

어 휘 ① occasion: 행사 (특히 특별한 행사)

예문1) The opening of a new school is always a great occasion.
(신설 학교의 개교식은 언제나 큰 행사이다.)

구 문 ① 행사 + be + on + 특정일: ~행사가 특정일에 열리다

예문1) His wedding is on July 22.
(그의 결혼식은 7월 22일이다.)

06

The celebration will begin at 6 pm.

(축하행사는 저녁 6시에 시작합니다.)

어 휘 ① celebration: 축하, 축하행사

예문1) We held a celebration for John's graduation from the university.
(우리는 존의 대학졸업을 기념하는 축하행사를 열었다.)

② begin: 시작하다

예문1) He began working here 5 months ago.
(그는 5개월 전 여기서 일하기 시작했다.)

07

General Information

This will be a momentous event because Mr. Dongho Choi is having his sixtieth birthday.

(최동호님께서 60번째 생일을 맞이하기 때문에 이 행사는 중요한 행사가 될 것입니다.)

어 휘 ① momentous: 중요한

예문1) We listened to the momentous news that the war had begun.
(우리는 전쟁이 시작되었다는 중요한 뉴스를 들었다.)

② event: 행사

구 문 ① 주어 + 동사 + because + 주어 + 동사: ~ 때문에 ~하다

예문1) I was angry because she was late.
(나는 그녀가 늦어서 화가 났다.)

08 Please bring your friends and family to enjoy the evening.
(당신의 친구와 가족을 동반하셔서 즐거운 저녁시간을 보내세요.)

어 휘 ① bring: ~를 데리고 오다, ~을 가져오다

예문1) Please bring your friend to the party.
(당신의 친구를 파티에 데려오세요.)

예문2) Will you bring me a cup of tea?
(저에게 차 한 잔 가져다주시겠습니까?)

② enjoy: 즐기다

예문1) I enjoy going to the movies.
(나는 영화 보러가는 것을 즐긴다.)

09 We are hoping for as many people as possible to come to the party.
(우리는 가능한 많은 사람들이 파티에 올 수 있기를 바랍니다.)

어 휘 ① hope for: ~을 바라다, 희망하다

예문1) Everyone is hoping for rain.
(모두는 비를 바라고 있다.)

예문2) We hope for him to pass the exam.
(우리는 그가 시험에 합격하기를 바란다.)

관용표현 ① as many + 명사 + as possible: 가능한 많은

예문1) Sue invited as many people as possible to her house warming.
(수는 가능한 많은 사람들을 그녀의 집들이에 초청했다.)

10

RSVP

We would like you to RSVP by May 20, 2013.

(2013년 5월 20일까지 회답을 부탁 드립니다.)

어 휘 ① RSVP: 회답하다

예문1) Please RSVP by June 12, 2013.
(2013년 6월 12일까지 회답을 주세요.)

구 문 ① would like + 목적어 + to-부정사: ~에게 ~을 부탁하다

예문1) I would like you to pick me up at the airport.
(나는 네가 공항에 차로 나를 마중 나와 줄 것을 부탁한다.)

11

Please call us at 010-555-**.**

(010-555-****로 우리에게 전화주세요.)

어 휘 ① call: 전화하다

예문1) She called me from London.
(그녀는 런던에서 나에게 전화했다.)

구 문 ① call + 목적어 + at + 전화번호: ~전화번호로 ~에게 전화하다

예문1) Feel free to call me at 010-2255-****.
(010-2255-**** 번호로 저에게 자유롭게 전화하세요.)

12 Directions

Please find directions on the enclosed map.

(행사장 교통안내는 동봉된 지도에 나와 있습니다.)

어 휘

① directions: 교통편 안내

예문1) She gave me directions to the fire station.

(그녀는 나에게 소방서로 가는 길을 알려주었다.)

② enclosed: 동봉된

예문1) What is enclosed in the letter?

(편지에 무엇이 동봉되어 있습니까?)

③ map: 지도

Practice 1 Vocabulary & Expression

초대장에 나왔던 어휘와 구문을 정리해 보겠습니다. 숨기기 버튼을 클릭하여 내용을 숨긴 후 연습장에 해당 내용을 입력하면서 암기해 보세요.

구분	어휘 & 구문	의미
어휘	celebrate	축하하다, 기념하다
	beautiful	아름다운
	moment	순간
	invite	초대하다
	birthday	생일
	hold	~을 개최하다, ~을 열다
	sixtieth	60번째의
	host	~을 주최하다
	eldest	제일 연상의, 장남 또는 장녀의
	occasion	(특별한)행사
	celebration	축하, 축하행사
	begin	시작하다
	momentous	중요한
	event	행사
	bring	~를 데리고 오다, ~을 가져오다
	enjoy	즐기다
	hope for	~을 바라다, 희망하다
	RSVP	회답하다
	call	전화하다
	directions	교통편 안내
	enclosed	동봉된
	map	지도
관용표현	as many + 명사 + as possible	가능한 많은
구문	It is time + to-부정사	~할 때다
	행사 + be + on + 특정일	~행사가 특정일에 열리다
	주어 + 동사 + because + 주어 + 동사	~때문에 ~이다
	would like + 목적어 + to부정사	~에게 ~을 부탁하다
	call + 목적어 + at + 전화번호	~전화번호로 ~에게 전화하다

Practice 1 Task 1

주어진 단어를 이용하여 문장을 완성하세요. 필요한 경우는 동사의 형태를 변형시키세요.

보기	invite	celebrate	hold	host

(1) It is time to ( ) a beautiful moment in life.
(2) Mr. Dongho Choi is ( ) you and your family to his birthday party.
(3) A party will be ( ) to celebrate Mr.Dongho Choi's sixtieth birthday.
(4) The party will be ( ) by the eldest daughter of Mr. Dongho Choi.

Practice 1 Task 2

빈 칸에 들어갈 적절한 단어를 입력하여 문장을 완성하세요.

(1) 행사는 2013년 6월 23일 저녁 최미순님의 댁에서 열립니다.

The ( ) will be ( ) the evening of June 23, 2013 at the home of Misoon Choi.

(2) 축하행사는 저녁 6시에 시작합니다.

The ( ) will begin ( ) 6 pm.

(3) 최동호님께서 60번째 생일을 맞이하기 때문에 이 행사는 중요한 행사가 될 것 입니다.

This will be a ( ) event ( ) Mr. Dongho Choi is ( ) his sixtieth birthday.

(4) 당신의 친구와 가족을 동반하셔서 즐거운 저녁시간을 보내세요.

Please ( ) your friends and family to ( ) the evening.

Practice 1 Task 3

(1) 우리는 가능한 많은 사람들이 파티에 올 수 있기를 바랍니다.

for are we hoping

( ) as many people as possible to come to the party.

(2) 2013년 5월 20일까지 회답을 부탁 드립니다.

RSVP to like would you we

( ) by May 20, 2013

(3) 010-555-****로 우리에게 전화주세요.

us at call please

( ) 010-555-****.

(4) 행사장 교통안내는 동봉된 지도에 나와있습니다.

directions the enclosed find map please on

( )

Olympic Facts

France created the Olympic flag in 1914. The Olympic flag has five interconnected rings on a white background. The five rings are the symbol of the five major continents, and they are connected to show friendship, which is made through the international competitions. The color of the rings on the flag are blue, yellow, black, green, and red. At least one of these colors is found on every flag in the world.

Olympic medals are the most important prizes given for each Olympic event. The last real gold medal given at an Olympic game was in 112. Now, the Olympic medals are made specially for each Olympic game. The gold medal now only has six grams of gold in the actual medal.

The Olympic Opening Ceremony is an important part of the Olympic Games. It brings all the countries and athletes together at one time to show their pride for their countries and citizens. The first opening ceremonies were held in the 1908 Olympic Games in London.

The order of the procession at the ceremony is important. The Greeks were the creators of the Olympic Games, so they get the honor of being the first country represented. After the Greeks, it is in alphabetical order from A to Z. The final team is always the host team.

Korea has had a great record at the Olympic Games in the past 30 years. The South Koreans have won 203 Olympic medals including 72 gold medals since 1976. In this time, South Korea has won more gold medals than Cuba, Venezuela, Portugal and Nigeria combined.

Coffee break

올림픽 이야기

오륜기는 1914년 프랑스에서 만들어졌다. 오륜기는 하얀 바탕 위에 5개의 원이 서로 연결되어있다. 이 5개의 원은 5개의 대륙을 상징하는데, 이것들은 서로 연결되어 국가 간 경쟁을 통해 만들어지는 국가 간의 우정을 보여준다. 원은 각각 파랑, 노랑, 검정, 초록, 빨강의 색으로 되어있다. 이 색 중 적어도 한 가지는 전 세계의 국기에서 모두 찾아볼 수 있다.

올림픽 메달은 각 올림픽 행사에서 주어지는 가장 중요한 상품이다. 서기 112년은 올림픽경기에서 실제 금으로 만들어진 금메달이 수여된 마지막 해였다. 요즘은 매 올림픽경기마다 특별히 메달을 제작한다. 현재 금메달에는 오직 6그램의 금만이 실제 포함되어있다.

개막행사는 올림픽의 중요한 부분 중 하나이다. 모든 국가의 선수들이 함께 모여 동시에 그들의 자신감을 자국과 국민들에게 뽐낸다. 첫 개막행사는 1908년 런던올림픽에서 시작되었다.

개막식 입장순서는 중요하다. 그리스는 올림픽경기를 창시한 국가이기 때문에, 첫 번째로 입장하는 영광을 얻었다. 그리스 이후는 국가 명 알파벳 A-Z의 순서 별로 입장하고, 마지막 입장은 항상 주최국이다.

한국은 지난 30년간 올림픽 경기에서 훌륭한 기록을 가지고 있다. 남한은 1976년 이래로 72개의 금메달을 포함 203개의 올림픽 메달을 지고 있다. 남한은 쿠바, 베네수엘라, 포르투갈, 나이지리아의 금메달을 모두 합한 것보다 많은 금메달을 가지고 있다.

Practice 2 Comprehension Check up

New Beginnings

We are honored to invite you and your wife to Jina Park's wedding.

Event

We are celebrating the union of Mincheol Kim and Jina Park.

Host

Mr. Hansoo Park and Mrs. Sojin Lee are proud to host this wedding ceremony.

Date and Place

The affair will be on August 17, 2013 at Seoul Wedding Plaza.

The ceremony will begin at 1 pm.

General Information

A wedding reception will follow this ceremony at 2 pm.

Food and drinks will be served at the reception.

RSVP

We would appreciate it if you would RSVP by August 12, 2013.

Please RSVP to Minseok Park at minseok@*****.com.

Directions

Please find directions on the reverse side of this invitation card.

1. What is the invitation about?

   ① Invitation to a birthday party
   ② Invitation to a wedding ceremony
   ③ Invitation to a graduation ceremony
   ④ Invitation to an exhibition

2. Who is hosting the event?

   ① Mr. Hansoo Park
   ② Mr. Hansoo Park and Mrs. Sojin Lee
   ③ Jina Park
   ④ Mincheol Kim

3. Where is the occasion taking place?

① At the home of Jina Park
② At the home of Mincheol Kim
③ At Seoul Wedding Plaza
④ To be announced later

4. When does the event begin?

① At 1 pm on August 12, 2013
② At 1 pm on August 17, 2013
③ At 2 pm on August 12, 2013
④ At 2 pm on August 17, 2013

5. How can guests reply to this invitation?

① By sending an email
② By sending a fax
③ By calling Seoul Wedding Plaza
④ By calling Minseok Park

새로운 시작
당신과 당신의 부인을 박지나 양의 결혼식에 초대하게 돼어 영광입니다.
행사
김민철군과 박지나 양의 결혼을 축하합니다.
주최
박한수 선생님과 이소진 여사께서 이 결혼식을 주최하게 되어 자랑스럽습니다.
날짜와 장소
행사는 2013년 8월 17일 서울웨딩플라자에서 거행됩니다. 식은 오후 1시에 시작됩니다.
안내사항
이 결혼식 후 결혼식 피로연이 오후 2시에 있을 예정입니다. 피로연에서 음식과 음료가 제공될 것입니다.
회답
2013년 8월 12일까지 회답을 주시면 감사하겠습니다.
minseok@*****.com으로 박민석에게 연락주세요.
행사장 교통 안내
이 초대장의 뒷면에 행사장 교통안내가 나와 있습니다.

1. 초대장의 내용은 무엇에 관한 것입니까?
   ① 생일파티에 초대
   ② 결혼식에 초대
   ③ 졸업식에 초대
   ④ 전시회에 초대

2. 행사는 누가 주최합니까?
   ① 박한수 선생님
   ② 박한수 선생님과 이소진 여사
   ③ 박지나 양
   ④ 김민철 군

3. 행사는 어디에서 거행됩니까?

① 박지나 양의 집
② 김민철 군의 집
③ 서울웨딩플라자
④ 추후공지예정

4. 행사는 언제 시작합니까?

① 2013년 8월 12일 오후 1시
② 2013년 8월 17일 오후 1시
③ 2013년 8월 12일 오후 2시
④ 2013년 8월 17일 오후 2시

5. 손님들은 이 초대에 어떻게 답장을 할 수 있습니까?

① 전자우편을 보낸다
② 팩스를 보낸다
③ 서울웨딩플라자에 전화한다
④ 박민석에게 전화한다

Practice 2 Lecture

01

New Beginnings

(새로운 시작)

어 휘

① new: 새로운

② beginnings: 시작

예문1) Everything has a beginning.

(모든 것은 시작이 있다.)

예문2) Confucianism has its beginnings in China.

(유교는 중국에서 시작되었다.)

02

We are honored to invite you and your wife to Jina Park's wedding.

(당신과 당신의 부인을 박지나 양의 결혼식에 초대하게 되어 영광입니다.)

어 휘

① invite: 초대하다

② wedding: 결혼식

예문1) Sam invited most of his friends to his wedding.

(샘은 자신의 친구들을 대부분 자신의 결혼식에 초대했다.)

구 문

① 주어 + be + honored + to-부정사: ~하게 되어 영광이다

예문1) I was honored to meet with the President.

(나는 대통령을 만나게 되어 영광이었다.)

03

Event

We are celebrating the union of Mincheol Kim and Jina Park.

(김민철 군과 박지나 양의 결혼을 축하합니다.)

어 휘

① celebrate: 축하하다

② union: 결혼, 일치

예문1) John and Mary's love can lead to a union.
(존과 메리의 사랑은 결혼으로 이어질 수 있다.)

04

Host

Mr. Hansoo Park and Mrs. Sojin Lee are proud to host this wedding ceremony.

박한수 선생님과 이소진 여사께서 이 결혼식을 주최하게 되어 자랑스럽습니다.

어 휘

① host: ~을 주최하다

② wedding ceremony: 결혼식

예문1) Have you ever been invited to a wedding ceremony in a church?
(당신은 교회에서 하는 결혼식에 초대된 적이 있습니까?)

구 문

① 주어 + be + proud + to-부정사: ~하게 되어 자랑스럽다

예문1) The athlete was very proud to win a gold medal.
(그 선수는 금메달을 따서 매우 자랑스러웠다.)

05

Date and Place

The affair will be on August 17, 2013 at Seoul Wedding Plaza.

(행사는 2013년 8월 17일 서울웨딩플라자에서 거행됩니다.)

어 휘

① affair: 행사

예문1) Christmas is an annual affair.
(크리스마스는 연중행사다.)

구 문

① 행사 + be + on + 특정일: ~행사가 특정일에 열리다

예문1) The presidential election is on December 20.
(대통령 선거는 12월 20일이다.)

06

The ceremony will begin at 1 pm.

(식은 오후 1시에 시작합니다.)

어 휘

① ceremony: 의식

예문1) He will attend a ceremony marking the 10th anniversary of the society.

(그는 그 학회의 창립 10주년 기념식에 참석할 것이다.)

② begin: 시작하다

07

General Information

A wedding reception will follow this ceremony at 2 pm.

(이 결혼식 후 결혼식 피로연이 오후 2시에 있을 예정입니다.)

어 휘

① reception: 피로연, 환영회

예문1) A reception was held for the new governor.

(신임 주지사를 위한 피로연이 개최되었다.)

구 문

① 행사a + will + follow + 행사b: 행사b 후 행사a가 있을 예정이다

예문1) The closing ceremony will follow the performance.

(공연 후 폐회식이 있을 예정이다.)

08

Food and drinks will be served at the reception.

(피로연에서 음식과 음료가 제공됩니다.)

어 휘

① food: 음식

② drinks: 음료

③ serve: 제공하다

예문1) Please serve the coffee now.

(커피를 지금 제공해주세요.)

예문2) What time is breakfast served in this hotel?
(이 호텔에서 아침식사는 몇 시에 제공되나요?)

09

RSVP

We would appreciate it if you would RSVP by August 12, 2013.
(2013년 8월 12일까지 회답을 주시면 감사하겠습니다.)

어 휘 ① RSVP: 회답하다

구 문 ① 주어 + would + appreciate it + if + 주어 + would + 동사: ~해주시면 감사하겠습니다

예문1) I would appreciate it if you would do me a favor.
(당신이 부탁을 들어 주시면 저는 감사하겠습니다.)

10

Please RSVP to Minseok Park at minseok@***.com.**
(minseok@*****.com으로 박민석님에게 연락주세요.)

구 문 ① RSVP + to + 목적어 + at + 전자우편주소: ~에게 ~로 연락하다

예문1) Please RSVP to me at jks1004@*****.net.
(저에게 jks1004@*****.net으로 연락주세요.)

11

Directions

Please find directions on the reverse side of this invitation card.
(이 초대장의 뒷면에 행사장 교통안내가 나와 있습니다.)

어 휘 ① directions: 교통편 안내

② reverse: 반대의, 거꾸로 된

예문1) He read the names on the list in reverse order.

(그는 목록에 있는 이름들을 뒤에서부터 읽었다.)

③ invitation card: 초대장

Practice 2 Vocabulary & Expression

구분	어휘 & 표현	의미
어휘	new	새로운
	beginnings	시작
	invite	초대하다
	wedding	결혼식
	celebrate	축하하다
	union	결혼, 일치
	host	~을 주최하다
	wedding ceremony	결혼식
	affair	행사
	ceremony	의식
	begin	시작하다
	reception	피로연, 환영회
	food	음식
	drinks	음료
	serve	제공하다
	RSVP	회답하다
	directions	교통편 안내
	reverse	반대로, 거꾸로 된
	invitation card	초대장
구문	주어 + be + honored + to + 동사원형	~하게 되어 영광이다
	주어 + be + proud + to + 동사원형	~하게 되어 자랑스럽다
	행사 + be + on + 특정일	~행사가 특정일에 열리다
	행사a + will + follow + 행사b	행사b 후에 행사a가 있을 예정이다
	주어 + would + appreciate it + if + 주어 + would + 동사	~해주시면 감사하겠습니다
	RSVP + to + 목적어 + at + 전자우편주소	~에게 ~로 연락하다

Practice 2 Task 4

보기에 있는 단어를 이용하여 문장을 완성하세요. 필요한 경우 단어를 변형하세요.

보기	honor union be affair

(1) We are (   ) to invite you and your wife to Jina Park's wedding.

(2) We are celebrating the (   ) of Mincheol Kim and Jina Park.

(3) Mr. Hansoo Park and Mrs. Sojin Lee (   ) proud to host this wedding ceremony.

(4) The (   ) will be on August 17, 2013 at Seoul Wedding Plaza.

Practice 2 Task 5

빈 칸에 들어갈 적절한 단어를 입력하여 문장을 완성하세요.

(1) 식은 오후 1시에 시작합니다.

The (   ) will (   ) at 1 pm.

(2) 이 결혼식 후 결혼식 피로연이 오후 2시에 있을 예정입니다.

A wedding (   ) will (   ) this ceremony at 2 pm.

(3) 피로연에서 음식과 음료가 제공될 것입니다.

(   ) and (   ) will be (   ) at the reception.

Practice 2 Task 6

제시되어 있는 단어와 구문을 활용하여 올바른 문장을 완성하세요.

(1) 2013년 8월 12일까지 회답을 주시면 감사하겠습니다.

it would appreciate we

( ) if you would RSVP by August 12, 2013.

(2) minseok@*****.com으로 박민석님에게 연락주세요.

please at minseok@*****.com RSVP to Minseok Park

( )

(3) 이 초대장의 뒷면에 교통안내가 나와 있습니다.

the on reverse this invitation card side of

Please find directions ( )

Practice 2 Vocabulary Game

celebrate	directions
occasion	reception
RSVP	host
hold	union
wedding	invite

개최하다	피로연
결혼식	결혼
축하하다.	회답하다
행사	초대하다
교통편 안내	주최하다

Exercise Writing

왼쪽의 글을 읽은 후 그를 바탕으로 초대장을 영작해 보세요. 영작 후 [확인] 버튼을 클릭하여 [모범 답안]과 비교해 보세요.

인생의 아름다운 순간을 축하할 때입니다. John Brown 선생님이 당신과 당신의 남편을 자신의 생일파티에 초대합니다.	
행사	**Event**
John Brown 선생님의 70번째 생일을 축하하기 위해서 파티가 열립니다.	( )
주최	**Host**
파티는 John Brown 선생님의 장남이 주최합니다.	( )
날짜와 장소	**Date and Place**
행사는 2013년 9월 17일 저녁에 John Brown 선생님의 집에서 열립니다. 축하행사는 오후 4시에 시작합니다.	( )
안내	**General Information**
당신의 아이들을 파티에 데려오세요.	( )
회답	**RSVP**
2013년 9월 10일까지 회답을 부탁드립니다. 010-2233-****로 우리에게 전화주세요.	( )
교통편 안내	**Directions**
교통편 안내는 동봉된 지도에 나와 있습니다.	( )

Exercise You be the editor

다음 초대장을 읽고 밑줄친 부분을 올바르게 고치세요.

New Beginnings

We are delighted to <u>invite you and your family at my daughter's wedding</u>.

Event

<u>We are celebrated</u> the union of Minsoo Kim and Younhee Seo.

Host

Mr. Jaeyoung Park and Mrs. Mijin Lee are proud to host this wedding ceremony.

Date and Place

The occasion will be <u>in July 17</u>, 2013 at Seoul Wedding Plaza. The ceremony will begin at 3 pm.

General Information

A wedding reception will follow this ceremony at 4 pm. Food and drinks <u>will served</u> at the reception.

RSVP

We would appreciate it if you would RSVP <u>until July 12, 2013</u>.

Please call us at 010-3320-****.

Directions

Please find directions on the reverse side of this invitation card.

Wrap up

Summary

1. The format of a invitation card

(1) Title

(2) Guest

(3) Event

(4) Host

(5) Date and Place

(6) General Information

(7) RSVP

(8) Directions

2. Key expressions for an invitation card

(1) We are honored to invite you and your wife to Jina Park's wedding.

(2) A party will be held to celebrate Mr. Dongho Choi's sixtieth birthday.

(3) Please RSVP to Minseok Park at minseok@*****.com.

(4) Please find directions on the enclosed map.

Wrap up

Assignment Ⅰ

오늘 학습한 주요 문형을 활용할 수 있는 문장을 작성하여 다른 학습자와 공유하세요.

It is time + to + 동사	~할 때다.
행사 + be + on + 특정일	~행사가 특정일에 열리다.
주어 + 동사 + because + 주어 + 동사	~ 때문에 ~이다.
would like + 목적어 + to + 동사	~에게 ~을 부탁하다.
call + 목적어 + at + 전화번호	~전화번호로 ~에게 전화하다.
주어 + be + honored + to + 동사원형	~하게 되어 영광이다.
주어 + be + proud + to + 동사원형	~하게 되어 자랑스럽다.
행사 + be + on + 특정일	~행사가 특정일에 열리다.
행사a + will + follow + 행사b	행사b 후 행사a가 있을 예정이다.
주어 + would + appreciate it + if + 주어 + would + 동사	~해주시면 감사하겠습니다.
RSVP + to + 목적어 + at + 전자우편주소	~에게 ~로 연락하다.

Wrap up

Assignment II

오늘 학습한 주요내용과 제시된 조건에 맞게 초대장을 작성해 봅시다. 영어(한글) 형태로 작성한 후 〔제출하기〕버튼을 클릭하면 〔과제방〉주관식 과제〕에 등록됩니다.

[조건]

1. 주제

 본인의 생일 파티 초대

2. 형식

 (1) Title
 (2) Guest
 (3) Event
 (4) Host
 (5) Date and Place
 (6) General Information
 (7) RSVP
 (8) Directions

3. (6) General Information은 3문장, 나머지는 각 1문장이 되도록 하세요.

Answers

Lesson 7. We are delighted to invite you to our wedding anniversary.

Warm up
Check up

1.
   A. Guest
   B. Event
   C. Host
   D. Date and Place
   E. General information
   F. RSVP
   G. Directions

2.
   1) 제목
   2) 회답
   3) 교통편 안내
   4) 안내
   5) 주최
   6) 날짜와 장소
   7) 초대손님
   8) 행사

3. ① Please reply

Practice 1 Comprehension Check up

1) ① Invitation to a birthday party
2) ④ Mr. Dongho choi's daughter
3) ① Because it is his 60th birthday
4) ① The evening of June 23, 2008
5) ③ By calling 010-555-****

Practice 1 Task 1

1) It is time to celebrate a beautiful moment in life.
2) Mr. Dongho Choi is inviting you and your family to his birthday party.
3) A party will be held to celebrate Mr. Dongho Choi's sixtieth birthday.
4) The party will be hosted by the eldest daughter of Mr. Dongho Choi.

Practice 1 Task 2

1) The occasion will be on the evening of June 23, 2013 at the home of Misoon Choi.
2) The celebration will begin at 6 pm.
3) This will be a momentous event because Mr. Dongho Choi is having his sixtieth birthday.
4) Please bring your friends and family to enjoy the evening.

Practice 1 Task 3

1) We are hoping for as many people as possible to come to the party.
2) We would like you to RSVP by May 20, 2013.
3) Please call us at 010-555-****.
4) Please find directions on the enclosed map.

Practice 2 Comprehension Check up

1) ② Invitation to a wedding ceremony
2) ② Mr. Hansoo Park and Mrs. Sojin Lee
3) ③ At Seoul Wedding Plaza
4) ② At 1 pm on August 17, 2013
5) ① By sending an email

Practice 2 Task 4

1) We are honored to invite you and your wife to Jina Park's wedding.
2) We are celebrating the union of Mincheol Kim and Jina Park.
3) Mr. Hansoo Park and Mrs. Sojin Lee are proud to host this wedding ceremony.
4) The affair will be on August 17, 2013 at Seoul Wedding Plaza.

Practice 2 Task 5

1) The ceremony will begin at 1 pm.

2) A wedding reception will follow this ceremony at 2 pm.
3) Food and drinks will be served at the reception.

Practice 2 Task 6

1) We would appreciate it if you would RSVP by August 12, 2013.
2) Please RSVP to Minseok Park at minseok@*****.com.
3) Please find directions on the reverse side of this invitation card.

Exercise Writing

It is time to celebrate a beautiful moment in life.

Mr. John Brown is inviting you and your husband to his birthday party.

Event A party will be held to celebrate Mr. John Brown's seventieth birthday

Host The party will be hosted by the eldest son of Mr. John Brown.

Date and Place The occasion will be on September 17, 2013 at the home of Mr. John Brown. The celebration will begin at 4 pm.

General Information Please bring your children to the party.

RSVP We would like you to RSVP by September 10, 2013. Please call us at 010-2233-****

Directions Please find directions on the enclosed map.

Exercise You be the editor

New Beginnings

We are delighted to invite you and your family to (invite A to B: A를 B에 초대하다.) my daughter's wedding.

Event

We are celebrating (주어 + be + celebrating: ~을 축하한다.) the union of Minsoo Kim and Younhee Seo.

Host

Mr. Jaeyoung Park and Mrs. Mijin Lee are proud to host this wedding ceremony.

Date and Place

The occasion will be on July 17, 2013 (on + 특정일) at Seoul Wedding Plaza. The ceremony will begin at 3 pm.

General Information

A wedding reception will follow this ceremony at 4 pm. Food and drinks will be served (주어 + will + be + served:~이 제공될 예정이다.) at the reception.

RSVP

We would appreciate it if you would RSVP by July 12, 2013 (by + 마감기간). Please call us at 010-3320-****.

Directions

Please find directions on the reverse side of this invitation card.

Business
Management
Writing
Basis and Application

Review Exercises

비즈니스영어작문 총정리 연습문제 (Lesson 1~7)

비즈니스 영어작문 총정리 연습문제 (Lesson 1~7)

Part 1. 다음 e-mail의 format을 잘 살펴보고 물음에 답하시오.

From sue@*****.com

To jina@*****.com

[(1) 제목] A favor

[(2) 첨부]

[(3) 잭슨 선생님께]:

I am doing my best, but we need some more time to finish the work. Can you extend the deadline to the end of this month? I am sorry for the delay. I have attached two report files for your information.

[(4)],

Jina Brown

[(5)추신] Even if the deadline is extended, I will try to finish the work ASAP.

1. 위 e-mail의 format에서 (1)에 들어갈 적절한 단어 또는 표현을 넣으시오. (첫 철자는 대문자로 시작하세요.)

2. 위 e-mail의 format에서 (2)에 들어갈 적절한 단어 또는 표현을 넣으시오. (첫 철자는 대문자로 시작하세요.)

3. 위 e-mail의 format에서 (3)에 들어갈 적절한 단어 또는 표현을 넣으시오.
(잭슨 선생님은 남자입니다.)

4. 위 e-mail의 format에서 (4)에 적절한 격식 체 closing을 넣으시오.

5. 위 e-mail의 format에서 (5)에 들어갈 적절한 단어 또는 표현을 넣으시오.

Part 2. 다음 영문일기의 **format**을 잘 살펴보고 물음에 답하시오.

A Visit to a Fire Station

[(6) 2013년 4월 25일 목요일 비]

Today we learned about a fire in class. After the class was over, we went to a fire station. It was [(7)]. When we arrived at the fire station, there were 14 fire fighters there. They showed us fire trucks and fire suits. We tried [(8)] the fire suits. They were very heavy.

I think fire fighters are heroes. They help to save people's lives. They are brave people. I respect them very much. [(9)] I grow up, I want to be a brave fire fighter. The trip to the fire station was [(10)]

6. 위 영문일기의 format에서 (6)에 들어갈 적절한 단어 또는 표현을 넣으시오.(생략형을 사용하지 말고 full version을 사용하세요.)

7. 위 영문일기의 format에서 (7)에 "~에 신나는 견학"이라는 의미를 표현하기 위해 필요한 4개의 영어단어를 기입하시오.

8. 위 영문일기의 format에서 (8)에 들어갈 적절한 단어를 기입하시오.

9. 위 영문일기의 format에서 (9)에 주된 사건과 배경사건을 나타낼 때 사용 할 수 있는 접속사를 기입하시오.

10. 위 영문일기의 format에서 (10)에 (7)에 "~에 좋은 경험이 이었다"라는 의미를 표현하기 위해 필요한 3개의 영어단어를 기입하시오.

Part 3. 다음 영문이력서의 **format**을 잘 살펴보고 물음에 답하시오.

Personal Information

Name: Mincheol Kim

Date of Birth: June 12, 1986

Address: 270 Imun-dong, Dongdaemun-gu, Seoul 130-791

Job Objective

[(11) 홍보부]

Work Experience

March 2010 - February 2013 GS Construction, Suwon

Intern, Department of Planning

[(12) 판매와 광고담당]

Education	
March 2003 - February 2012	Sejong University, Seoul Major: Computer Engineering, Minor: [(13) 경영학]
March 2000 - February 2003	Sejong High School, Seoul

Special Skills	
Foreign Language	Fluent in English and Japanese [(14) FLEX에서 750점 취득함]
Computer	Proficient in Excel, MS Word, and Internet searching

Licenses and Certificates	
March 2008	Data Processing Engineer Certification, Grade 2
February 2004	Translation Certification, Grade 1

Activities	
May 2005 - February 2006	President of English Club, Sejong University
March 2004 - February 2005	[(15) 어학연수로 하버드대학교 방문함]

11. 위 영문이력서 format의 (11)에 들어갈 적절한 단어나 표현을 쓰시오.

12. 위 영문이력서 format의 (12)에 들어갈 적절한 단어나 표현을 쓰시오.

13. 위 영문이력서 format의 (13)에 들어갈 적절한 단어나 표현을 쓰시오.

14. 위 영문이력서 format의 (14)에 들어갈 적절한 단어나 표현을 쓰시오.

15. 위 영문이력서 format의 (15)에 들어갈 적절한 단어나 표현을 쓰시오.

Part 4. 다음 영문자기소개서를 잘 살펴보고 물음에 답하시오.

Personal History

My family includes my parents, my elder brother, my elder sister, and me. I am the youngest child in my family. I was home-educated to work well in a team environment. So since childhood I have been getting along with others.

School Days

In high school, social studies was my favorite subject. Because of my interest in social studies, I majored in Business Administration at university. After graduating from university I entered graduate school and majored in Marketing.

Strengths and Weaknesses

I am an idealistic person, but I am also a good natured person. I always try to help others with their work.

Career Objectives

I will improve my English [(20)   ]. In addition, I will work hard to make better products for the company.

16. 위 영문자기소개서 저자의 가족은 총 몇 명인가?

① 3명 ② 4명 ③ 5명 ④ 6명 ⑤ 7명

17. 위 영문자기소개서 저자가 고등학교 때 좋아했던 과목은 무엇인가?

① 사회 ② 영어 ③ 국어 ④ 세계사 ⑤ 지리

18. 위 영문자기소개서 저자의 대학원 전공은 무엇인가?

① 경영학 ② 회계학 ③ 국제무역 ④ 마케팅 ⑤ 국제무역

19. 위 영문자기소개서 저자의 약점은 무엇인가?

① 소극적 성격 ② 이상주의자
③ 이기적인 성격 ④ 넓은 포용력

20. 위 영문자기소개서 (20)에 "토익에서 900점을 받을 때까지"라는 의미를 나타낼 수 있는 영어표현을 완성하시오. ("until"을 사용하시오.)

Part 5. 다음 영문입사지원서의 format을 살펴보고 물음에 답하시오.

23 Yonghun-dong, Nam-gu
Incheon 402-751

March 27, 2013
Mr. Minsoo Kim
Manager, Department of Human Resources
New World Corporation
275 Yeoksam-dong, Gangnam-gu
Seoul 823-333
(21) 담당선생님께 :

[(22) 저는 당신 회사의 회계원 자리에 지원하기 위해 편지를 씁니다.] [(23) 저는 저의 이력서를 동봉했습니다.] I hope that my application will be of interest to you. I would like to schedule an interview with you. [(24) 아무 때라도 자유롭게 저에게 연락하세요.]
I look forward to hearing from you soon.

Sincerely,

Haemin Park
Haemin Park
(25) 동봉물

21. 위 영문이력서 format의 (21)에 들어갈 적절한 표현을 쓰시오.

22. 위 영문이력서 format의 (22)에 들어갈 적절한 문장을 쓰시오.

23. 위 영문이력서 format의 (23)에 들어갈 적절한 문장을 쓰시오.

24. 위 영문이력서 format의 (24)에 들어갈 적절한 문장을 쓰시오. ("Please"를 사용하세요)

25. 위 영문이력서 format의 (25)에 들어갈 적절한 단어나 표현을 쓰시오.

Part 6. 다음 영문팩스의 format을 잘 살펴보고 물음에 답하오.

FAX

Date:	April 1, 2013
To:	Keechol Park Mirae Electronics
From:	Minyoung Kim World Tour

Subject:	[(26) Your rent is overdue]
Reference:	Foreign Exchange Bank account number: 100-65-4357-557
Number of pages:	[(27) 1페이지]
Message:	[(28) 당신의 월세가 3개월 연체되어있습니다.] [(29) 이번 주 말까지 완불해주세요.] [(30) 당신의 신속한 응답을 고대하겠습니다.]

26. 위 영문팩스 제목 (26)을 팩스형식으로 수정하세요.

27. 위 영문팩스 (27)에 들어갈 적절한 영문을 쓰시오.

28. 위 영문팩스 (28)에 들어갈 적절한 영어문장을 쓰시오.

29. 위 영문팩스 (29)에 들어갈 적절한 영어문장을 쓰시오.("Please"를 사용하세요.)

30 위 영문팩스 (30)에 들어갈 적절한 영어문장을 쓰시오.("look forward"를 사용하세요.)

Part 7. 다음 영문초대장의 format을 잘 살펴보고 물음에 답하시오.

A Beautiful Moment in Time

We are delighted to invite you and your family to the wedding anniversary of the lovely Mr. and Mrs. Park.

Event

(31) 박선생님 부부는 결혼 30주년 축하합니다.

Host

The party will be hosted by the youngest daughter of the honored couple.

Date and Place

The affair will be [(32)   ] at the home of Jina Park. The night will begin at 6 pm.

General Information

[(33)   ] and dinner is provided for all the guests. We hope that you can share this special and fun evening with our family.

RSVP

We would like you to RSVP by April 30. [(34)   ] at jina@*****.com.

Directions:

Please find directions on the enclosed map.

31. 위 영문초대장 (31)에 들어갈 적절한 영어문장을 쓰시오. ("The Parks", "celebrating", "30 years"를 사용하시오.)

32. 위 영문초대장 (32)에 "2013년 5월 6일 저녁에"에 해당하는 영문표현을 쓰시오.

33. 위 영문초대장의 (33)에 "정장을 입고 올 필요가 없습니다"라는 의미를 표현하기 위해서 들어가야 할 적절한 영어문장을 쓰시오.("The party"를 사용해서 문장을 완성하시오.)

34. 위 영문초대장의 (34)에 "박지나에게 회답하세요"라는 의미의 영문표현을 쓰세요. ("Please", "RSVP"를 사용하세요.)

35. 위 영문초대장의 내용과 일치하지 않는 것을 고르시오.

① 초대장의 제목 "A Beautiful Moment in Time"은 박선생님 부부의 결혼 30주년을 의미한다.

② 결혼기념일 행사는 저녁 6시에 시작한다.

③ 참석한 모든 이에게 저녁식사가 제공된다.

④ 행사장 안내는 초대장에 동봉되어있다.

⑤ 참석여부는 박 선생님 부부에게 전자우편으로 알린다.

Answers

비즈니스 영어작문 총정리 연습문제 (Lesson 1~7)

Part 1.

1. Subject
2. Attachment
3. Dear Mr. Jackson
4. (1) Sincerely yours (2) Sincerely (3) Cordially (4) Cordially yours
5. P.S.

Part 2.

6. (1) Rainy, Thursday, April 25, 2013 (2) Wet, Thursday, April 25, 2013
7. a very exciting trip
8. wearing
9. When
10. a good experience

Part 3.

11. Department of Public Relations
12. (1) Responsibilities include sales and advertising.
13. Business Administration
14. Scored 750 on the FLEX
15. (1) Visited Harvard University for a Language Program

Part 4.

16. (3)

17. (1)

18. (4)

19. (2)

20. (1) until I achieve a score of 900 on the TOEIC

Part 5.

21. (1) To whom it may concern
(2) To whom it may concern:
(3) To whom it may concern,

22. (1) I am writing to apply for the accountant position at your company.
(3) I am writing this letter to apply for the accountant position at your company.

23. (1) I have enclosed my resume.
(3) I am enclosing my resume.

24. (1) Please feel free to contact me at any time.

25. (1) Enclosure

Part 6.

26. (1) Overdue rent

27. This page only

28. (1) Your rent is three months overdue.

29. (1) Please make full payment by the end of this week.

30. I look forward to your prompt response.

Part 7.

31. (1) The Parks are celebrating 30 years of marriage.

32. on the evening of May 6, 2013

33. (1) The party is casual.

34. (1) Please RSVP to Jina Park

35. (5)

Lesson 08

I am happy to recommend Michael Kim.

Lesson 08

I am happy to recommend Michael Kim.

Introduction

Lesson objectives

1. Writing a recommendation letter
2. Learning the key expressions for a recommendation letter
   (1) It is with great pleasure that I recommend Mr. Michael Kim for the position of English teacher.
   (2) He was one of the best teachers that we have had at our school.
   (3) I am very pleased to write this letter of recommendation for Jamie Park.
   (4) She will be a valuable asset to your company.

Warm up

The format of a recommendation letter

① Return Address

Juniper Yang
23-5 Sangji-dong, Sang-gu Daejeon 113-447

② Date

May 21, 2013

③ Inside Address

Mr. John H. Petry
Manager, Department of Personnel
Cell System Corporation
12-4 Myongryoon-dong, Chongno-gu
Seoul 130-551

④ Greeting

Dear Mr. Petry:

⑤ Body

I am happy to recommend Rachel Lee for employment at your company.

I had the pleasure of working with Rachel Lee at Dream Enterprise in Daejeon where she was the administrative coordinator of the marketing division. She was organized, efficient, and willing to do whatever was needed to get a particular task finished.

Rachel deserves serious consideration as a potential employee, and I recommend her highly.

⑥ Closing

Sincerely,

⑦ Signature

Juniper Yang

⑧ Name

Juniper Yang

⑨ Job Title

Vice Principal

① 발신인 주소

• 추천서를 쓰는 사람의 주소를 기재합니다. 추천인, 번지수, 동, 구, 시, 그리고 우편번호를 기재합니다.

② 날짜

• 추천서를 쓰는 날짜를 기재합니다. 날짜는 월 + 일, 연도 순서로 기재합니다.

③ 수신인 주소

• 추천서를 받는 사람의 주소를 기재합니다. 수신인 주소는 수신인, 직책, 부서, 회사, 번지 +동, 구, 도시, 우편번호 순서로 기재합니다.

수신인	내용
남성	Mr. + 이름 + 성
기혼여성	Mrs. + 이름 + 성
미혼여성	Miss + 이름 + 성
기혼 또는 미혼여성	Ms. + 이름 + 성

④ 인사

수신인	내용
남성	Dear Mr. + 수신인의 성:
기혼여성	Dear Mrs. + 수신인의 성:
미혼여성	Dear Miss +수신인의 성:
기혼 또는 미혼여성	Dear Ms. + 수신인의 성:

• 지원서의 인사는 격식체 인사를 사용합니다.

⑤ 본문

• 첫 번째 문단은 추천서를 쓰는 사람의 자세에 대해서 기재합니다. 두 번째 문단은 피추천인의 장점과 능력에 대해서 기재합니다. 세 번째 문단은 피추천인에 대한 추천인의 입장을 정리합니다.

⑥ 끝인사

격식체	Sincerely, Sincerely yours, Cordially, Cordially yours,

• 추천서의 끝인사는 격식체를 사용합니다.

⑦ 서명

• 추천서를 쓰는 사람의 서명을 기재합니다.

⑧ 이름

• 추천서를 쓰는 사람의 이름을 기재합니다.

⑨ 직책

• 추천서를 쓰는 사람의 직책을 기재합니다.

Warm up

Check up

추천서의 구조와 내용에 대한 다음 문제를 풀어보겠습니다.

1. 추천서의 본문에 들어가는 내용을 순서에 맞게 배열하세요. 항목을 선택한 후 화살표를 클릭하여 위 아래로 항목 위치를 이동 후 확인 버튼을 클릭하세요.

A. It is with great pleasure that I recommend Sally Forth for the position of history teacher at Seoul International High School. B. Her primary responsibilities were teaching social studies and general history. C. She taught at Mirae High School from March 4, 2007 to February 25, 2012, during which time I was principal. D. I strongly recommend her and am sure that you will be more than satisfied with her performance in the classroom.

1) [ ] → 2) [ ] → 3) [ ] → 4) [ ]

2. 다음 중 추천서에서 사용되는 Greeting과 Closing에 가장 적절한 스타일은?

① 격식체
② 비격식체
③ 약식체

Practice 1 Comprehension Check up

다음 추천서를 읽고 질문에 대한 답을 선택한 후 확인 버튼을 클릭하세요.

1-27 Myongryoon-dong
Chongno-gu, Seoul 110-521

March 21, 2013

Mr. Minwoo Song
Principal
Incheon Foreign Language High School
434 Kaja-dong, Seo-gu
Incheon 404-250

Dear Mr. Song:

It is with great pleasure that I recommend Mr. Michael Kim for the position of English teacher at Incheon Foreign Language High School.

Mr. Michael Kim taught at Seoul International High School from March 2, 2006 to February 28, 2013. His primary responsibilities were teaching English Grammar and English Composition. He was one of the best teachers that we have had at our school. We were deeply saddened when he and his family moved to Incheon. I can assure you that you will be more than satisfied with his performance in the classroom.

He is conscientious, professional, and diligent. I strongly recommend him for the position of English teacher at your school.

Sincerely,

Dongmin Yang

Dongmin Yang

Vice Principal

1. What is the job title of the person who wrote the recommendation letter?
① English teacher
② Principal
③ Vice Principal
④ Coordinator

2. Who is the recommendation letter addressed to?
① Mr. Minwoo Song
② Mr. Dongmin Yang
③ Mr. Michael Kim
④ Mr. Michael Kim's wife

3. What did Mr. Michael Kim teach at Seoul International High School? (Choose two)
① English Conversation
② English Grammar
③ English Composition
④ English discussion

4. Why did Mr. Michael Kim have to quit his job at Seoul International High School?
① Because he wanted a different job.
② Because he wanted to make more money.
③ Because he moved to Incheon.
④ Because he left Korea.

5. How did Mr. Dongmin Yang describe Mr. Michael?
① diligent
② cooperative
③ creative
④ ambitious

서울 종로구
명륜동 1-27번지 11-521

2013년 3월 21일

인천시 서구
가좌동 434번지 404-250
인천외국어고등학교
송민우 교장 선생님

송선생님께

저는 김마이클 선생님을 인천외국어고등학교 영어선생님으로 추천하게 되어 매우 기쁩니다. 김마이클 선생님은 2006년 3월 2일부터 2013년 2월 28일까지 서울국제고등학교에서 가르치셨습니다. 그의 주된 업무는 영문법과 영작문을 가르치는 일이었습니다. 그는 우리 학교에 계셨던 최고의 선생님들 중에 한 분이었습니다. 그리고 우리는 그와 그의 가족들이 인천으로 이사가서 몹시 안타까웠습니다. 저는 당신이 그의 교실에서의 수행능력에 기대 이상으로 만족할 것이라고 당신에게 확신할 수 있습니다.
그는 성실하고 전문적이며 근면합니다. 저는 그를 당신 학교의 영어교사로 적극 추천합니다.

양동민 교감

1. 추천서를 쓴 사람의 직책은 무엇입니까?
   ① 영어교사
   ② 교장
   ③ 교감
   ④ 코디네이터

2. 추천서는 누구에게 보내졌습니까?
   ① 송민우 선생님
   ② 양동민 선생님
   ③ 김마이클 선생님
   ④ 김마이클 선생님의 부인

3. 마이클 김선생님은 국제고등학교에서 무슨 과목을 가르쳤습니까? (둘을 고르시오)

① 영어회화
② 영어문법
③ 영어작문
④ 영어토론

4. 마이클 김 선생님은 왜 서울국제고등학교 교사를 그만두셨습니까?

① 다른 직업을 원했기 때문에
② 돈을 더 벌기 위해서
③ 인천으로 이사갔기 때문에
④ 한국을 떠났기 때문에

5. 양동민 선생님은 송민우 선생님이 어떻다고 말했나요?

① 근면한
② 협력적인
③ 창조적인
④ 야심 있는

Practice 1 Lecture

01

Dear Mr. Song:

(송선생님께)

관용표현 Dear + title + family name: ~선생님께

예문1) Dear Mrs. Lee: (이선생님께)

02

It is with great pleasure that I recommend Mr. Michael Kim for the position of English teacher at Incheon Foreign Language High School.

(저는 김마이클 선생님을 인천외국어고등학교 영어선생님으로 추천하게 되어 기쁩니다.)

어 휘

① pleasure: 기쁨

② recommend: 추천하다

예문1) I recommended her for the job.

(나는 그 직업에 그녀를 추천했다.)

③ position: 일자리

구 문

① It is with great pleasure that + 주어 + 동사: ~하게 되어 매우 기쁘다

예문1) It is with great pleasure that I had an opportunity to talk with her.

(나는 그녀와 이야기 할 수 있는 기회가 있어서 매우 기쁘다.)

03 Mr. Michael Kim taught at Seoul International High School from March 2, 2006 to February 28, 2013.

(김마이클 선생님은 2006년 3월 2일에서 2013년 2월 28일까지 서울국제고등학교에서 가르치셨습니다.)

어 휘

① teach: 가르치다

예문1) She teaches politics to college students.
(그녀는 대학생들에게 정치학을 가르친다.)

② position: 일자리

구 문

① from A to B: ~부터 ~까지

예문1) My mom was deeply saddened by the early retirement of my father.
(엄마는 아빠가 일찍 퇴직하게 되어 몹시 안타까웠다.)

04 His primary responsibilities were teaching English Grammar and English Composition.

(그의 주된 업무는 영문법과 영작문을 가르치는 일이었습니다.)

어 휘

① primary: 주된, 주요한

② responsibilities: 업무, 책임

예문1) The father of a family has many responsibilities.
(가족을 부양하는 아버지는 많은 책임이 있다.)

구 문

① One's primary responsibility was ~: 담당업무는 ~ 였습니다

예문1) Her primary responsibility was managing the restaurant.
(그녀의 주된 업무는 레스토랑을 경영하는 것이었습니다.)

05 **He was one of the best teachers that we have had at our school.**

(그는 우리학교에 계셨던 최고의 선생님들 중에 한 분이었습니다.)

어 휘 ① area: 분야, 영역

예문1) He is an expert in the area of linguistics.
(그는 언어학 분야에 전문가다.)

관용표현 ① 주어 + be + one + of + the + best + 복수명사: 최고의 ~중에 하나다

예문1) He is one of the best scholars in Korea.
(그는 한국의 최고의 학자 중에 한 분이다.)

06 **We were deeply saddened when he and his family moved to Incheon.**

(우리는 그와 그의 가족들이 인천으로 이사가서 몹시 안타까웠습니다.)

어 휘 ① deeply: 몹시, 강하게

② saddened: 안타까운, 슬픈

예문1) My mom was deeply saddened by the early retirement of my father.
(엄마는 아빠가 일찍 퇴직하게 되어 몹시 안타까웠다.)

③ when: ~할 때

예문1) When he comes, tell him to wait in my office.
(그가 오면 내 사무실에서 기다리라고 말해줘.)

④ move: 이사 가다

예문1) Their present house is too small, so they have decided to move.
(그들이 현재 살고 있는 집은 너무 작아서 그들은 이사가기로 결정했다.)

07 I can assure you that you will be more than satisfied with his performance in the classroom.

(저는 당신이 그의 교실에서의 수행능력에 기대 이상으로 만족할 것이라는 것을 당신에게 확신시킬 수 있습니다.)

어 휘

① performance: 수행, 이행, 성취

예문1) Our soccer team's performance has been excellent this year.
(올해 우리 축구팀의 성적이 우수하다.)

구 문

① assure + 간목 + 직목: ~에게 ~을 확신시키다

예문1) I assure you that this medicine will not harm you.
(저는 이 약이 당신에게 해를 주지 않는다는 것을 당신에게 확신 시킬 수 있습니다.)

② be more than satisfied with: ~에 매우 만족하다, 기대이상으로 만족하다

예문1) Lyman was more than satisfied with the results.
(라이만은 그 결과에 매우 만족했다.)

08 He is conscientious, professional, and diligent.

(그는 성실하고 전문성이 있으며 근면합니다.)

어 휘

① conscientious: 양심적인, 성실한

② professional: 전문적인

③ diligent: 근면한, 열심히 일하는

예문1) Though he is not quick, he is a diligent worker.
(그는 빠르지는 않지만 열심히 일한다.)

09 **I strongly recommend him for the position of English teacher at your school.**
(저는 그를 당신 학교의 영어교사로 적극 추천합니다.)

구 문

① strongly: 적극적으로, 강하게
② recommend: 추천하다

예문1) They strongly recommended her as a good lawyer.
(그들은 그녀를 좋은 변호사라고 적극 추천했다.)

Practice 1 Vocabulary & Expression

추천서에 나왔던 어휘와 구문을 정리해 보겠습니다.
숨기기 버튼을 클릭해서 내용을 숨긴 후 연습장에 해당 내용을 입력하면서 암기해 보세요.

구분	어휘 & 구문	의미
어휘	pleasure	기쁨
	recommend	추천하다.
	position	일자리
	teach	가르치다.
	primary	주된, 주요한
	responsibilities	업무, 담당업무
	English Grammer	영문법
	English Composition	영작문
	deeply	몹시, 강하게
	saddened	안타까운, 슬픈
	when	~ 할 때
	move	이사가다
	performance	수행, 이행, 성취
	conscientious	양심적인
	professional	전문적인
	diligent	근면한, 열심히 일하는
	strongly	적극적으로, 강하게
	recommend	추천하다
관용표현	from A to B	~부터 ~까지
	주어 + be + one + of + the + best + 복수명사	최고의 ~중에 하나다
구문	It is with great pleasure that + 주어 + 동사	~하게 되어 매우 기쁘다
	assure + 간목 + 직목	~에게 ~을 확신시키다
	be more than satisfied with	~ 에 매우 만족하다

Practice 1 Task 1

주어진 단어를 이용하여 문장을 완성하세요. 필요한 경우는 동사의 형태를 변형시키세요.

보기	primary from for recommend to responsibilities

(1) It is with great pleasure that I (　　　) Mr. Michael Kim (　　　) the position of English teacher at Incheon Foreign Language High School.

(2) Mr. Michael Kim taught at Seoul International High School (　　　　　) March 2, 2006 (　　　　　) February 28, 2013.

(3) His (　　　　　) (　　　　　) were teaching English Grammar and English Composition.

Practice 1 Task 2

빈칸에 들어갈 적절한 단어를 입력하여 문장을 완성하세요.

(1) 그는 우리 학교에 계셨던 최고의 선생님들 중에 한 분이었습니다.
He was (　　　　) of the (　　　　) teachers that we have (　　　) at our school.

(2) 우리는 그와 그의 가족들이 인천으로 이사 가서 몹시 안타까웠습니다.
We were (　　　　　)(　　　　　)(　　　　　) he and his family moved to Incheon.

(3) 저는 당신이 그의 교실에서의 수행능력에 매우 만족할 것이라고 당신에게 확신 드립니다.

I can (　　　)(　　　)(　　　) you will be more than satisfied with his performance in the classroom.

Practice 1 Task 3

제시되어 있는 단어를 활용하여 문장을 만들어 보세요.

(1) 그는 성실하고 전문적이며 근면합니다. (콤마를 2번 사용하세요)

① professional　② diligent　③ conscientious

(　　　　　　　　　　　　　　　　　　　　)

(2) 저는 그를 당신 학교의 영어교사로 적극 추천합니다.

① recommend　② strongly　③ the position of English teacher

(　　　　　　　　　　　　　　　　　　　　)

Coffee break

A Tip for Living a Healthy Life

Everyone knows that staying in good physical shape is important for health, long life, and for simply feeling good. But did you know that helping your brain get in shape is also immensely important? It's true; if you get your brain back in shape, you'll be on the path to a better body as well, and there are seven easy ways to get started.

First of all, try mixing things up. Instead of doing the same things every day in the same ways, change your patterns. If you usually use your right hand to brush your teeth, try using your left hand. If you walk to work, try a different route. Doing things in a different way helps to wake up your brain and makes your mind ready to face new challenges in life. Secondly, exercise your brain with mental activities like logic puzzles or math problems. Doing mental exercises for just 10 minutes a day will make you feel better and increase your creativity and memory.

Are you a big fan of music? Then why not try learning a new instrument? Playing or writing music exercises both sides of your brain, and it's something you can do at any age. Similar to learning a new instrument is learning a new language. This forces your brain to store and retrieve information, speeding up processing. Another good exercise is reading aloud. It's easy, yet it causes your mind to scan ahead, analyze, decide on inflection and tone, determine pronunciation, and understand word meanings.

If that makes you tired, then move on to the next idea, which is adding "superfoods" like salmon, blueberries, green tea and espresso to your diet. Not only can these foods increase your mental clarity, but they also have physical benefits. Finally, don't forget to sweat! Exercising for 30 minutes a day can help you think better, increase your energy, and make you look better. And if you look better, you'll have more motivation to do the other six mental exercises as well.

Coffee break

건강한 삶을 위한 비결

사람들은 건강을 위하고 장수를 하기 위해 그리고 단순히 기분이 좋도록 몸에 균형이 잡혀져 있어야 좋다는 사실을 알고 있다. 그러나 두뇌 또한 균형이 잡히도록 만드는 것이 굉장히 중요하고 신체적 건강과 용모도 더 돋보이게 한다는 놀라운 사실을 알고 있는가 이것은 사실이다. 그리고 이것을 시작하기 위해서는 일곱 가지의 간단한 방법들이 있다.

우선, 해야 할 일들을 섞어보자. 매일 똑같은 일을 같은 방식으로 하는 것 보다 양식을 바꿔보자. 만약 양치질을 하기 위해 오른쪽 손을 사용한다면 왼쪽을 사용해보자. 도보로 출근을 한다면 다른 항로를 시도해보자. 일을 다른 방식으로 한다면 두뇌를 깨워주고 인생에 있어서의 새로운 도전들을 준비할 수 있는 정신을 길러준다. 둘째, 논리적인 퍼즐이나 수학문제 같은 지능 활동을 통해 자신의 두뇌를 훈련 시켜보자. 하루에 10분만이라도 지능 활동을 한다면 기분도 좋아지고 창의력과 기억력 또한 좋아질 것이다.

당신은 음악을 매우 좋아하는가? 그렇다면 새로운 악기 연주를 배워보는 것이 어떠한가 음악 연주나 작곡하여 두뇌 양쪽을 사용하는 것은 어느 연령대에서나 할 수 있는 일이다. 새로운 악기를 배우는 것은 새로운 언어를 배우는 것과 같다. 이것은 당신의 두뇌에 지식을 축적하고 다시 되찾고 그리고 처리의 속도를 높이게 만든다.
또 다른 좋은 운동은 크게 글을 읽는 것이다. 이것은 매우 쉬운 일이지만 당신은 앞서 사고하게 되고 분석하고 어형 변화, 음성의 소절과 억양을 결정하고 단어의 의미를 이해하게 된다.

만약 이것이 당신을 피로하게 한다면 다음 아이디어로 이동하라. 그것은 연어, 블루베리, 녹차 그리고 에스프레소 커피를 당신의 식단에 더하는 것이다.
이런 음식들은 당신의 두뇌를 명석하게 만들 뿐만 아니라 신체적 이득을 증가시킨다. 끝으로 땀을 흘리는 것을 잊지 말아라! 하루에 30분씩 운동을 하면 더 나은 사고를 하게 되고 에너지가 증가하고 또한 용모가 더 나아질 것이다. 또한 당신이 더 아름다워 보인다면 더욱 활기가 생겨 나머지 여섯 가지의 정신 운동을 할 의욕이 생길 것이다.

Practice 2 Comprehension Check up

331-27 Kasan-dong
Geumcheon-gu, Seoul 110-521

June 11, 2013
To whom it may concern:

I am very pleased to write this letter of recommendation for Jenny Park. She worked with me in the Sales Department at Dell Electronics for 5 years. She was a hard worker. She began her employment as an entry-level sales employee. After three years, she was promoted to team leader. She was organized, efficient, and goal-oriented. She was punctual and dedicated to the work at hand.

I strongly recommend her for the position of sales manager in your company. She will be a valuable asset to your company.

Sincerely yours,
Jimmy Kind
Jimmy Kind
Sales Manager

1. Who was the recommendation letter written for?
   ① Jimmy Kind
   ② Jenny Park
   ③ Jimmy Kind's coworker
   ④ Jenny Park's coworker

2. What was Jenny Park's job title when she began her employment at Dell?
   ① Entry-level employee
   ② Team leader
   ③ Sales Manager
   ④ Sales Agent

3. How long did it take for Jenny to get a promotion to team leader?

① Three months
② Three years
③ Five months
④ Five years

4. How long did Jimmy Kind and Jenny Park work together at Dell?

① Three months
② Three years
③ Five months
④ Five years

5. What type of person did Jimmy Kind say Jenny Park was?

① Organized and efficient
② Egocentric and creative
③ Hard-working and ambitious
④ Sociable and cooperative

서울 금천구

가산동 331-27번지 110-521

2013년 6월 11일

담당 선생님께

저는 박제니를 위한 이 추천서를 쓰게 되어 매우 기쁩니다.
그녀는 델전자의 판매부에서 5년 동안 저와 함께 일했습니다. 그녀는 열심히 근무했습니다. 그녀는 말단 판매직원으로 직무를 시작했습니다. 3년 후 그녀는 팀장으로 승진했습니다. 그녀는 조직적이며, 능률적이고, 목표 지향적이었습니다. 그는 시간을 엄수했고 주어진 일에 헌신했습니다.
저는 그녀를 당신 회사의 판매과장 자리에 적극적으로 추천합니다. 그녀는 당신 회사에 소중한 재산이 될 것입니다

안녕히 계십시오.

판매과장 지미 카인드

1. 누구를 위한 추천서인가요?
   ① 지미 카인드
   ② 박제니
   ③ 지미 카인드의 동료
   ④ 박제니의 동료

2. 박제니는 델 전자에서 직무를 시작했을 때 직책이 무엇이었습니까?
   ① 평사원
   ② 팀장
   ③ 판매과장
   ④ 판매원

3. 박제니는 팀장이 되는데 얼마의 기간이 걸렸습니까?
   ① 3개월
   ② 3년
   ③ 5개월
   ④ 5년

4. 지미 카인드와 박제니는 델 전자에서 얼마 동안 함께 일했습니까?
① 3개월
② 3년
③ 5개월
④ 5년

5. 지미 카인드는 박제니가 어떤 유형의 사람이라고 말했습니까?
① 조직적이고 능률적인 사람
② 자기중심적이고 창조적인 사람
③ 일을 열심히 하고 야심 있는 사람
④ 사교적이고 협조적인 사람

Practice 2 Lecture

01

To whom it may concern:

(담당 선생님께)

관용표현 To whom it may concern: 수신인이 누구인지 모를 때 사용하는 인사

02

I am very pleased to write this letter of recommendation for Jenny Park.

(저는 박제니를 위해 이 추천서를 쓰게 되어 매우 기쁩니다.)

어 휘 ① letter of recommendation: 추천서

예문1) Professor Smith wrote a letter of recommendation for his student.
(스미스 교수는 자신의 학생을 위해서 추천서를 써줬다.)

구 문 ① pleased to-부정사: ~하게 되어 기쁘다

예문1) He was very pleased to win a scholarship.
(그는 장학금을 타서 매우 기뻤다.)

03

She worked with me in the Sales Department at Dell Electronics for 5 years.

(그녀는 델 전자의 판매부에서 5년 동안 저와 함께 일했습니다.)

어 휘 ① work: 근무하다, 일하다

예문1) She worked in the Department of Public Relations at Samsung Electronics for two years.
(그녀는 삼성전자 홍보부에서 2년 동안 근무했다.)

② Sales Department: 판매부

04 She was a hard worker.

(그녀는 열심히 근무했습니다.)

어 휘 ① hard worker: 열심히 일하는 사람

예문1) She is a hard worker.
(그녀는 열심히 일한다.)

구 문 ① 주어 + be + a + 형용사 + 동사 파생명사: ~게 ~하다

예문1) He is a good singer
(그는 노래를 잘한다.)

05 She began her employment as an entry-level sales employee.

(그녀는 말단 판매부 평사원으로 직무를 시작했습니다.)

어 휘 ① employment: 직무, 근무, 일

예문1) His son is seeking employment.
(그의 아들은 일자리를 찾고 있다.)

② entry level: 말단의, 평사원의

③ employee: 직원, 고용인

06 After three years, she was promoted to team leader.

(3년 후 그녀는 팀장으로 승진했습니다.)

어 휘 ① after: ~ 후

예문1) We will leave after breakfast.
(우리는 아침식사 후 떠날 것이다.)

② team leader: 팀장

관용표현

① be promoted to: ~으로 승진하다

예문1) She was promoted to senior manager.
(그녀는 차장으로 승진했다.)

07 She was organized, efficient, and goal-oriented.

(그녀는 조직적이며, 능률적이고, 목표 지향적이었습니다.)

어 휘

① organized: 조직적인

② efficient: 능률적인

예문1) She is a quick and efficient worker.
(그녀는 일을 빠르고 능률적으로 한다.)

③ goal-oriented: 목표지향적인

08 She was punctual and dedicated to the work at hand.

(그녀는 시간을 엄수했고 주어진 일에 헌신했습니다.)

어 휘

① punctual: 시간을 엄수하는

예문1) Kant was punctual to the minute.
(칸트는 1분도 시간을 어기지 않았다.)

② at hand: 가까이에 있는, 주어진

예문1) Election day is at hand. (선거가 다가왔다.)

관용표현

① be dedicated to: ~에 헌신하다

예문1) She is dedicated to her work.
(그녀는 자신의 일에 헌신한다.)

09 **I strongly recommend her for the position of sales manager in your company.**

(저는 당신 회사의 판매과장 자리에 그녀를 적극적으로 추천합니다.)

어 휘

① strongly: 적극적으로, 강하게

② recommend: 추천하다

예문1) I have no hesitation in recommending him for the sales position.

(나는 그를 판매직에 추천하는데 망설임이 없다.)

10 **She will be a valuable asset to your company.**

(그녀는 당신 회사에 소중한 재산이 될 것입니다.)

어 휘

① valuable: 소중한, 값비싼

예문1) She has a valuable diamond.

(그녀는 값비싼 다이아몬드를 가지고 있다.)

② asset: 재산, 자산

예문1) A sense of humor is a great asset.

(유머 감각은 큰 재산이다.)

Practice 2 Vocabulary & Expression

추천서에 나왔던 어휘와 구문을 정리해 보겠습니다.

구분	어휘 & 표현	의미
어휘	letter of recommendation	추천서
	work	일하다
	Sales Department	판매부
	hard worker	열심히 일하는 사람
	employment	직무, 근무, 일
	entry level	말단의, 평사원의
	employee	직원, 고용인
	after	~ 후
	team leader	팀장
	organized	조직적인
	efficient	능률적인
	goal oriented	목표지향적인
	punctual	시간을 엄수하는
	the work at hand	주어진 일
	strongly	적극적으로, 강하게
	recommend	추천하다
	valuable	소중한, 값비싼
	asset	재산, 자산
관용표현	pleased + to-부정사	~하게 되어 기쁘다
구문	be promoted to	~으로 승진하다
	be dedicated to	~에 헌신하다

Practice 2 Task 4

보기에 있는 단어를 이용하여 문장을 완성하세요.

보기	pleased worked write worker hard for

(1) I am very (　　　　　) to (　　　　　) this letter of recommendation for Jenny Park.

(2) She (　　　　　) with me in the sales Department at Dell Electronics (　　　　　) 5 years.

(3) She was a (　　　　　) (　　　　　).

Practice 2 Task 5

빈칸에 들어갈 적절한 표현을 입력하여 문장을 완성하세요.

(1) 그녀는 판매부 평사원으로 직무를 시작했습니다.
She (　　　　) her (　　　　) (　　　　) an entry-level sales employee.

(2) 3년 후 그는 팀장으로 승진했습니다.
(　　　　) three years, she was (　　　　)(　　　　) team leader.

(3) 그녀는 조직적이며, 능률적이고, 목표 지향적이었습니다.
She was (　　　　　), (　　　　　), and (　　　　　).

Practice 2 Task 6

제시되어 있는 단어를 배열하여 올바른 문장을 만들어 보세요. (첫 단어는 대문자로 시작하세요.)

(1) 그녀는 시간을 엄수했고 주어진 일에 헌신했습니다.

was punctual she dedicated the work to at hand and

( )

(2) 저는 판매과장 자리에 그녀를 적극적으로 추천합니다.

strongly sales manager her recommend for of the position I a

( )

(3) 그녀는 당신 회사에 소중한 재산이 될 것입니다.

company valuable asset your she be will a to

( )

Exercise Writing

글을 읽은 후 그를 바탕으로 추천서의 본문을 영작해 보겠습니다. 영작 후 확인 버튼을 클릭하여 모범 답안과 비교해 보세요.

저는 John Smith를 위한 이 추천서를 쓰게 되어 매우 기쁩니다.

그는 판매부에서 5년 동안 저와 함께 일했습니다.
그는 열심히 근무했습니다.

그는 시간을 엄수했고 주어진 일에 헌신했습니다.
저는 그를 판매과장 자리에 추천합니다.
그는 당신 회사에 소중한 재산이 될 것입니다.

Exercise You be the editor

다음 추천장을 읽고 밑줄친 부분을 올바르게 고치세요. 이를 찾아 오른쪽박스의 내용을 올바르게 고친 후 확인 버튼을 클릭하여 정답과 비교하세요.

Dear Mr. Jackson: It is with great pleasure that I recommend Mr. John Smith <u>at</u> the position of history teacher at your school. Mr. John Smith taught at Mokpo High School from March 1, 2007 to February 20, 2013. His primary <u>responsibility</u> were teaching World History and Korean History. He was one of the best teachers that we have <u>have</u> at our school. I can <u>sure</u> you that you will be more than <u>satisfy</u> with his performance in the classroom. I strongly recommend him for the position of history teacher at your school. Sincerely, *Soomin Han* Soomin Han Principal	Dear Mr. Jackson: It is with great pleasure that I recommend Mr. John Smith at the position of history teacher at your school. Mr. John Smith taught at Mokpo High School from March 1, 2007 to February 20, 2013. His primary responsibility were teaching World History and Korean History. He was one of the best teachers that we have have at our school. I can sure you that you will be more than satisfy with his performance in the classroom. I strongly recommend him for the position of history teacher at your school. Sincerely, *Soomin Han* Soomin Han Principal

Wrap up
Summary

1. The format of a recommendation letter

(1) Return Address

(2) Date

(3) Inside Address

(4) Greeting

(5) Body

(6) Closing

(7) Signature

(8) Name

(9) Job Title

2. The key expressions

(1) It is with great pleasure that I recommend Mr. Michael Kim for the position of English teacher.

(2) He was one of the best teachers that we have had at our school.

(3) I am very pleased to write this letter of recommendation for Jamie Park.

(4) She will be a valuable asset to your company.

Wrap up

Assignment I

오늘 학습한 주요 문형을 활용할 수 있도록 문장을 작성하세요.

It is great pleasure that + 주어 + 동사	~하게 되어 매우 기쁘다
assure + 간목 + 직목	~에게 ~을 확신시키다
be more than satisfied with	~에 매우 만족하다
pleased to + 동사원형	~하게 되어 기쁘다

Answers

Lesson 8. I am happy to recommend Michael Kim.

Warm up

Check up

1. A. It is with great pleasure that I recommend Sally Forth for the history teacher position at Seoul International High School.

   C. She taught at Mirae High School from March 4. 2007 to Feburary 25. 2012, during which time I was principal.

   B. Her primary responsibilities were teaching social studies and general history.

   D. I strongly recommend her and am sure that you will be more than satisfied with her performance in the classroom.

2. ① 격식체

Practice 1 Comprehension Check up

1) ③ Vice Principal
2) ① Mr. Minwoo Song
3) ② English Grammar ③ English Composition
4) ③ Because he moved to Incheon.
5) ① diligent

Practice 1 Task 1

1) It is with great pleasure that I recommend Mr. Michael Kim for the position of English teacher at Incheon Foreign Language High School.
2) Mr. Michael Kim taught at Seoul International High School from March 2, 2006 to February 28, 2013.
3) His primary responsibilities were teaching English Grammar and English Composition.

Practice 1 Task 2

1) He was one of the best teachers we have had at our school.
2) We were deeply saddened when he and his family moved to Incheon.
3) I can assure you that you will be more than satisfied with his performance in the classroom.

Practice 1 Task 3

1) He is conscientious, professional, and diligent.
2) I strongly recommend him for the position of English teacher in your school.

Practice 2 Comprehension Check up

1) ② Jenny Park
2) ① Entry-level employee
3) ② Three years
4) ④ Five years
5) ① organized and efficient

Practice 2 Task 4

1) I am very pleased to write this letter of recommendation for Jenny Park.
2) She worked with me in the Sales Department at Dell Electronics for 5 years.
3) She was a hard worker.

Practice 2 Task 5

1) She began her employment as an entry-level sales employee.
2) After three years, she was promoted to team leader.
3) She was organized, efficient, and goal oriented.

Practice 2 Task 6

1) She was punctual and dedicated to the work at hand.
2) I strongly recommend her for the position of a sales manager.
3) She will be a valuable asset to your company.

Exercise Writing

I am very pleased to write this letter of recommendation for John Smith. He worked with me in the Sales Department for five years. He was a hard worker. He was punctual and dedicated to the work at hand. I recommend him for the position of sales manager. He will be a valuable asset to your company.

Exercise You be the editor

Dear Mr. Jackson:

It is with great pleasure that I recommend Mr. John Smith for (recommend A for B: A를 B에 추천하다) the history teacher position in your school.

Mr. John Smith taught at Mokpo High School from March 1, 2007 to February 20, 2013. His primary responsibilities (responsibilities: 업무,책임/복수형) were teaching World History and Korean History. He was one of the best teachers we have had (have had 현재완료/이제까지~해 온) at our school. I can assure (assure 간목 + 직목: ~에게 ~을 확신시키다) you that you will be more than satisfied (be satisfied with: ~에 만족하다) with his performance in the classroom.

I strongly recommend him for the history teacher position in your school.

Sincerely,
Soomin Han
Soomin Han
Principal

Business
Management
Writing
Basis and Application

Lesson 09

Thank you for the opportunity to make your travel arrangements.

Lesson 09

Thank you for the opportunity to make your travel arrangements.

Introduction

Lesson objectives

1. Writing a thank you letter

2. Learning key expressions for writing a thank you letter
   (1) Thank you for giving us the opportunity to make your travel arrangements.
   (2) We hope that you were pleased with the air travel and the hotel accommodations.
   (3) We hope that you will afford us the opportunity to help you plan your next vacation.
   (4) Thank you very much for having taken the time to meet with me.

Warm up

The format of a thank you letter

① Keely Pyle
1504 Egger Avenue
Rockville, Vermont 29939

②
May 12, 2013

③
Molly Jumper
472-1 Hoegi-dong, Dongdaemun-gu
Seoul 340-309
South Korea

④
Dear Mrs. Jumper,

⑤
Thank you for the time and consideration you extended to me during my interview with you yesterday.
I appreciate having had the opportunity to speak with you about my experience in related fields and my future goals.
I look forward to hearing from you and wish to thank you again for your courtesy.

⑥
Best regards,

⑦
Keely Pyle

⑧
Keely Pyle

① 발신인 주소

감사편지를 쓰는 사람의 주소를 기재합니다. 미국주소의 경우는 감사편지를 쓰는 사람의 이름, 번지수 + 거리명, 도시명, 주명, 그리고 우편번호 순서로 기재합니다. 도시명과 주명 사이에는 쉼표가(,) 들어갑니다.

미국주소의 예

Martin Baron
2207 South Avenue
San Francisco, California 92654

② 날짜

감사편지를 쓰는 날짜를 기재합니다. 날짜를 기재할 때는 기수로 기재 할 수 도 있고 서수로 기재 할 수 도 있습니다. 하지만 읽을 때는 거의 언제나 서수로 읽습니다.

③ 수신인 주소

감사편지를 받는 사람의 주소를 기재합니다. 한국주소의 경우 감사편지를 받는 사람의 이름, 번지수 + 동, 구, 시, 그리고 우편번호를 기재합니다. 국제우편인 경우는 우편번호 다음에 국가명을 기재합니다. 동의 명칭과 구의 명칭 사이에는 쉼표(,)가 들어갑니다.

국가명이 들어가는 한국주소의 예

Cheosoo Kim
66 Guro-dong, Guro-gu
Seoul 152-050
South Korea

국가명의 예

미국 : USA
영국 : UK
캐나다 : Canada
일본 : Japan
중국 : China
프랑스 : France
독일 : Germany
스위스 : Switzerland
태국 : Thailand
대만 : Taiwan
베트남 : Vietnam

④ 인사

감사편지의 인사는 격식체 또는 비격식체를 사용합니다. 격식체와 비격식체의 인사는 다음과 같습니다.

격식체

수신인	내용
남성	Dear Mr. + 수신인의 성:
기혼여성	Dear Mrs. + 수신인의 성:
미혼여성	Dear Miss + 수신인의 성:
기혼 또는 미혼여성	Dear Ms. + 수신인의 성:

비격식체

수신인	내용
남성	Dear Mr. + 수신인의 성,
기혼여성	Dear Mrs. + 수신인의 성,
미혼여성	Dear Miss + 수신인의 성,
기혼 또는 미혼여성	Dear Ms. + 수신인의 성,

⑤ 본문

본문은 감사편지에 가장 중요한 부분입니다. 감사편지의 본문에는 감사편지를 보내는 이유에 대해서 기재합니다.

⑥ 끝인사

감사편지의 끝인사는 격식체 또는 비격식체를 사용합니다. 격식체와 비격식체의 끝인사는 다음과 같습니다.

구 분	형식
격식체	Sincerely, Sincerely yours, Cordially, Cordially yours
비격식체	Regards, Best regards, Best wishes, With best wishes

⑦ 서명

감사편지를 쓰는 사람의 서명을 기재합니다.

⑧ 이름

감사편지를 쓰는 사람의 이름을 기재합니다.

Warm up

Check up

감사편지의 구조와 내용에 대한 다음 문제를 풀어보겠습니다.

1. 감사편지의 본문에 들어가는 내용을 순서에 맞게 배열하세요.

보기	A. I am looking forward to hearing from you and wish to thank you again for your courtesy. B. Sincerely, C. Thank you for the time and consideration you extended to me during my interview with you yesterday. D. I appreciate having had the opportunity to speak with you about my experience in related fields and my future goals. E. Dear Mr. Williamson,

1. [ ] 2. [ ] 3. [ ] 4. [ ] 5. [ ]

2. 보기를 보고 발신인의 주소를 순서대로 배열하세요.

보기	Arlington Sue Thomson 239 Willson Boulevard Virginia 28835,

1. [ ]
2. [ ]
3. [ ] 4. [ ] 5. [ ] 6. [ ]

3. 수신인의 주소를 순서대로 배열하세요.

보기	South Korea　　Molly Kim　　Nowon-gu　　Seoul 051-090　　,　　233-2 Wolgye-dong

1. [　　　　]
2. [　　　　] 3. [　　] 4. [　　　　]
5. [　　　　] 6. [　　　　]
7. [　　　　]

Practice 1 Comprehension Check up

다음 감사편지를 읽고 질문에 답을 선택 한 후 [확인] 버튼을 클릭 하세요.

Ben Faller
337 Wilson Boulevard
San Francisco, CA 19237

December 27, 2013
Martin Fisher
259 Sixth Avenue
Honolulu, Hawaii 90073

Dear Mr. Fisher:

Thank you for giving us the opportunity to make your travel arrangements for your recent trip to Beijing, China. We hope that you were pleased with the air travel and the hotel accommodations that we arranged for you. We encourage your comments. This is the best means for us to learn, first hand, if the amenities that we represent to our clients are offered by the hotel.

We look forward to hearing from you. We hope that in the near future you will afford us the opportunity to help you plan your next vacation or business trip. Thank you very much.

Sincerely,
Ben Faller
Ben Faller

1. Where does the person who wrote the letter live?

① San Francisco
② Beijing
③ Tokyo
④ Honolulu

2. Where does the recipient of the letter live?

① San Francisco
② Beijing
③ Tokyo
④ Honolulu

3. What is this letter about?

① Thanking the client for the business
② Informing the client of the travel schedule
③ Asking the client to pay the bill
④ Canceling the reservation that the client has made

4. Which country did Mr. Fisher make a tour of recently?

① Japan
② Italy
③ Switzerland
④ China

5. What does Ben Faller ask Martin Fisher?

① His comments about the travel arrangements
② His comments about China
③ His plan for the next trip to China
④ His plan for the next business

캘리포니아 샌프란시스코
윌슨 불르바드 337번지 91237
벤 폴러

2013년 12월 27일
하와이 호놀룰루
식스 애버뉴 259번지 90073
마틴 피셔

피셔 선생님께

당신의 최근 중국 베이징 여행을 준비할 기회를 우리에게 주셔서 감사합니다. 우리가 당신을 위해 준비한 항공여행과 호텔숙박시설에 당신이 만족했기를 바랍니다. 당신의 논평을 부탁드립니다. 이것은 우리가 고객들에게 제시한 시설이 호텔에 의해서 제공되었는지를 직접 확인할 수 있는 가장 좋은 방법입니다.
우리는 당신으로부터 연락을 고대합니다. 우리는 당신이 가까운 미래에 당신의 다음 휴가나 출장을 계획하는 것을 도울 수 있는 기회를 우리에게 주기를 바랍니다.
대단히 감사합니다.
안녕히 계십시오.

벤 폴러

1. 편지를 쓴 사람은 어디에서 살고 있습니까?
   ① 샌프란시스코
   ② 베이징
   ③ 도쿄
   ④ 호놀룰루

2. 편지를 받은 사람은 어디에서 살고 있습니까?
   ① 샌프란시스코
   ② 베이징
   ③ 도쿄
   ④ 호놀룰루

3. 편지는 무엇에 관한 내용입니까?
① 비즈니스에 대해서 고객에 감사하기
② 고객에게 여행계획을 알려주기
③ 고객에게 청구비용 지불을 요청하기
④ 고객의 예약을 취소하기

4. 마틴 피셔는 최근에 어떤 나라를 여행했나요?
① 일본
② 이탈리아
③ 스위스
④ 중국

5. 벤 폴러는 마틴 피셔에게 무엇을 요청하나요?
① 여행준비에 대한 그의 의견
② 중국에 대한 그의 의견
③ 다음 중국여행에 대한 그의 계획
④ 다음 사업에 대한 그의 계획

Practice 1 Lecture

01

Thank you for giving us the opportunity to make your travel arrangements for your recent trip to Beijing, China.

(당신의 최근 중국 베이징 여행을 준비할 기회를 우리에게 주셔서 감사합니다.)

어 휘

① opportunity : 기회

예문1) I had no opportunity to see her.

(나는 그녀를 볼 기회가 없었다.)

② arrangements : 준비, 채비

예문1) Please make arrangements for the furniture to be delivered right away

(그 가구를 곧 배달하도록 해주세요.)

③ recent : 최근의

④ trip : 여행

구 문

① thank + A + for + B : B에 대해서 A에게 감사하다

예문1) I thanked Jim for inviting me to his birthday party.

(나는 짐에게 자신의 생일파티에 나를 초대해준 것에 대해서 감사했다.)

02

We hope that you were pleased with the air travel and the hotel accommodations that we arranged for you.

(우리가 당신을 위해 준비한 항공여행과 호텔 숙박시설에 당신이 만족했기를 바랍니다.)

어 휘

① hope : 바라다, 희망하다

② pleased with : ~에 만족하다

예문1) He was pleased with the exam results.

(그는 시험결과에 만족했다.)

③ air travel : 항공여행

④ accommodations : 숙박, 숙박시설

예문1) The hotel affords accommodations for two hundred guests.
(그 호텔은 200명을 수용할 수 있는 숙박시설을 갖추고 있다.)

03 **We encourage your comments.**
(우리는 당신의 논평을 부탁 드립니다.)

어 휘

① encourage: 격려하다, 부탁하다

예문1) Banks encourage people to borrow money.
(은행은 사람들에게 돈을 빌리도록 적극 권장하고 있다.)

② comment: 논평

04 **This is the best means for us to learn, first hand, if the amenities that we represent to our clients are offered by the hotel.**
(이것은 우리가 고객들에게 제시한 시설이 호텔에 의해서 제공되었는지를 직접 확인 할 수 있는 가장 좋은 방법입니다.)

어 휘

① means: 방법, 수단

예문1) The quickest means of travel is by plane.
(여행 할 수 있는 가정 빠른 수단은 비행기이다.)

② learn: 알게 되다

예문1) Her mother learned of her daughter's success in the newspapers.
(그녀의 어머니는 신문에서 그녀의 딸의 성공을 알게 되었다.)

③ amenities: 시설

예문1) Parks and swimming pools are some of the town's amenities.
(공원과 수영장은 마을의 시설의 일부다.)

④ represent: 제시하다, 나타내다

⑤ client: 고객

05 We look forward to hearing from you.

(우리는 당신으로부터 소식 듣기를 고대합니다.)

어 휘

① hear from: ~로부터 소식을 듣다

예문1) I heard from her last week.
(나는 지난 주에 그녀의 소식을 들었다.)

06 We hope that in the near future you will afford us the opportunity to help you plan your next vacation or business trip.

(우리는 당신이 다음 휴가나 출장을 계획하는 것을 우리가 도울 수 있는 기회를 조만간 우리에게 주기를 희망합니다.)

어 휘

① opportunity: 기회

② afford: ~주다

예문1) The roof afforded us the shelter from the rain.
(그 지붕은 우리에게 비를 피할 수 있는 피난처를 제공해 주었다.)

③ plan: 계획하다

예문1) We have been planning this visit for months.
(우리는 여러 달 동안 이 방문을 계획해 왔다.)

구 문

① 주어 + help + 목적어 + 동사원형: ~가 ~하는 것을 돕다

예문1) Could you help me lift this box?
(내가 이 상자 드는 것을 도와 줄 수 있나요?)

07 Thank you very much

(대단히 감사합니다.)

어 휘 ① thank : 감사하다

예문1) I thank you for your kindness.

(당신의 친절에 감사드립니다.)

Practice 1 Vocabulary & Expression

구분	어휘 & 표현	의미
어휘	opportunity	기회
	arrangements	준비, 채비
	recent	최근의
	trip	여행
	hope	바라다, 희망하다
	pleased with	~에 만족하다
	air travel	항공여행
	accommodations	숙박, 숙박시설
	arrange	준비하다, 계획하다
	encourage	격려하다, 조장하다
	comments	의견, 논평, 비평
	means	수단
	first hand	직접적으로
	representations	설명, 진술, 주장
	amenities	시설
	learn	~을 알게되다
	if	~인지 아닌지
	accurate	정확한
	hear from	소식을 듣다
	afford	~주다
	plan	계획하다
	thank	감사하다
관용표현	look forward to	~을 고대하다
구문	thank + A + for + B	B에 대해서 A에게 감사하다
	주어 + 동사 + because + 주어 + 동사	~때문에 ~하다
	주어 + help + 목적어 + 동사원형	~가 ~하는 것을 돕다

Practice 1 Task 1

빈 칸에 들어갈 적절한 단어를 입력하여 문장을 완성하세요.

(1) 당신의 최근 중국 베이징 여행을 준비할 기회를 우리에게 주셔서 감사합니다.

Thank you ( ) giving us the ( ) to make your travel ( ) for your recent trip to Beijing, China.

(2) 우리가 당신을 위해 준비한 항공여행과 호텔 숙박시설에 당신이 만족했기를 바랍니다.

We hope that you were ( )( ) the air travel and the hotel ( ) that we ( ) for you.

(3) 우리는 당신의 논평을 부탁드립니다.

We ( ) your comments.

Practice 1 Task 2

빈 칸에 들어갈 적절한 단어를 입력하여 문장을 완성하세요.

(1) 이것은 우리가 고객들에게 제시한 시설이 호텔에 의해서 제공되었는지를 확인 할 수 있는 가장 좋은 방법입니다

This is the best ( ) for us to ( ) if the ( ) that we ( ) to our clients are offered by the hotel.

(2) 우리는 당신으로부터 소식 듣기를 고대합니다.

We ( ) ( ) ( ) hearing from you.

(3) 우리는 당신이 다음 휴가나 출장을 계획하는 것을 우리가 도울 수 있는 기회를 조만간 우리에게 주기를 희망합니다.

We (   ) that in the near future you will (   ) us the opportunity to help you (   ) your next vacation or business trip.

(4) 대단히 감사합니다.

(   ) (   ) very much.

Coffee break

Being Thankful for Life's Blessings

Be thankful for what you have; you'll end up having more. If you concentrate on what you don't have, you will never, ever have enough. - Oprah Winfrey

If you are thankful, you have the possibility of receiving wonderful blessings. If you are grateful, you will have a positive energy that will attract others. But what does being thankful really mean? It's more than saying, "Thank you" to someone who does a kind thing for you. It's a deep feeling of appreciation for all of the important things in your life.

One way to focus on being thankful is to keep a journal. Every night before you go to bed, think about the positive aspects of your day. Even on your worst day, if you have a positive outlook you will be able to find something to be thankful for. At first it might be hard, but eventually you will be surprised how many positive things you start thinking of every night.

If you start living your life with a thankful heart, you will notice you have fewer bad moods. As a result, more people will want to be around you and spend time with you. After all, it doesn't take much energy to be around someone who is always positive. An optimistic person has a spark of energy and joy that others are attracted to.

Even though life isn't perfect, we can control our attitudes and our reactions when things don't go our way. Focus on what you are thankful for, and that will help you press on. If you can get past today's troubles, you can receive tomorrow's blessings.

What are you waiting for? Get started today! Take out a piece of paper and start making a list. Write down everything you are thankful for, no matter how small it is. When you start to focus on the good things in life, you will be able to change your mindset and accomplish your dreams.

Coffee break

삶의 축복에 감사하라.

가진 것들에 대해 감사하라, 그렇다면 더욱 많이 갖게 될 것이다. 만약 당신이 가지지 못한 것에만 집중을 한다면 당신은 절대 만족하지 못 할 것이다. - 오프라 윈프리

만약 당신이 감사 하다면 축복을 받을 권리가 있다. 만약 당신이 감사하다면 다른 사람들을 매료시키는 긍정적인 에너지가 있을 것이다. 하지만 감사라는 뜻은 무슨 의미인가?

당신에게 친절한 일을 한다고 해서 "감사합니다."라고 말하는 것의 이상이다. 이것은 당신의 삶 속에서 중요한 일들에 대한 깊은 감사의 표현이다.

감사하는 마음을 가지려는 한 가지 방법은 감사 일기를 쓰는 것이다. 매일 밤 잠에 들기 전 하루 동안의 긍정적인 측면을 생각해보라. 가장 괴로운 날에도 긍정적인 측면을 찾는다면 감사할 일들이 있을 것이다. 처음에는 힘들 수 있지만 나중에는 얼마나 감사하는 일들을 많이 생각하는지

놀랄 것이다.

당신의 인생을 감사함으로 살기 시작한다면 기분 나쁜 일들이 더 적은 것을 알게 될 것이다. 결과적으로는 더 많은 사람들은 너의 곁에 있길 원하고 너와 시간을 보내길 바랄 것이다. 결국은 긍정적인 사람과 함께 있는 것은 그다지 힘든 일이 아니다. 긍정적인 사람은 다른 이들이 매료되는 에너지의 활기를 가지고 있다.

인생이 완벽하지 않더라도 우리는 일이 뜻대로 되지 않을 때 우리의 감정들과 반응을 조절할 수 있게 된다. 하지만 고난의 시기에는 낙심하지 말라. 감사한 것에 대해 집중하면 더 나아갈 수 있게 힘이 될 것이다. 만약 오늘의 고난을 이긴다면 내일의 축복을 받을 수 있게 된다.

무엇을 기다리는가? 오늘부터 시작하자! 종이 한 장을 꺼내 목록을 만들어라. 아무리 작은 일이라도 감사할 일들을 적어라. 만약 좋은 일들에 대해 집중한다면 당신의 사고방식을 바꾸게 되고 꿈을 성취하게 될 것이다.

Practice 2 Comprehension Check up

Jacob Vest
7346 Longhorn Blvd.
Boston, MA 77345

May 9, 2013

Geoffrey T. Cartwright
594 West Avenue
Scranton, Pennsylvania 77378

Dear Mr. Cartwright,

Thank you very much for having taken the time to meet with me during my recruiting trip to Scranton. I was most favorably impressed with you. As a result, our recruiting committee has concurred in my recommendation that we invite you to meet more members of our company.

If you are still interested in our company, please call our recruiting coordinator, Janice Mars, to arrange a mutually convenient time to visit us.

We look forward to hearing from you. Again, thank you for your interest in our organization and for having taken the time to talk with me.

Best wishes,
Jacob Vest
Jacob Vest

1. Who is the letter addressed to?
   ① Mr. Jacob Vest
   ② Mr. Geoffrey Cartwright
   ③ Mr. Janice Mars
   ④ Mr. Janice Mars's friend

2. When was the letter written?
   ① March 4, 2013
   ② April 7, 2013
   ③ May 9, 2013
   ④ June 10, 2013

3. What is this letter about?
   ① Expressing gratitude for taking the time to talk
   ② Offering to join the next trip
   ③ Asking the client to pay the bill
   ④ Announcing that the reservation has been canceled

4. What is the purpose of Mr. Jacob Vest's trip to Scranton?
   ① To recruit people
   ② To go sightseeing
   ③ To meet with the recruiting coordinator
   ④ To arrange a convenient time for the next meeting

5. If Cartwright is interested in the company, what is he supposed to do?
   ① Visit Mr. Jacob Vest
   ② Contact Ms. Janice Mars
   ③ Write a letter to Mr. Jacob Vest
   ④ Meet more members of the recruiting committee

메사추세츠 보스턴
롱혼 불르바드 7346번지
야곱 베스트

2013년 5월 9일

펜실베니아 스크랜튼
웨스트 에버뉴 594번지
조프레이 카트라이트

카트라이트 씨에게

스크랜튼으로 갔던 직원채용을 위한 저의 여행 동안에 저를 만나기 위해 시간을 내주셔서 매우 감사합니다. 저는 당신에게 매우 호의적인 인상을 받았습니다. 결과적으로 우리가 당신에게 우리 회사의 더 많은 사원들을 만나도록 요청하자는 저의 제안에 우리 사원모집 위원회는 동의하였습니다.

만약 당신이 우리 회사에 여전히 관심이 있다면 우리 직원채용 코디네이터 제니스 말스에게 전화해서 우리를 만날 수 있는 서로에게 편리한 시간을 정하기 바랍니다. 우리는 당신으로부터 소식 듣기를 고대합니다.

우리 조직에 관심을 보여주시고 저와 이야기 할 수 있는 시간을 내주셔서 다시 한번 감사 드립니다. 안녕히 계십시오.

야곱베스트

1. 이 편지는 누구에게 보내진 편지입니까?
   ① 야곱 베스트
   ② 조프레이 카트라이트
   ③ 제니스 말스
   ④ 제니스 말스의 친구

2. 편지는 언제 쓰여졌습니까?
   ① 2013년 3월 4일
   ② 2013년 4월 7일
   ③ 2013년 5월 9일
   ④ 2013년 6월 10일

3. 편지의 내용은 무엇에 관한 것 입니까?
   ① 시간을 내 준 것에 대한 감사
   ② 다음 여행에 합류하자는 제안
   ③ 고객에게 청구비용 지불 요청
   ④ 예약이 취소되었음을 알리기

4. 야곱 베스트 씨가 스크랜튼으로 출장을 간 목적은 무엇입니까?
   ① 직원 채용을 위해서
   ② 관광하기 위해서
   ③ 채용 코디네이터를 만나기 위해서
   ④ 다음 모임을 위한 편리한 시간을 정하기 위해서

5. 만약 카트라이트 씨가 그 회사에 관심이 있다면 어떻게 해야 하나요?
   ① 야곱 베스트 씨를 찾아간다
   ② 제니스 말스 씨에게 연락한다
   ③ 야곱 베스트 씨에게 편지를 쓴다
   ④ 사원모집 위원회의 더 많은 위원들을 만난다

Practice 2 Lecture

01

Thank you very much for having taken the time to meet with me during my recruiting trip to Scranton.

(스크랜튼으로 갔던 직원 채용을 위한 저의 여행 동안에 저를 만나기 위해 시간을 내주셔서 매우 감사합니다.)

어 휘

① meet with : ~를 만나다

예문1) Our representative met with the governor.

(우리 대표는 주지사와 만났다.)

② recruit : 신입직원을 모집하다

예문1) The company is recruiting new employees.

(그 회사는 신입직원을 모집하고 있습니다.)

③ during : 동안

예문1) They lived abroad during the war.

(그들은 전쟁 동안에 해외에서 살았다.)

관용표현

① take the time : ~하기 위해 시간을 내다

예문1) She took the time to help me with my homework.

(그녀는 나의 숙제를 도와주기 위해 시간을 내줬다.)

02

I was most favorably impressed with you.

(저는 당신께 매우 호의적인 인상을 받았습니다.)

어 휘

① most : 매우

예문1) It was a most enjoyable party.

(그 파티는 매우 즐거운 파티였다.)

② favorably : 호의적인, 호의적으로, 호의를 가지고(부사)

예문1) She gave a favorable answer.

(그녀는 호의적인 대답을 하였다.)

③ impressed with : 인상을 받다

예문1) I was very impressed with their new house.
(나는 그들의 새 집에 큰 인상을 받았다.)

03

As a result, our recruiting committee has concurred in my recommendation that we invite you to meet more members of our company.

(그래서 우리 회사의 직원채용 위원회는 당신에게 우리 회사의 다 많은 직원들을 만나보도록 하자는 저의 제안에 동의하였습니다.)

어 휘

① committee : 위원회

예문1) He is on a lot of committees.
(그는 많은 위원회에 소속되어 있다.)

② concur in : ~에 동의하다.

예문1) They all concurred in giving him the prize.
(그들은 모두 그에게 상을 주는 것에 동의 했다.)

③ recommendation : 제안, 추천

예문1) They bought the car on Paul's recommendation.
(그들은 폴의 제안으로 그 자동차를 샀다.)

④ invite: 요청하다

예문1) I invited her to go for a walk.
(나는 그녀에게 산책을 가자고 요청했다.)

04

If you are still interested in our company,

(만약 당신이 우리 회사에 여전히 관심이 있다면,)

어 휘

① still : 여전히, 아직도

예문1) Sue: Have you finished your dinner?
(저녁식사 끝나셨어요?)

Mary: No, I still haven't finished it yet
(아니요 아직 끝나지 않았습니다.)

② interested in : ~에 관심이 있다

예문1) He is interested in astronomy.
(그는 천문학에 관심이 있다.)

③ company : 회사

예문1) Which company do you work for?
(당신은 어느 회사에서 근무하나요?)

05

please call our recruiting coordinator, Janice Mars, to arrange a mutually convenient time to visit us.

(우리 직원채용 코디네이터 제니스 말스에게 전화해서 우리를 만날 수 있는 서로에게 편리한 시간을 정하기 바랍니다.)

어 휘

① coordinator : 코디네이터, 조정하는 사람

② call : 전화하다

③ arrange : 계획하다, 준비하다

예문1) The secretary arranged for her boss to meet the guest at 11 am.
(그 비서는 자신의 사장님이 손님을 오전 11시에 만나도록 준비했다.)

④ mutually : 서로, 상호적으로

예문1) I do not understand their mutual dislike.
(나는 그들 서로 싫어하는 것을 이해하지 못한다.)

⑤ convenient : 편리한

예문1) When would it be convenient for you to come?
(당신이 언제 오는 게 편하시겠습니까?)

구 문

① please + 동사원형: ~하기 바랍니다

예문1) Please turn off your cellular phone.
(휴대전화를 끄기 바랍니다.)

06 We look forward to hearing from you.

(우리는 당신으로부터의 소식 듣기를 고대합니다.)

어 휘 ① hear from : 소식을 듣다

예문1) I have not heard from him for a long time.
(나는 오래 동안 그의 소식을 듣지 못했다.)

관용표현 ① look forward to : ~을 고대하다

예문1) She is looking forward to hearing from her son.
(그녀는 자신의 아들의 소식을 듣기를 고대하고 있다.)

07 Again, thank you for your interest in our organization and for having taken the time to talk with me.

(우리 조직에 관심을 보여주시고 저와 이야기 할 수 있는 시간을 내주셔서 다시 한 번 감사 드립니다.)

어 휘 ① again : 또, 다시 한 번

예문1) When can I see you again?
(언제 또 만날 수 있나요?)

② interest : 관심, 흥미

③ organization : 조직

④ talk with : ~와 이야기하다

예문1) She was talking over an important matter with her father.
(그녀는 중요한 문제에 대해서 그녀의 아버지와 이야기하고 있었다.)

관용표현 ① take the time : 시간을 내다

예문1) I can't take the time to meet her.
(나는 그녀를 만날 시간을 낼 수 없다.)

Practice 2 Vocabulary & Expression

구분	어휘 & 표현	의미
어휘	meet with	~를 만나다
	recruit	신입사원을 모집하다
	during	동안
	most	매우
	favorably	호의적으로
	impressed	인상을 받다
	committee	위원회
	concur in	~에 동의하다
	recommendation	제안, 추천
	invite	요청하다
	continue	계속해서 ~하다
	interested in	~에 관심이 있다
	company	회사
	coordinator	코디네이터, 조정하는 사람
	call	전화하다
	arrange	계획하다, 준비하다
	mutually	서로, 상호적으로
	convenient	편리한
	hear from	소식을 듣다
	again	또, 다시 한 번
	interest	관심, 흥미
	organization	조직
	talk with	~와 이야기하다
구문	I would appreciate it + if + 주어 + 동사	~한다면 감사하겠습니다
관용표현	Take the time	시간을 내다
	Look forward to	~을 고대하다

Practice 2 Task 3

보기에 있는 단어를 이용하여 문장을 완성하세요. 필요한 경우는 단어의 형태를 변형시키세요.

보기	time the take impress in with concur

(1) Thank you very much for having (   )(   )(   ) to meet with me during my recruiting trip to Scranton.

(2) I was most favorably (   )(   ) you.

(3) As a result, our recruiting committee has (   )(   ) my recommendation that we invite you to meet more members of our company.

Practice 2 Task 4

빈 칸에 적절한 단어를 입력하여 문장을 완성하세요.

(1) 만약 당신이 우리 회사에 여전히 관심이 있는 경우라면,

If you are (   ) (   ) (   ) our company,

(2) 우리 사원모집 코디네이터 제니스 말스에게 전화해서 우리를 만날 수 있는 서로에게 편리한 시간을 정하기 바랍니다.

please (   ) our recruiting coordinator, Janice Mars, to (   ) a (   ) (   ) time to visit us.

(3) 우리는 당신으로부터 소식 듣기를 고대합니다.

We (　　　　) (　　　　) to (　　　　) (　　　　) you.

(4) 우리 조직에 관심을 보여주시고 저와 이야기 할 수 있는 시간을 내주셔서 다시 한번 감사 드립니다.

Again, thank you for your (　　　　) (　　) (　　) (　　　　) and for (　　　　) (　　　　) (　　) (　　　) to talk with me

Exercise Writing

감사편지의 본문을 영작해 보겠습니다.

당신의 최근 중국 여행을 준비할 기회를 우리에게 주셔서 감사합니다.

우리가 당신을 위해 준비한 호텔 숙박시설에 만족하셨기를 바랍니다.

우리는 당신이 당신의 다음 중국 여행을 계획하는 것을 도울 수 있는 기회를 우리에게 주기를 바랍니다.

대단히 감사합니다.

Exercise You be the editor

다음 감사편지를 읽고 밑줄친 부분을 올바르게 고치세요.

Thank you very much for having took the time to meet with me during my recent trip to New York.

I was most favorable impressed with you.

As a result, our recruiting committee has concurred in my recommendation that we employed you for our company.

I would appreciate it if you would call our recruiting coordinator, John Smith, to arrange a mutual convenient time to visit us.

We look forward to hearing from you.

Wrap up

Summary

1. The format of a thank you letter.

① 발신인 주소
② 날짜
③ 수신인 주소
④ 인사
⑤ 본문
⑥ 끝 인사
⑦ 서명
⑧ 이름

2. The key expressions for writing a thank you letter

(1) Thank you for giving us the opportunity to make your travel arrangements.

(2) We hope that you were pleased with the air travel and the hotel accommodations.

(3) We hope that you will afford us the opportunity to help you plan your next vacation.

(4) Thank you very much for having taken the time to meet with me.

Wrap up

Assignment I

오늘 학습한 주요 문형을 활용하여 영어문장을 작성하여 봅시다.

thank + A + for + B	B에 대해서 A에게 감사하다
주어 + 동사 + because + 주어 + 동사	~ 때문에 ~하다
주어 + help + 목적어 + 동사원형	~가 ~하는 것을 돕다
I would appreciate it + if + 주어 + 동사	~한다면 감사하겠습니다

Wram up

Assignment II

오늘 학습한 주요 문형을 활용하여 제시된 조건에 맞게 감사편지를 작성해 봅시다.

[조건]	[과제]
1. 사용문형 (1) thank you for (2번 사용가능) (2) very pleased with (3) hope (4) again 2. 각 문장에 한글 해석을 첨가할 것 3. 문장 개수 5~10문장(최소 5문장, 최대 10문장)	

Answers

Lesson 9. Thank you for the opportunity to make your travel arrangements.

Warm up

Check up

1. E. Dear Mr. Williamson,

   C. Thank you for the time and consideration you extended to me during my interview with you yesterday.

   D. I appreciate having had the opportunity to speak with you about my experience in related fields and my future goals.

   A. I am looking forward to hearing from you and wish to thank you again for your courtesy.

   B. Sincerely,

2. 1) Sue Thomson
   2) 239 Wilson Boulevard
   3) Arlington
   4) ,
   5) Virginia 28835
   6) 28835

3. 1) Molly Kim
   2) 233-2 Wolgye-dong
   3) ,
   4) Nowon-gu
   5) Seoul
   6) 051-090
   7) South Korea

Practice 1 Comprehension Check up

1) ① San Francisco
2) ④ Honolulu
3) ① Thanking the client for the business
4) ④ China
5) ① His comments about the travel arrangements

Practice 1 Task 1

1) Thank you for giving us the opportunity to make your travel arrangements for your recent trip to Beijing, China.
2) We hope that you were pleased with the air travel and the hotel accommodations that we arranged for you.
3) We encourage your comments.

Practice 1 Task 2

1) This is the best means for us to learn if the amenities that we represent to our clients are offered by the hotel.
2) We look forward to hearing from you.
3) We hope that in the near future you will afford us the opportunity to help you plan your next vacation or business trip.
4) Thank you very much.

Practice 2 Comprehension Check up

1) ② Mr. Geoffrey Kartwright
2) ③ May 9, 2013
3) ① Expressing gratitude for taking the time to talk
4) ① To recruit people
5) ② Contact Ms. Janice Mars

Practice 2 Task 3

1) Thank you very much for having taken the time to meet with me during my recruiting trip to Scranton.
2) I was most favorably impressed with you.
3) As a result, our recruiting committee has concurred in my recommendation that we invite you to meet more members of our company.

Practice 2 Task 4

1) If you are still interested in our company,
2) Please call our recruiting coordinator, Janice Mars, to arrange a mutually convenient time to visit us.
3) We look forward to hearing from you.
4) Again, thank you for your interest in our organization and for having taken the time to talk with me.

Exercise Writing

Thank you for giving us the opportunity to make your travel arrangements for your recent trip to China.
We hope that you were pleased with the hotel accommodations that we arranged for you.
We hope that you will afford us the opportunity to help you plan your next trip to China.
Thank you very much.

Exercise You be the editor

Thank you very much for having taken (전치사 + having + 완료형 과거분사: 본동사 보다 앞선 시제를 나타냄) the time to meet with me during my recent trip to New York.

I was most favorably impressed with (be impressed: ~에 인상을 받다) you.

As a result, our recruiting committee has concurred in my recommendation that we employ (recommendation + that + 주어 + 동사원형: ~하자는 제안) you for our company.

I would appreciate it if you would call our recruiting coordinator, John Smith, to arrange a mutually (부사 + 형용사) convenient time to visit us.

We look forward to hearing from you.

Lesson 10

Congratulations on your acceptance to university.

Lesson 10

Congratulations on your acceptance to University

Introduction

Lesson objectives

1. Writing a letter to express congratulations

2. Learning key expressions for writing a letter of congratulation
   (1) I offer congratulations on your new position.
   (2) It is our pleasure to have you join our company.
   (3) We recognize the importance of your decision.
   (4) My best wishes to you for your successful collegiate life.

Warm up

The format of a letter of congratulations

① Leslie Rocker
3992 San Antonio Blvd.
Santa Barbra, California 15702

② January 4, 2013

③ Jin Lee
Rose Apt. 3-323
Seongbuk-dong, Seongbuk-gu
Seoul 136-020
South Korea

④ Dear Mr. Lee, → 격식체

⑤ Congratulations on your acceptance to the University of California, Los Angeles. We know how hard you have worked to prepare for the exam. Please accept our best wishes for your success in your college life.

⑥ Sincerely, → 격식체에 사용 * practice 1 & 2 참고
⑦ *Leslie Rocker*
⑧ Leslie Rocker
Admissions Counselor

① 발신인 주소

축하편지를 쓰는 사람의 주소를 기재합니다. 미국주소의 경우는 축하편지를 쓰는 사람의 이름, 번지수, 거리명, 도시명, 주명, 그리고 우편번호 순서로 기재합니다. 도시명과 주명 사이에는 쉼표(,)가 들어갑니다.

② 날짜

축하편지를 쓰는 날짜를 기재합니다. 날짜를 기재할 때는 기수로 기재 할 수 도 있고 서수로 기재 할 수 도 있습니다. 하지만 읽을 때는 거의 언제나 서수로 읽습니다.

③ 수신인 주소

축하편지를 받는 사람의 주소를 기재합니다. 국내주소인 경우는 축하편지를 받는 사람의 이름, 아파트 이름, 아파트 동, 아파트 호수, 동, 구, 도시, 그리고 우편번호를 기재합니다. 동의 명칭과 구의 명칭 사이에는 쉼표가 들어갑니다. 국제 우편인 경우는 우편번호 뒤에 국가명을 기재합니다.

④ 인사

축하편지의 인사는 격식체 또는 비격식체를 사용합니다. 격식체와 비격식체는 다음과 같은 형식을 사용합니다.

수신인	격식체	비격식체
남성	Dear Mr. + 수신인의 성:	Dear Mr. + 수신인의 성,
기혼여성	Dear Mrs. + 수신인의 성:	Dear Mrs. + 수신인의 성,
미혼여성	Dear Miss + 수신인의 성:	Dear Miss + 수신인의 성,
기혼 또는 미혼여성	Dear Ms. + 수신인의 성:	Dear Ms. + 수신인의 성,

⑤ 본문

- 본문은 축하편지에서 가장 중요한 부분입니다. 축하편지의 본문에는 무엇에 대해서 축하하는지를 명시합니다.

⑥ 끝 인사

- 축하편지의 끝인사는 격식체 또는 비격식체를 사용합니다.

구분	형식
격식체	Sincerely,
	Sincerely yours,
	Cordially,
	Cordially yours,
비격식체	Regards,
	Best regards,
	Best wishes,
	With best wishes,

⑦ 서명

- 축하편지를 쓰는 사람의 서명을 기재합니다.

⑧ 이름

- 축하편지를 쓰는 사람의 이름을 기재합니다.

⑨ 직책

- 축하편지를 쓰는 사람의 직책을 기재할 수도 있습니다.

Warm up

Check up

축하 편지의 구조와 내용에 대한 다음 문제를 풀어보겠습니다.

1. 축하편지의 본문에 들어가는 내용을 순서에 맞게 배열하세요.

보기	A. Sincerely, B. I have heard the news from your parents. C. Please accept our best wishes for your success in your new position. D. I know how hard you have worked to earn the recognition you presently enjoy at Samsung. E. Dear Ms. Jang, F. Congratulations on your recent promotion to District Manager.

1. ______ → 2. ______ → 3. ______ → 4. ______ → 5. ______ → 6. ______

2. 다음은 축하편지를 읽고 무엇에 대한 축하편지인지 기술하세요.

> Congratulations on your promotion. We are very pleased that you received a promotion to the position of Managing Director in your company. We wish you a success in your new position. We look forward to working closely with you in the future.

____

3. 보기에 주어진 축하문장의 생략형을 잘 이해하고 문제에 주어진 문장을 생략형으로 바꾸세요.

보기	a. Let me congratulate you on having passed the exam. → b. Congratulations on having passed the exam.

a. Let me congratulate you on the birth of your son.
→

b. (　　　　　　　　　　　　　　　　　　　　)

Practice 1 Comprehension Check up

다음 축하편지를 읽고 질문에 답을 선택한 후 [확인] 버튼을 클릭하세요.

Mary Stephens
1992 San Antonio Blvd.
Austin, TX 77925

March 4, 2013

Jinsoo Kim
Samsung Apt. 5-224, Gyesan-dong
Seo-gu, Incheon 407-050
South Korea

Dear Mr. Kim,

Congratulations on your acceptance to the University of Texas at Austin. You are now challenged with making the very important decision of selecting which college you are going to attend. We know that this can often be an extremely difficult decision for young men or women about to enter college.

We at the University of Texas recognize the importance of your decision. This decision may well have an impact on the quality of your life.

My best wishes to you for a successful collegiate life. And I sincerely hope you will be joining us here at the University of Texas in the fall.

Sincerely,
Mary Stephens
Mary Stephens
Admissions Counselor

1. What is the letter about?
   ① Congratulations on the applicant's acceptance to university
   ② Confirming a reservation that the client has made
   ③ Scheduling a flight for the client
   ④ Rescheduling a flight for the client

2. What is the job tile of the person who wrote this letter?
   ① Dean of the Department of Admission
   ② Admissions Counselor
   ③ Chairperson of the Department
   ④ Dean of the college

3. Where does the applicant live?
   ① Seoul
   ② Incheon
   ③ Austin
   ④ California

4. What decision does the applicant have to make?
   ① Which job to accept
   ② Which college to attend
   ③ Which adviser to select
   ④ Which city to live

5. When does the next semester begin at the University of Texas?
   ① In the spring
   ② In the summer
   ③ In the fall
   ④ In the winter

텍사스 오스틴
산안토니오 블르바드 1992 번지 77925
메리 스티픈슨

2013년 3월 4일

대한민국
인천 서구
계산동 삼성 아파트 5동 224호 407-050
김진수

진수님께

텍사스 대학교 오스틴 캠퍼스에 입학 허락된 것을 축하 드립니다.
당신은 이제 어느 대학에 다닐지를 선택해야 하는 중요한 결정에 직면해있습니다. 우리는 대학에 막 입학하려고 하는 남자나 여자에게 있어서 이러한 일이 종종 매우 어려운 결정이라는 것을 알고 있습니다.
우리 텍사스 대학교에서는 당신의 결정의 중요성을 인식하고 있습니다. 이 결정은 당신의 인생의 질에 당연히 영향을 미칠 것입니다.
저는 당신에게 당신의 성공적인 대학생활을 진심으로 기원합니다. 그리고 가을에 여기 텍사스 대학에서 우리와 함께 하기를 진정으로 바랍니다.

안녕히 계십시오.

메리 스테픈슨
입학 카운슬러

1. 이 편지는 무엇에 관한 내용입니까?
   ① 지원자의 대학입학허락을 축하
   ② 고객의 예약 확인
   ③ 고객의 항공여행 계획
   ④ 고객의 항공여행 조정

2. 이 편지를 쓴 사람의 직책은 무엇입니까?
① 입학처장
② 입학카운슬러
③ 학과장
④ 대학 학장

3. 지원자는 어디에서 살고 있습니까?
① 서울
② 인천
③ 오스틴
④ 캘리포니아

4. 지원자는 어떠한 결정을 해야 하나요?
① 어떤 직업을 선택할 지
② 어느 대학을 선택할 지
③ 어느 지도교수를 선택할지
④ 어느 도시에 살지

5. 텍사스 오스틴 대학의 다음 학기는 언제 시작하나요?
① 봄
② 여름
③ 가을
④ 겨울

Practice 1 Lecture

01

Congratulations on your acceptance to the University of Texas at Austin.

(텍사스대학교 오스틴캠퍼스에 입학 허락된 것을 축하 드립니다.)

어 휘

① acceptance : 입학 허락, 수용, 수락

예문1) She won acceptance in her new job through a lot of efforts.
(그녀는 많은 노력을 통하여 그녀의 새로운 직장에 받아들여졌다.)

예문2) He was informed of his acceptance to Harvard University.
(그는 하버드 대학에 입학 허락이 되었음을 통보 받았다.)

구 문

① Congratulations on + 목적어 : ~을 축하하다

예문1) Congratulations on your having passed the exam.
(시험에 합격한 것을 축하 드립니다.)

예문2) Congratulations on your sixtieth birthday.
(당신의 60번째 생일을 축하 드립니다.)

02

You are now challenged with making the very important decision of selecting which college you are going to attend.

(당신은 어느 대학에 다닐지를 선택해야 하는 중요한 결정에 직면해 있습니다.)

어 휘

① challenged with : ~에 직면하다

예문1) He is challenged with a difficult problem.
(그는 어려운 문제에 직면해 있다.)

② select : 선택하다

예문1) He selected a shirt to match his suit.
(그는 자신의 옷에 어울리는 셔츠를 선택했다.)

③ attend : ~를 다니다

예문1) His son started attending school at the age of 6.

(그의 아들은 6살 때 학교에 다니기 시작했다.)

관용표현

① make the decision : 결정을 내리다

예문1) Who made the decision to employ him?

(누가 그를 고용하기로 결정했나요?)

03

We know that this can often be an extremely difficult decision for young men or women about to enter college.

(우리는 대학에 막 입학하려고 하는 남자나 여자에게 있어서 이러한 일이 종종 매우 어려운 결정이라는 것을 알고 있습니다.)

어 휘

① know : 알다

예문1) He knows how to drive a truck.

(그는 트럭을 운전할 줄 안다.)

② extremely : 매우, 대단히, 몹시

예문1) I am extremely sorry.

(나는 정말 미안하다.)

③ difficult : 어려운

④ decision : 결정

관용표현

① about to-부정사 : 막 ~하려고 하는

예문1) We were about to leave when it started to rain.

(우리가 막 떠나려고 하는데 비가 내리기 시작했다.)

04

We at the University of Texas recognize the importance of your decision.

(우리 텍사스 대학교에서는 당신의 결정의 중요성을 인식하고 있습니다.)

어 휘

① recognize : ~을 인식하다, 인지하다

예문1) He recognized the boy as his own son.
(그는 그 소년이 자신의 아들이라는 것을 인식했다.)

예문2) I was able to recognize Mary in the photograph.
(나는 사진에서 메리를 알아볼 수 있었다.)

05 **This decision may well have an impact on the quality of your life.**
(이 결정은 당신의 인생의 질에 당연히 영향을 미칠 것입니다.)

어 휘

① quality : 자질, 질

예문1) She has qualities of leadership.
(그는 리더의 자질을 가지고 있다.)

구 문

① have an impact on : ~에 영향을 미치다

예문1) The new theory had a great impact on English education.
(새로운 이론은 영어교육에 큰 영향을 미쳤다.)

관용표현

① may well + 동사 : ~당연히 할 것이다

예문1) He may well ask why.
(그가 이유를 묻는 것은 당연하다.)

06 **My very best wishes to you for your successful collegiate life.**
(저는 당신에게 성공적인 대학생활을 진심으로 기원합니다.)

어 휘

① successful: 성공적인

② collegiate: 대학의

예문1) She bought a collegiate dictionary.
(그녀는 대학생 용 사전을 샀다.)

구 문 ① My best wishes to + A + for + B : A에게 B를 진심으로 기원하다

예문1) My best wishes to you for your happiness.
(저는 당신에게 당신의 행복을 진심으로 기원합니다.)

07 **And I sincerely hope that you will be joining us here at the University of Texas in the fall.**
(그리고 저는 당신이 가을에 여기 텍사스 대학에서 우리와 함께 하기를 진정으로 바랍니다.)

어 휘 ① sincerely: 진정으로

② hope: 바라다, 희망하다

예문1) We are hoping to visit Switzerland next year.
(우리는 내년에 스위스를 방문하기를 바라고 있다.)

③ join: 합류하다, 가담하다

예문1) Will you join me for a drink?
(저와 술 한잔 하시겠습니까?)

예문2) He joined an English club.
(그는 영어회화 서클에 가입했다.)

④ fall: 가을

Practice 1 Vocabulary & Expression

축하편지에 나왔던 어휘와 구문을 정리해 보겠습니다.
[숨기기] 버튼을 클릭하여 내용을 숨긴 후 연습장에 해당 내용을 입력하면서 암기해 보세요

구분	어휘 & 표현	의미
어휘	acceptance	입학 허락, 수용, 수락
	challenged with	~에 직면하다
	select	선택하다
	attend	~를 다니다
	know	알다
	extremely	매우, 대단히, 몹시
	difficult	어려운
	decision	결정
	recognize	~을 인식하다, 인지하다
	quality	자질, 질
	successful	성공적인
	collegiate	대학의
	sincerely	진정으로
	hope	바라다, 희망하다
	join	합류하다, 가담하다
	fall	가을
관용표현	make the decision	결정을 내리다
	about to + 동사	막 ~하려고 하는
	may well + 동사	당연히 할 것이다
구문	Congratulations on + 목적어	~을 축하하다
	have an impact on	~에 영향을 미치다
	My best wishes to + A + for + B	A에게 B를 진심으로 기원하다

Practice 1 Task 1

필요한 경우는 동사의 형태를 변화시켜보세요. 첫 단어는 대문자로 시작합니다.

보기	challenged with　congratulations on　about to　for

(1) (   ) your acceptance to the University of Texas at Austin.

(2) You are now (   ) making the very important decision of selecting which college you are going to attend.

(3) We know that this can often be a difficult decision (   ) young men or women (   ) enter college.

Practice 1 Task 2

빈 칸에 들어갈 적절한 단어를 입력하여 문장을 완성하세요.

(1) 우리 텍사스 대학교에서는 당신의 결정의 중요성을 인식하고 있습니다.
We, at the University of Texas, (   ) the (   ) of your (   ).

(2) 이 결정은 당신의 인생의 질에 당연히 영향을 미칠 것입니다.
This decision may well (   ) an (   )(   ) the quality of your life.

Practice 1 Task 3

빈칸에 해당하는 표현을 입력하여 문장을 완성하세요. 문장의 첫 단어는 대문자로 입력하세요.

(1) 저는 당신에게 당신의 성공적인 대학생활을 진심으로 기원합니다.

( ) ( ) ( ) ( ) ( ) for your successful collegiate life.

(2) 그리고 가을에 여기 텍사스 대학에서 우리와 함께 하기를 진정으로 바랍니다.

I sincerely hope that ( ) ( ) ( ) ( ) ( ) here at the University of Texas in the fall.

Creative Congratulations

The reasons and occasions for offering congratulations never end. Most of the time we give a greeting card or flowers to congratulate someone, but being a bit more creative in the way you give congratulations can make others feel even more special. If you can do it in a way different from other people, your congratulations will seem more genuine and heartfelt.

First, you should think about the person you want to congratulate. What is that person like? Every person is unique, and your congratulations should be as unique as the individual. If you can celebrate the person as an individual, it will show your love and thoughtfulness. So when you think about your friends, keep in mind their preferences, their hobbies, and the parts that make them different from other people.

If you have a friend that loves music, instead of buying a CD, why not buy him some private music lessons? If you have a friend that loves writing letters, consider getting a fancy pen with a personal engraving. Thinking of creative gifts isn't that hard. It only takes a little effort, but in the end it is worth the extra time because it makes the person feel special.

The next time you want to congratulate someone in your life, don't be lazy. Put some thought into it, and do a good job. Be creative. Think outside the box. The people in your life are irreplaceable, and you should show them with creative congratulations. Give the best that you can by giving with your heart and your creativity.

Coffee break

창의적인 축하

축하를 표하는 이유와 경우는 끝이 없다. 대부분의 경우 우리는 축하 카드나 꽃을 주어 다른 이들을 축하해 주지만 축하 하는 방법을 조금만 달리 한다면 받는 사람은 더 특별하게 느낄 것이다. 다른 사람들과 다른 방법으로 한다면 당신의 축하는 더 진실되고 진심으로 우러나오는 것으로 보이게 될 것이다.
첫째, 축하해주고 싶은 사람을 먼저 생각해봐야 한다. 그 사람은 어떤 사람인가? 모든 사람은 유일무이하고 당신의 축하는 개개인처럼 유일해야 한다. 만약 그 사람을 개인적으로 축하해줄 수 있다면 당신의 사랑과 배려가 보일 것이다. 그래서 만약 친구들에 대해서 생각한다면 그들의 취향, 그들의 취미, 그리고 그들은 다른 사람들과 다르게 만드는 부분을 생각해 보아라.
음악을 좋아하는 친구가 있다면 CD를 사는 대신 음악 교습 수강비를 내주는 것이 어떠한가? 편지를 쓰는 것을 좋아하는 친구가 있다면 개인의 이름을 새긴 화려한 펜을 선물하는 것을 고려해보라. 창의적인 선물들을 생각하는 것은 어려운 일이 아니다. 이것은 작은 노력이 필요하지만 결국 그 사람을 특별하게 느끼게 해주기 때문에 시간을 더 쓸 가치가 있다.
다음에 당신이 축하해주고 싶은 사람이 있다면 게을리 하지 마라. 생각을 하여 훌륭하게 하여라. 창의적으로 생각하라. 당신 인생에 있는 사람들은 대체할 수 없다 그리고 그들에게 창의적인 축하를 보여주어야 한다. 정성과 창의력을 사용하여 줄 수 있는 최고의 선물을 선물하라.

Practice 2 Comprehension Check up

다음 축하편지를 읽고 질문에 답을 선택하세요.

Inyoung Jung
Mirae Imports, Inc.
34-6 Miwon-dong, Jung-gu
Seoul 304-347

July 1, 2013

Geoffrey T. Kartwright
594 Wealth Avenue
New orleans, Louisiana 02177
USA

Dear Mr. Kartwright,

I offer congratulations on your new position. We are very pleased that you have accepted the position of Sales Director at the monthly salary of 3 million won.
We hope that this will be a mutually rewarding and long-lasting relationship. I hope that you can relocate to Seoul and start work on August 1. Then you can sign our contract, and I can orient you to our company and Korean culture. Once again, it is our pleasure to have you join our company.
If you have any questions, please call me.

Best regards,
Inyoung Jung
Inyoung Jung
President

1. Who is the letter addressed to?
① Geoffrey Kartwright
② Inyoung Jung
③ Geoffrey Kartwright's secretary
④ Inyoung Jung's secretary

2. What is the letter about?
① Informing the applicant that that he was accepted to the university
② Congratulations on the applicant's acceptance to the new position
③ Arranging a meeting with a client
④ Rescheduling the appointment with a client

3. What is the applicant's job title in the new position?
① Sales Assistant
② Salesman
③ Sales Director
④ Clerk

4. Where does the applicant have to move to start his new job?
① Orleans
② His hometown
③ Incheon
④ Seoul

5. When will the applicant start his new job?
① July 1
② August 1
③ December 1
④ December 25

서울시 중구
미원동 34-6번지
미래수출 주식회사 304-347
정인영

2013년 7월 1일

미국
루이지애나주 뉴올리언스
웰스 애버뉴 594번지 02177
조프레이 카트라이트

카트라이트 씨께

저는 당신의 새로운 일자리를 축하합니다. 우리는 당신이 300만 원의 월급을 받는 판매과장자리를 수락해서 매우 기쁩니다.

우리는 이것이 서로에게 유익하고 오래 지속되는 관계가 되길 바랍니다. 저는 당신이 서울로 이주하여 8월 1일부터 업무를 시작하기를 바랍니다. 그때 당신은 우리의 계약서에 서명할 수 있으며, 저는 당신에게 우리회사와 한국문화에 대해 안내할 수 있습니다. 다시 한번 말씀 드리지만 당신이 우리 회사에 합류하게 된 것은 우리의 기쁨입니다.

혹시 문의 사항이 있으면 저에게 전화하세요.

안녕히 계십시오.

정인영
사장

1. 이 편지는 누구에게 보내진 편지입니까?
   ① 조프레이 카트라이트
   ② 정인영
   ③ 조프레이 카트라이트의 비서
   ④ 정인영의 비서

2. 이 편지는 무엇에 관한 내용입니까?
① 지원자에게 대학입학이 허락되었음을 통보
② 지원자의 새로운 일자리를 축하
③ 고객과의 만남을 주선
④ 고객과의 약속을 조정

3. 지원자가 새로운 일자리에서 갖게 되는 직책은 무엇입니까?
① 판매보조원
② 판매원
③ 판매과장
④ 점원

4. 지원자는 그의 새로운 직무를 시작하기 위해서 어디로 이사해야 하나요?
① 뉴올리언스
② 자신의 고향
③ 인천
④ 서울

5. 지원자는 자신의 직무를 언제 시작합니까?
① 7월 1일
② 8월 1일
③ 12월 1일
④ 12월 25일

Practice 2 Lecture

01

I offer congratulations on your new position.

(당신이 새로운 일자리를 갖게 된 것에 대해 축하합니다.)

어 휘

① position : 일자리

예문1) He has a good position in an oil company.

(그는 정유회사에서 좋은 일자리를 가지고 있다.)

구 문

① 주어 + offer + congratulations + on + 목적어 : ~을 축하하다

예문1) I offer congratulations on your achievement.

(저는 당신의 업적에 대해 축하드립니다.)

02

We are very pleased that you have accepted the position of Sales Director at the monthly salary of 3 million won.

(우리는 당신이 300만 원의 월급을 받는 판매과장 자리를 수락해서 매우 기쁩니다.)

어 휘

① accept : 수락하다, 받아들이다

예문1) She accepted my present with hearty thanks.

(그녀는 나의 선물을 진심으로 감사하며 받았다.)

② Sales Director: 판매과장

③ monthly salary: 월 급여

④ million: 100만

예문1) His monthly salary is 2.5 million won.

(그의 월 급여는 250만 원이다.)

구 문

① pleased + that + 주어 + 동사 : ~해서 기쁘다

예문1) I am very pleased that you have decided to come back home.

(나는 네가 집으로 돌아오도록 결정해서 매우 기쁘다.)

03 **We hope that this will be a mutually rewarding and long-lasting relationship.**

(우리는 이것이 서로에게 유익하고 오래 지속되는 관계가 되길 바랍니다.)

어 휘

① mutually : 서로에게, 상호적으로

예문1) The two countries are mutual enemies.

(그 두 국가는 서로 적이다.)

② rewarding : 유익한, 보답이 있는

예문1) The trip to the fire station was a rewarding experience.

(소방서 견학은 유익한 경험이었다.)

③ long lasting : 오래 지속되는

④ relationship : 관계

04 **I hope that you can relocate to Seoul and start work on August 1.**

(저는 당신이 서울로 이주하여 8월 1일부터 업무를 시작하기를 바랍니다.)

어 휘

① relocate : 이주하다, 이사하다

예문1) We will relocate outside Seoul next year.

(우리는 내년에 서울 밖으로 이주한다.)

② start : 시작하다, 출발하다

예문1) I can't start the car.

(나는 자동차 시동을 걸 수 없다.)

05 **Then you can sign our contract, and I can orient you to our company and Korean culture.**

(그때 당신은 우리의 계약서에 서명할 수 있으며, 그리고 저는 당신에게 우리회사와 한국문화에 대해 안내할 수 있습니다.)

어 휘

① sign : 서명하다

예문1) He signed the contract to work for the company for 2 years.
(그는 그 회사의 2년 근로계약에 서명했다.)

② orient : 안내하다, 설명하다

예문1) We helped freshmen to orient themselves to new college life.
(우리는 신입생들이 새로운 대학생활에 적응할 수 있도록 도움을 주었다.)

③ culture : 문화

06 Once again, it's a pleasure to have you join our company.

(다시 한 번 말씀 드리지만 당신이 우리 회사에 합류하게 된 것은 우리의 기쁨입니다.)

어 휘

① once again : 다시 한 번

예문1) We have to repeat the same process once again.
(우리는 같은 절차를 다시 한 번 반복해야 한다.)

② join : 합류하다, 가담하다

구 문

① It is a pleasure to부정사 : ~하게 되어 기쁘다

예문1) It is a pleasure to talk with you.
(당신과 이야기하게 되어 기쁩니다.)

② have + 목적어 + 동사원형 : ~을 맞이하다, 하게 되다

예문1) I am so happy to have you come back home.
(나는 네가 집에 돌아와서 매우 기쁘다.)

07 If you have any questions, please call me.

(혹시 문의 사항이 있으면 저에게 전화하세요.)

어 휘

① call : 전화하다

예문1) She called me early in the morning.
(그녀가 나에게 아침 일찍 전화했다.)

구 문

① If + 주어 + 동사, 주어 + 동사: ~한다면 ~ 할 것이다

예문1) If it rains tomorrow, I will stay home.
(내일 비가 오면 나는 집에 있을 것이다.)

Practice 2 Vocabulary & Expression

축하편지에 나왔던 어휘와 구문을 정리해 보겠습니다.

구분	어휘 & 표현	의미
어휘	position	일자리
	accept	수락하다, 받아들이다
	Sales Director	판매책임자
	monthly salary	월급
	million	100만
	mutually	서로에게, 상호적으로
	rewarding	유익한, 보답이 있는
	long lasting	오래 지속되는
	relationship	관계
	relocate	이사하다, 이주하다
	start	시작하다, 출발하다
	sign	서명하다
	orient	안내하다, 설명하다
	culture	문화
	once again	다시 한 번
	join	합류하다, 가담하다
	if	~라면
	call	전화하다.
구문	주어 + offer + congratulations on + 목적어	~을 축하하다
	pleased + that + 주어 + 동사	~해서 기쁘다
	It is a pleasure to + 동사	~하게 되어 기쁘다
	have + 목적어 + 동사원형	~하게 되다

Practice 2 Task 4

보기에 있는 단어를 이용하여 문장을 완성하세요. 필요한 경우는 단어의 형태를 변형시키세요.

보기	congratulations offer accepted pleased at

(1) I ( ) ( ) on your new position.

(2) We are very ( ) that you have ( ) the position of Sales Director ( ) the monthly salary of 3 million won.

Practice 2 Task 5

빈 칸에 들어갈 적절한 단어를 입력하여 문장을 완성하세요.

(1) 우리는 이것이 서로에게 유익하고 오래 지속되는 관계가 되길 바랍니다.
We hope that this will be a ( ) ( ) and ( ) relationship.

(2) 저는 당신이 서울로 이주하여 8월 1일부터 업무를 시작하기를 바랍니다.
I hope that you can ( ) to Seoul and start work ( ) August 1.

(3) 그때 당신은 우리의 계약서에 서명할 수 있으며, 저는 당신에게 우리회사와 한국문화에 대해 안내할 수 있습니다.
Then you can ( ) our contract, and I can ( ) you to our company and Korean culture.

Practice 2 Task 6

제시되어 있는 단어를 배열하여 올바른 문장을 만들어 보세요. 첫 글자의 첫 철자는 대문자로 쓰세요.

(1) 다시 한번 말씀 드리지만 당신이 우리회사에 합류하게 된 것은 우리의 기쁨입니다.

once again　　　our pleasure　　　have you join our company

(　　　　　　　　　　　　　　　　　　　　　　　　　　　　)

(2) 혹시 문의사항이 있으면 저에게 전화하세요.

have any questions　　　　　　call me

(　　　　　　　　　　　　　　　　　　　　　　　　　　　　)

Exercise Writing

1. 글을 읽은 후 그를 바탕으로 축하편지의 본문을 영작해 보세요.

당신의 새로운 일자리를 축하합니다. 우리는 당신이 디자이너 자리를 수락해서 매우 기쁩니다. 저는 당신이 10월 1일부터 일을 시작할 수 있기를 바랍니다. 우리 회사에 당신이 합류할 수 있게 된 것은 우리의 기쁨입니다. 혹시 문의사항이 있으면 저에게 전화하세요.	

Exercise You be the editor

2. 감사편지의 내용을 읽고 밑줄친 부분을 올바르게 고치세요.

I offer congratulations <u>in</u> your acceptance to the University of Illinois.

You are <u>challenging</u> with making the decision of selecting which college you are going to attend. We know that this can often be a difficult decision for <u>the</u> young men or women about to enter college.
We, at the University of Illinois, recognize the importance of you decision. This decision may well <u>has</u> an impact on your life.
My best wishes to you for <u>successful collegiate life.</u>
And I sincerely hope that you will be joining us here at the University of Illinois in the fall.

Wrap up

Summary

1. The format of a congratulations letter

[1] Return Address
[2] Date
[3] Inside Address
[4] Greeting
[5] Body
[6] Closing
[7] Signature
[8] Name
[9] Job Title

2. The key expressions for a letter of congratulations

(1) I offer congratulations on your new position.
(2) It is our pleasure to have you join our company.
(3) We recognize the importance of your decision.
(4) My best wishes to you for your successful collegiate life.

Wrap up

Assignment I

오늘 학습한 주요 문형을 활용하여 영어문장을 작성하여 봅시다.

Congratulations on + 목적어	~을 축하하다.
have an impact on	~에 영향을 미치다.
My best wishes to + A + for + B	A에게 B를 진심으로 기원하다.
주어 + offer + congratulations on + 목적어	~을 축하하다.
pleased + that + 주어 + 동사	~해서 기쁘다.
It is a pleasure to +동사	~하게되어 기쁘다.
have + 목적어 + 동사원형	~하게되다.

Answers

Lesson 10. Congratulations on your acceptance to University.

Warm up
Check up

1. 1) E. Dear Ms. Jang,
   2) F. Congratulations on your recent promotion to District Manager.
   3) B. I have heard the news from your parents.
   4) D. I know how hard you have worked to earn the recognition you presently enjoy at Samsung.
   5) C. Please accept our best wishes for your success in your new position.
   6) A. Sincerely,
2. 상무이사(전무이사)로 승진 한 것에 대한 축하편지
3. Congratulations on the birth of your son.

Practice 1 Comprehension Check up

1) ① Congratulations on the applicant's acceptance to the University
2) ② Admissions Counselor
3) ② Incheon
4) ② Which college to attend
5) ③ In the fall

Practice 1 Task 1

1) Congratulations on your acceptance to the University of Texas at Austin.
2) You are now challenged with making the very important decision of selecting which college you are going to attend.
3) We know that this can often be a difficult decision for young men or women about to enter college.

Practice 1 Task 2

1) We, at the University of Texas, recognize the importance of your decision.
2) This decision may well have an impact on the quality of your life.

Practice 1 Task 3

1) My best wishes to you for your successful collegiate life.
2) I sincerely hope that you will be joining us here at the University of Texas in the fall.

Practice 2 Comprehension Check up

1) ① Geoffrey Kartwright
2) ② Congratulations on the applicant's acceptance to the new position
3) ③ Sales Director
4) ④ Seoul
5) ② August 1

Practice 2 Task 4

1) I offer congratulations on your new position.
2) We are very pleased that you have accepted the position of Sales Director at the monthly salary of 3 million won.

Practice 2 Task 5

1) We hope that his will be a mutually rewarding and long-lasting relationship.
2) I hope that you can relocate to Seoul and start work on August 1.
3) Then you can sign our contract, and I can orient you to our company and Korean culture.

Practice 2 Task 6

1) Once again, it is our pleasure to have you join our company.
2) If you have any questions, please call me.

Exercise Writing

I offer congratulations on your new position. (또는 Congratulations on your new position.) We are very pleased that you have accepted the position of a designer. I hope that you can start work on October 1. It is our pleasure to have you join our company. If you have any questions, please call me.

Exercise You be the editor

I offer congratulations on (offer congratulations on + 목적어: ~에 대해서 축하하다) your acceptance to the University of Illinois.

You are challenged with (challenged with: ~에 직면하다) making the decision of selecting which college you are going to attend. We know that this can often be a difficult decision for young men or women about to enter college.
We, at the University of Illinois, recognize the importance of your decision. This decision may well have (may well + 동사원형: 당연히 ~하다) an impact on your life.
My best wishes to you for your successful collegiate life (for + 한정사 + 형용사 + 명사). And I sincerely hope that you will be joining us here at the University of Illinois in the fall.

Lesson 11

We cannot comply with your request at this time.

Lesson 11

We cannot comply with your request at this time.

Introduction

Lesson objectives

1. Writing a letter to express rejection
2. Learning key expressions for writing a letter of rejection
   (1) We cannot comply with your request at this time.
   (2) We have found that we do not have an appropriate position for you.
   (3) We will keep you in mind for future opportunities.
   (4) We do not believe that a raise is appropriate at this time.

Warm up

The format of a letter of rejection

① Mijin Kim
349-1 Guui-dong, Gwangjin-gu
Seoul 834-939

② December 15, 2013

③ Jung In Seong
367 Gajeong-dong
Daejeon 994-348

④ Dear Mr. Jung,

⑤ Thank you for your recent request for a credit line increase on your Mastercard account. Regrettably, we cannot comply with your request at this time.
We are not able to increase your credit line, as we have discovered that the amounts you presently owe are sufficient, taking into consideration your income.
In the event that you experience a change in your financial situation and you wish to be reconsidered for a credit line increase, please contact us again.
It is our pleasure to serve you.

⑥ Sincerely,
⑦ *Mijin Kim*
⑧ Mijin Kim
⑨ Senior Manager

① 발신인 주소

- 거절편지를 쓰는 사람의 주소를 기재합니다. 편지를 쓰는 사람의 이름, 번지수, 동, 구, 시, 그리고 우편번호를 기재합니다. 동의 명칭과 구의 명칭 사이에 쉼표(,)가 들어갑니다.

② 날짜

- 거절편지를 쓰는 날짜를 기재합니다. 날짜를 기재할 때는 기수로 기재 할 수 도 있고 서수로 기재 할 수 도 있습니다. 하지만 읽을 때는 거의 언제나 서수로 읽습니다.

③ 수신인 주소

- 수신인 주소에는 거절편지를 받는 사람의 이름과 주소를 기재합니다. 거절편지를 쓰는 사람의 이름, 번지수 + 동, 구, 도시, 그리고 우편번호를 기재합니다. 동의 명칭과 구의 명칭 사이에 쉼표(,)가 들어갑니다.

④ 인사

- 거절편지의 인사는 격식체 또는 비격식체를 사용합니다. 격식체와 비격식체의 인사는 다음과 같습니다.

수신인	격식체	비격식체
남성	Dear Mr. + 수신인의 성:	Dear Mr. + 수신인의 성,
기혼여성	Dear Mrs. + 수신인의 성:	Dear Mrs. + 수신인의 성,
미혼여성	Dear Miss + 수신인의 성:	Dear Miss + 수신인의 성,
기혼 또는 미혼 여성	Dear Ms. + 수신인의 성:	Dear Ms. + 수신인의 성,

⑤ 본문

- 본문은 거절편지에서 가장 중요한 부분입니다. 거절편지의 본문에는 무엇에 대해서 거절하는지 그리고 거절하는 이유가 무엇인지 명시합니다. 거절편지는 가능한 부드럽게 쓰는 것이 바람직합니다.

⑥ 끝인사

- 거절편지의 끝인사는 격식체 또는 비격식체를 사용합니다.

구분	형식
격식체	Sincerely,
	Sincerely yours,
	Cordially,
	Cordially yours,
비격식체	Regards,
	Best regards,
	Best wishes,
	With best wishes,

⑦ 서명

- 거절편지를 쓰는 사람의 서명을 기재합니다.

⑧ 이름

- 거절편지를 쓰는 사람의 이름을 기재합니다.

⑨ 직책

- 필요에 따라서 거절편지를 쓰는 사람의 직책을 기재할 수 있습니다.

Warm up

Checkup

1. 거절편지의 본문에 들어가는 내용을 순서에 맞게 배열하세요. 주어진 항목을 읽어 본 후 순서에 맞게 배열하세요.

보기	Dear Mrs. Lim, A: However, we regret to inform you that because of the very intense competition for a limited number of slots, we are unable to offer you admittance. B: The Admissions Committee has carefully reviewed your application to the sophomore class in our school in March 3, 2009 C: I wish you every success in the future and hope you find a suitable institution to meet your needs. D: Good luck in your future endeavors. Sincerely yours.

1. ______ → 2. ______ → 3. ______ → 4. ______ → 5. ______ → 6. ______

2. 다음은 거절편지의 본문이다. 무엇에 대한 거절인지 내용을 입력하세요.

Thank you for your credit card application at Lotte Department Store. Your references are good and your employment record shows a promising future. However, your current financial status does not meet our requirements. Therefore, we cannot grant you the credit card you requested.
In the event that you experience a change in your financial situation and you wish to be reconsidered for a credit card, please contact us again.
It is our pleasure to serve you.

---

3. 다음 두 문장의 의미를 번역하세요.

1) We regret to inform you that we cannot comply with your request.

---

2) We regretted informing you that we could not comply with your request.

Practice 1 Comprehension Check up

다음 거절 편지를 읽고 질문에 답을 선택한 후 [확인] 버튼을 클릭하세요.

Jinsoo Park
890-16 Daechi-dong, Gangnam-gu,
Seoul 400-103

December 3, 2013

Jinjoo Choi
Dasol Apt. 102-1007
Gu-dong, Yuseong-gu
Daejeon 305-335

Dear Miss Choi:

Thank you for giving us the chance to consider you for employment. We are always looking for quality people like you. We are really grateful for your interest in Heinz.

Our team has carefully evaluated your background and credentials, and we found that we do not have an appropriate position for you at this time. While we understand this is unwelcome news, we would like to keep your application on file for future openings.

If an opportunity becomes available, we will be pleased to contact you. We appreciate your applying for a position at Heinz and will keep you in mind for future opportunities. We wish you success in your search.

Cordially yours,
Jinsoo Park
Jinsoo Park
Human Resources Manager

1. What is the letter about?

① Informing the applicant that she was accepted to the company
② Informing the applicant that she was not accepted to the company
③ Arranging an interview with the applicant
④ Canceling the appointment with the applicant

2. What is Miss Jinjoo Choi interested in?

① A position at Heinz
② Moving to Seoul
③ Starting a business with Heinz
④ Recruiting people for Heinz

3. What is the job tile of the person who wrote this letter?

① Human Resources Manager
② Human Resources Secretary
③ Human Resources Associate
④ Human Resources Managing Director

4. Which city does the applicant live?

① Seoul
② Incheon
③ Mokpo
④ Daegu

5. Why can't Mr. Jinsoo Park offer Miss Jinjoo Choi a position?

① Because there is no appropriate position for her.
② Because she is not old enough for the position.
③ Because he has already employed a person for the position.
④ Because she does not live in Seoul.

서울시 강남구 대치동 890-16
400-103
박진수

2013년 12월 3일

유성구 구동
다솔 APT 102-1007 305-335
최진주

최진주 님께.

고용을 위해서 당신을 고려해볼 수 있는 기회를 저희에게 주셔서 감사합니다. 우리는 항상 당신과 같은 자질이 우수한 사람들을 찾고 있습니다. 우리는 당신의 하인즈에 대한 관심에 대해 정말로 감사합니다.

우리 팀이 주의 깊게 당신의 경력과 증명서를 평가하였습니다. 그리고 우리는 현재로서는 당신을 위한 적절한 일자리가 없다는 것을 알았습니다. 우리는 이것이 달갑지 않은 소식이라는 것을 이해하지만 우리는 당신의 지원서를 추후 자리가 날 경우를 대비해서 철하여 보관하려고 합니다. 만약 기회가 생기면 우리는 기꺼이 당신에게 연락하겠습니다. 우리는 하인즈의 일자리에 당신이 지원한 것에 감사드리며 추후에 생길 기회를 위해서 당신을 기억하겠습니다. 우리는 당신의 구직에 성공을 기원합니다.

안녕히 계십시오.

박진수

인사부 과장

1. 이 편지는 무엇에 관한 내용입니까?
   ① 지원자에게 회사에 입사되었음을 알리기
   ② 지원자에게 회사에 입사되지 않았음을 알리기
   ③ 지원자와의 면접을 약속하기
   ④ 지원자와의 약속을 취소하기

2. 최진주 양은 무엇에 관심이 있습니까?

① 하인즈 회사의 일자리
② 서울로 이사
③ 하인즈 회사와의 업무 시작
④ 하인즈 회사를 위해 사원모집하기

3. 이 편지를 쓴 사람의 직책은 무엇입니까?

① 인사부 과장
② 인사부 비서
③ 인사부 평사원
④ 인사부 상무이사

4. 지원자는 어느 시에서 살고 있습니까?

① 서울
② 인천
③ 목포
④ 대구

5. 박진수 씨는 왜 최진주 양에게 일자리를 줄 수 없나요?

① 그녀에게 적합한 일자리기 없기 때문에
② 그 일을 담당할 나이가 되지 않아서
③ 그가 이미 그 일을 담당할 사람을 고용했기 때문에
④ 그녀가 서울에 살지 않기 때문에

Practice 1 Lecture

01

Thank you for giving us the chance to consider you for employment.
(고용을 위해서 당신을 고려해볼 수 있는 기회를 저희에게 주셔서 감사합니다.)

어 휘

① chance : 기회

② consider : 고려하다

예문1) I considered changing my job, but in the end I decided not to.
(나는 직업을 바꾸는 것을 고려해 보았으나 결국에는 바꾸지 않기로 결정했다.)

③ employment : 고용

예문1) He is in employment. (그는 취직 상태이다.)

구 문

① thank A for B : A에게 B에 대해서 감사하다

예문1) The old man thanked me for helping him.
(그 노인은 도움을 준 것에 대해서 나에게 고마워했다.)

② give + 간목 + 직목 : ~에게 ~을 주다

예문1) Give me the chance to try the job.
(그 일을 시도해볼 수 있는 기회를 저에게 주세요.)

02

We are always looking for quality people like you.
(우리는 항상 당신과 같은 자질이 우수한 사람들을 찾고 있습니다.)

어 휘

① always : 언제나, 항상

② look for : 을 찾다

예문1) She is looking for a job.
(그녀는 일자리를 찾고 있습니다.)

③ quality : 자질이 우수한

예문1) The store deals in quality goods.
(그 가게는 우량품을 취급한다.)

03 **We are really grateful for your interest in Heinz.**

(우리는 당신의 하인즈에 대한 관심에 대해 정말로 감사합니다.)

어 휘

① grateful for : ~에 대해 감사하다

예문1) I was grateful to John for his kindness.

(나는 존에게 그의 친절에 대해 감사했다.)

② interest : 관심, 흥미

예문1) My nephew is showing an interest in music.

(나의 조카는 음악에 관심을 보이고 있다.)

예문2) She has no interest in politics.

(그녀는 정치에 관심이 없다.)

04 **Our team has carefully evaluated your background and credentials,**

(우리 팀이 주의 깊게 당신의 경력과 증명서를 평가하였습니다.)

어 휘

① carefully : 주의 깊게

② evaluate : 평가하다

예문1) The school has only been open for six months, so it's too early to evaluate its success.

(그 학교는 개교한지 단지 6개월 되었으므로 성공을 평가하기는 너무 이르다.)

③ background : 경력, 학력

예문1) The man got a job because of his excellent background.

(그 남자는 자신의 훌륭한 경력 때문에 직업을 구했다.)

④ credential : 증명서 (성적증명서, 추천서 등)

05 **and we found that we do not have an appropriate position for you at this time.**

(그리고 우리는 현재로서는 당신을 위한 적절한 일자리가 없다는 것을 알았습니다.)

어 휘 ① appropriate : 적절한

예문1) Her bright colors were not appropriate for a funeral.
(그녀의 밝은 옷은 장례식에 적절하지 않았다.)

② position : 일자리

구 문 ① find that + 주어 + 동사 : ~임을 알게 되다

예문1) We went to her house but found that she was out.
(우리는 그녀의 집에 갔으나 그녀가 외출했다는 것을 알았다.)

06 **While we understand this is unwelcome news, we would like to keep your application on file for future openings.**
(우리는 이것이 반갑지 않은 소식이라는 것을 이해하지만 우리는 당신의 지원서를 추후 자리가 날 경우를 대비해서 보관하려고 합니다.)

어 휘 ① understand : 이해하다

② unwelcome : 반갑지 않은, 달갑지 않은

예문1) She was an unwelcome guest.
(그녀는 반갑지 않은 손님이었다.)

③ application : 지원서

④ opening : 빈자리

예문1) There is an opening for a secretary in our company.
(우리 회사에 비서 자리가 비어있다.)

관용표현 ① keep on file : 철하여 보관하다

예문1) I will keep your report on file.
(나는 너의 보고서를 철하여 보관할 것이다.)

구 문 ① while + 주어 + 동사, 주어 + 동사 : 비록 ~하지만, ~하다

예문1) While they do not agree, they still like each other.
(그들이 의견이 다르지만 여전히 서로를 좋아한다.)

07 If an opportunity becomes available, we will be pleased to contact you.

(만약 기회가 생기면 우리는 기꺼이 당신에게 연락하겠습니다.)

어 휘

① opportunity : 기회
② available : 이용할 수 있는
③ contact : 연락하다

구 문

① 주어 + become + 형용사 : ~하게 되다

예문1) The weather became colder
(날씨가 더 추워졌다.)

② 주어 + will + be + pleased + to부정사 : 기꺼이 ~하겠다

예문1) I will be pleased to drive you to your hotel.
(나는 기꺼이 당신을 호텔까지 차로 태워주겠다.)

③ If + 주어 + 동사, 주어 + will + 동사 : 만약 ~하면 ~하겠다

예문1) If it rains tomorrow, I will stay home.
(만약 내일 비가 오면 나는 집에 있겠다.)

08 We appreciate your applying for a position at Heinz and will keep you in mind for future opportunities.

(우리는 하인즈의 일자리에 당신이 지원한 것에 감사 드리며 추후에 생길 기회를 위해서 당신을 기억하겠습니다.)

어 휘

① appreciate : ~을 감사하다

예문1) I deeply appreciate her kindness.
(나는 그녀의 친절에 깊이 감사한다.)

② apply for : ~에 지원하다

예문1) She will apply for a new job.
(그녀는 새로운 직업에 지원할 것이다.)

관용표현 ① keep in mind: ~을 기억하다

예문1) I will always keep your suggestion in mind.
(나는 너의 제안을 항상 기억하겠다.)

09 We wish you success in your search.
(우리는 당신의 구직에 성공을 기원합니다.)

어 휘 ① success : 성공
② search : 탐구, 추구

예문1) Birds are flying south in search of the warm weather.
(새들은 따뜻한 날씨를 찾아서 남쪽으로 날아가고 있다.)

구 문 ① wish + 간목 + 직목 : ~에게 ~을 바라다

예문1) I wish you a merry Christmas.
(즐거운 성탄절 되십시오.)

Practice 1 Vocabulary & Expression

구분	어휘 & 구문	의미
어휘	chance	기회
	consider	고려하다
	employment	고용
	always	언제나, 항상
	look for	~을 찾다
	quality	자질이 우수한
	grateful for	~에 대해 감사하다
	interest	관심, 흥미
	carefully	주의 깊게
	evaluate	평가하다
	background	경력
	credential	증명서
	appropriate	적절한
	position	일자리
	understand	이해하다
	unwelcome	달갑지 않은, 반갑지 않은
	application	지원서
	opening	빈자리
	opportunity	기회
	available	이용할 수 있는
	contact	연락하다
	appreciate	~을 감사하다
	apply for	~에 지원하다
	success	성공
	search	탐구, 추구
관용표현	keep on file	철하여 보관하다
	keep in mind	~을 기억하다

구분	어휘 & 구문	의미
구문	thank A for B	A에게 B에 대해서 감사하다
	give + 간목 + 진목	~에게 ~을 주다
	find that + 주어 + 동사	~을 알게 되다
	while + 주어 + 동사, 주어 + 동사	비록 ~하지만, ~하다
	주어 + become + 형용사	~이 되다
	주어 + will + be + pleased + to + 동사	기꺼이 ~하겠다
	if + 주어 + 동사, 주어 + will + 동사	만약 ~하면 ~하겠다
	wish + 간목 + 진목	~에게 ~을 바라다

Practice 1 Task 1

보기에 있는 단어를 이용하여 문장을 완성하세요. 필요한 경우는 단어의 형태를 변형시키세요.

보기	for	look	thank	grateful

(1) (　　) you (　　) giving us the chance to consider you for employment.
(2) We are always (　　)(　　) quality people such as you.
(3) We are really (　　)(　　) your interest in Heinz.

Practice 1 Task 2

빈 칸에 들어갈 적절한 단어를 입력하여 문장을 완성하세요.

(1) 우리 팀이 주의 깊게 당신의 경력과 증명서를 평가하였습니다.
Our team has (　　　　)(　　　　) your background and credentials.

(2) 우리는 현재로서는 당신을 위한 적절한 일자리가 없다는 걸을 알았습니다.
We (　　　　)(　　　　) that we do not have an (　　　　) (　　　　) for you at this time.

(3) 우리는 이것이 반갑지 않은 소식이라는 것을 이해하지만 우리는 당신의 지원서를 추후 자리가 날 경우를 대비해서 보관하려고 합니다.
(　　　　) we understand that this is unwelcome news, we would like to (　　　　) your application (　　)(　　) for future openings.

Practice 1 Task 3

제시되어 있는 단어를 배열하여 올바른 문장을 만들어 보세요. 문장의 첫 철자는 대문자로 입력하세요.

(1) 만약 기회가 생기면 우리는 기꺼이 당신에게 연락하겠습니다.

if opportunity an becomes available

( ), we will be pleased to contact you.

(2) 우리는 하인즈의 일자리에 당신이 지원한 것에 감사드리며 추후에 생길 기회를 위해서 당신을 기억하겠습니다.

keep in mind you future for opportunities will

We appreciate your applying for a position at Heinz and

( ).

(3) 우리는 당신의 구직에 성공을 기원합니다.

wish you success in search we your

( )

Coffee break

Hangover Cures

In many cultures, drinking is an important social custom. Not only is it a way to bond with other people, but drinking also provides a way to relax and unwind after a hard day's work. When you are really stressed, you may find that drinking alcohol helps you temporarily forget about your problems and enables you to feel at ease. If you drink too much, though, the following morning you might find yourself reconsidering whether or not it was worth it.

When you wake up after a night of drinking and you have a monstrous headache, feel like your body has been crushed by a car, and are too dizzy to do anything useful, you are experiencing a hangover. Because alcohol causes you to urinate, your body becomes dehydrated. This also causes your brain to temporarily shrink, resulting in a headache. Also, when you urinate too much, your body loses important minerals that keep your heart beating at a normal rate. Needless to say, having a hangover makes you feel tired, and you end up yawning all day long, unable to concentrate.

Many people claim to have magical cures for hangovers. For example, American Indian tribes believed that running would help sweat out the alcohol's poison. In the middle ages, people ate almonds and dried eel to ward off the effects of a hangover. Puerto Ricans rub lemon under their arms, and some Mongolians drink tomato juice with a sheep's eye in it as a hangover cure.

While these ideas are all very entertaining, there is not actually a magical cure for a hangover. The best advice is to drink a lot of water. You can also drink Gatorade to put the important minerals back in your body, and when you're feeling tired, you should get back in bed. Of course, the wisest idea is just not to drink so much!

Coffee break

숙취 치료법

여러 문화에서는 음주는 중요한 사회 풍습이다. 다른 사람들과 묶어줄 뿐만 아니라 편안히 쉬게 하고 힘든 업무 후 긴장을 풀어준다. 스트레스를 매우 받았을 때, 알코올을 마시는 것이 일시적으로 문제를 잊게 하고 편안하게 만들어 준다는 것을 알게 된다. 만약 너무 과하게 마신다면 그 다음 아침 이것이 가치 있는지 다시 한 번 생각하게 된다.

밤에 술을 마신 후 일어나면 당신은 끔찍한 두통이 있고 몸이 차에 치인 것 같은 느낌을 받고, 쓸모 있는 일을 하기에는 너무나 어지럽다면 당신은 숙취를 경험하는 것이다. 알코올은 오줌을 누게 만들기 때문에 몸에 수분이 빠지게 된다. 이것은 또한 두뇌가 일시적으로 줄어들게 만들고 결과로서 두통이 생긴다. 또한, 오줌을 너무 많이 누게 되면 심장을 정상 속도로 뛰게 해주는 중요한 미네랄이 몸에서 빠져나가게 된다. 두 말할 나위없이 숙취는 당신을 피곤하게 만들어 결국 하루종일 하품하게 만들고 집중할 수 없게 한다.

많은 사람들은 숙취에 마법적인 치료법이 있다고 주장한다. 예를 들어 미국 인디안 부족은 뛰는 것이 알코올의 독소를 빼내게 한다고 믿었다. 중세시대에는 사람들은 숙취의 결과들을 막기 위해 아몬드와 말린 뱀장어를 먹었다. 푸에르토리코 사람들은 팔 아래 레몬을 문지르고 몽골 사람들은 숙취해소법으로 토마토 주스에 양의 눈을 넣어 마셨다.

이 아이디어들은 매우 흥미롭지만 숙취에 마법 같은 치료는 실제로 없다. 가장 좋은 조언은 물을 많이 마시는 것이다. 미네랄을 다시 몸에 넣기 위해서는 게토레이와 같은 스포츠 음료를 마시고 피곤하다면 잠을 자야 한다. 당연히 가장 지혜로운 방법은 술을 너무 많이 마시지 않는 것이다.

Practice 2 Comprehension Check up

다음 거절편지를 읽고 질문에 답을 선택한 후 [확인] 버튼을 클릭하세요.

June Kang
HiVol Sound Systems
234 Guui 5-dong, Gwangjin-gu
Seoul 399-956

March 8, 2013

Minwoo Hyun
Samik Apt. 3-224
Jisan-dong, Seo-gu
Seoul 305-390

Dear Mr. Hyun:

Thank you for taking the time to send us a letter detailing your accomplishments at our company. HiVol definitely values your efforts, your good work ethic, and your sales experience. That is why we have been pleased to have you working with us for the past few months.

While HiVol sympathizes with all the points that you have mentioned in your letter, we do not believe that a raise is appropriate at this time. It is HiVol's practice to review employee benefits and compensation at the end of each year. At that time we will take an increase in your salary into consideration, assuming the sales figures for your store are increased. I appreciate your understanding in this matter and hope that you will continue to contribute to HiVol's success.

Sincerely,
June Kang
June Kang
District Manager

1. What is the letter about?
① Informing the employee that his request was accepted
② Informing the employee that his request was not accepted
③ Informing the job applicant when he should come to the interview
④ Informing the job applicant that the interview was cancelled

2. What did Mr. Hyun request?
① Opening a new account
② Issuing a credit card
③ A Pay raise
④ A loan from the bank

3. Why was Mr. Hyun's request not granted?
① He is heavily in debt.
② He has too many credit cards.
③ His financial status is not stable
④ Time is not appropriate for a raise

4. What is the job title of Mr. June Kang?
① President
② Human Resources Manager
③ District Manager
④ Admissions Counselor

5. When will Mr. Hyun's request be considered again?
① At the beginning of April
② At the beginning of May
③ At the end of August
④ At the end of the year

서울 광진구
구의 5동 234번지 399-956
하이볼 사운드 시스템
강준

2013년 3월 8일

서울 서구
지산동 삼익 아파트 3동 224호 305-390
현민우

현 선생님께:

시간을 내어 우리 회사에서의 당신의 업적을 상세히 열거하는 편지를 보내주셔서 감사합니다. 하이볼은 명백히 당신의 노력, 좋은 업무 도덕, 그리고 판매 경험을 소중하게 생각합니다. 그 이유 때문에 우리는 지난 몇 개월 동안 당신이 우리와 함께 일하게 된 것을 기뻐했습니다.
하이볼은 당신이 편지에 언급한 모든 점들에 동감하지만 우리는 이 시점에서 급여 인상은 적절하다고 생각하지 않습니다. 매 년 말에 고용인들의 복지와 보수를 재고하는 것이 하이볼의 관행입니다. 그때에는 당신의 매장 판매 수치가 증가했다는 전제 하에 우리는 당신의 월급 인상을 고려할 것입니다. 이 일에 있어서 당신이 이해해주는 것에 감사드리며 당신이 계속해서 하이볼의 성공에 기여하길 바랍니다.

안녕히 계십시오.

강준
지사장

1. 편지는 무엇에 관한 내용입니까?
   ① 직원에게 그의 요청이 받아들여졌음을 알리는 내용
   ② 직원에게 그의 요청이 받아들여지지 않았음을 알리는 내용
   ③ 취업지원자에게 언제 면접 보러 오는지를 통보하는 내용
   ④ 취업지원자에게 면접이 취소되었음을 통보하는 내용

2. 현민우님은 무엇을 요구했나요?

① 은행구좌 개설
② 신용카드 발급
③ 월급 인상
④ 은행으로부터의 대출

3. 현민우님의 요구가 받아들여 지지 않은 이유는 무엇입니까?

① 빚이 많아서
② 신용카드가 많아서
③ 그의 재정 상태가 안정적이지 않아서
④ 월급 인상 시기가 아니기 때문에

4. 강준 씨의 직책은 무엇입니까?

① 사장
② 인사부 과장
③ 지사장
④ 입학 카운슬러

5. 현민우님의 요청은 언제 다시 고려될까요?

① 4월 초
② 5월 초
③ 8월 말
④ 연 말

Practice 2 Lecture

01

Thank you for taking the time to send us a letter detailing your accomplishments in our company.

(시간을 내어 우리 회사에서의 당신의 업적을 상세히 열거하는 편지를 보내주셔서 감사합니다.)

어 휘

① send : 보내다

예문1) If you need money, I will send you some.

(당신이 돈이 필요하면 내가 당신에게 좀 보내주겠소.)

② detail : 상세히 열거하다

예문1) He was detailing the reasons why he was absent at that time.

(그는 그때 그가 결석한 이유를 상세히 열거하고 있었다.)

③ accomplishments : 업적, 성과

예문1) He achieved lots of accomplishments as a scientist.

(그는 과학자로서 많은 업적을 이루었다.)

구 문

① thank A for B : A에게 B에 대해서 감사하다

예문1) We thanked the old man for his kindness.

(우리는 그 노인에게 그 친절에 대해서 감사했다.)

02

HiVol definitely values your efforts, your good work ethic, and your sales experience.

(하이볼은 명백히 당신의 노력, 훌륭한 직업 윤리, 그리고 판매 경험을 소중하게 생각합니다.)

어 휘

① definitely : 명백히

② value : 중요시하다, 소중하게 생각하다

예문1) We should value manual labor as well as mental labor.

(우리는 정신노동뿐만 아니라 육체노동도 중요시 해야 한다.)

③ effort : 노력

예문1) The prisoner made efforts to escape, but he failed.
(그 죄수는 탈출하려고 시도했으나 실패했다.)

④ ethic : 도덕, 윤리

예문1) They learn the ethic of dining at school.
(그들은 식사 예법을 학교에서 배운다.)

⑤ experience : 경험

03

That is why we have been pleased to have you working with us for the past few months.
(그 이유 때문에 우리는 지난 몇 개월 동안 당신이 우리와 함께 일하게 된 것을 기뻐했습니다.)

어 휘

① pleased to + 동사원형 : ~해서 기쁘다

예문1) He was very pleased to pass the driving test.
(그는 운전면허 시험을 합격해서 매우 기뻤다.)

② past : 지난

예문1) I haven't been feeling well for the past few days.
(나는 지난 며칠 동안 몸이 좋지 않았다.)

구 문

① that is why + 주어 + 동사 : 그 이유 때문에 ~하다

예문1) That is why I was late to the meeting.
(그 이유 때문에 나는 모임에 늦었다.)

② have + 목적어 + 현재분사 : ~하게 하다

예문1) The boss had his employees working until 5 pm.
(사장님은 직원들을 오후 5시까지 일하도록 했다.)

04

While HiVol sympathizes with all the points that you have mentioned in your letter,
(하이볼은 당신이 편지에 언급한 모든 점들에 동감하지만,)

어 휘

① sympathize with : 동감하다

예문1) It is really hard to sympathize with her political opinions.
(그녀의 정치적인 의견에 동감하기는 정말 어렵다.)

② points : 요점, 항목

예문1) There are two points in his speech that I don't understand.
(그의 연설에서 내가 이해하지 못한 두 가지 점이 있다.)

③ mention : 언급하다

예문1) He mentioned that he was interested in the lady.
(그는 그가 그 여인에게 관심 있다고 언급했다.)

구 문

① while + 주어 + 동사, 주어 + 동사 : ~하지만 ~하다

예문1) While John is a pianist, his brother is an engineer.
(존은 피아니스트 이지만 그의 형은 엔지니어다.)

05 We do not believe that a raise is appropriate at this time.

(우리는 이 시점에서 급여 인상은 적절하다고 생각하지 않습니다.)

어 휘

① raise : 급여 인상

예문1) I got a raise last month.
(나는 지난 달에 급여가 인상되었다.)

② appropriate : 적절한

예문1) The gloomy music was not appropriate to the wedding.
(그 우울한 음악은 결혼식에 적합하지 않았다.)

구 문

① 주어 + do + not + believe + that 주어 + 동사 ~ : ~라고 생각하지 않는다

예문1) I do not believe that he is telling the truth.
(나는 그가 진실을 말하고 있다고 생각하지 않는다.)

06 It is HiVol's practice to review employee benefits and compensation at the end of each year.

(매 년 말에 직원들의 복지와 보수를 재고하는 것이 하이볼의 관행입니다.)

어 휘 ① practice : 관행

예문1) It is not the usual practice for offices to stay open after 5 pm.
(사무실이 오후 5시 이후에 업무를 보는 것은 일상적인 관행은 아니다.)

② review : 재고하다

예문1) The government should review its education policy.
(정부는 교육정책을 재고해야 한다.)

③ benefit : 보조금, 복지

④ compensation : 보수

07 **At that time we will take an increase in your salary into consideration, assuming the sales figures for your store are increased.**

(그때에는 당신의 매장 판매 수치가 증가했다는 전제 하에 우리는 당신의 월급 인상을 고려할 것입니다.)

어 휘 ① increase : 증가, 증가시키다

예문1) Crime is on the increase.
(범죄가 증가하고 있다.)

예문2) The price of oil was increased again.
(기름값이 다시 증가되었다.)

② figures : 수치

예문1) Write the amount in figures.
(금액을 수치로 쓰시오.)

관용표현 ① take into consideration : ~을 고려하다

예문1) We took her recent illness into consideration when judging her accomplishments.
(우리는 그녀의 업적을 심사할 때 그녀가 최근에 아팠다는 점을 고려하였다.)

구 문 ① assuming that + 주어 + 동사 : ~한다는 전제 하에

예문1) She prepared for the party, assuming all the invited people would come.
(초대받은 사람들이 모두 온다는 전제하에 그녀는 파티를 준비했다.)

08 **I appreciate your understanding in this matter and hope that you will continue to contribute to HiVol's success.**

(이 일에 있어서 당신이 이해해주는 것에 감사드리며 당신이 계속해서 하이볼의 성공에 기여하길 바랍니다.)

어 휘

① appreciate : ~을 감사하게 생각하다

예문1) I appreciate your help.

(나는 당신의 도움에 감사드립니다.)

② continue to + 동사 : 계속 ~하다

예문1) Will you continue to play the game after lunch?

(당신은 점심식사 후에도 게임을 계속할 것입니까?)

③ contribute to + 목적어 : ~에 기여하다, 공헌하다

예문1) Fresh air contributes to good health.

(신선한 공기는 좋은 건강에 기여한다.)

Practice 2 Vocabulary & Expression

거절 편지에 나왔던 어휘와 구문을 정리해 보겠습니다.

구분	어휘 & 구문	의미
어휘	send	보내다
	detail	상세히 열거하다
	accomplishments	업적, 성과
	value	소중하게 생각하다, 중요시하다
	effort	노력
	ethic	윤리, 도덕
	experience	경험
	pleased to + 동사원형	~해서 기쁘다
	past	지난
	sympathize with	동감하다.
	points	요점, 항목
	mention	언급하다
	raise	급여 인상
	appropriate	적절한
	increase	증가, 증가시키다
	figures	수치
	appreciate	~을 감사하게 생각하다
	continue to + 동사	계속 ~하다
	contribute to + 동사	~에 기여하다, 공헌하다
구문	thank A for B	A에게 B에 대해서 감사하다
	that is why + 주어 + 동사	그 이유 때문에 ~ 하다
	have + 목적어 + 현재분사	~하게 하다
	while + 주어 + 동사, 주어 + 동사	~하지만 ~하다
	주어 + do + not + believe + that + 주어 + 동사	~라고 생각하지 않는다

Practice 2 Task 4

보기에 있는 단어를 이용하여 문장을 완성하세요. 필요한 경우는 단어의 형태를 변형시키세요.

보기	working please take detail value

(1) Thank you for (   ) the time to send us a letter (   ) your accomplishments at your company.

(2) HiVol definitely (   ) your efforts, your ethic, and your sales experience.

(3) That is why we have been (   ) to have you (   ) with us for the past few months.

Practice 2 Task 5

빈 칸에 들어갈 적절한 단어를 입력하여 문장을 완성하세요.

(1) 하이볼은 당신이 편지에 언급한 모든 점들에 동감하지만 이 시점에서 급여 인상은 적절하다고 생각하지 않습니다.

(   ) Hivol (   )(   ) all the points that you have mentioned in your letter, we do not believe that a raise is appropriate at this time.

(2) 매 년 말에 직원들의 복지와 보수를 재고하는 것이 하이볼의 관행입니다.

It is HiVol's (   ) to review employee (   ) and (   ) at the end of each year.

Practice 2 Task 6

제시되어 있는 난어와 구를 배열하여 올바른 문장을 만들어 보세요.

(1) 그때에는 당신의 매장 판매 실적이 증가했다면 우리는 당신의 급여 인상을 고려할 것입니다.

an increase in your salary, take into consideration, will, we

At that time (   ).

(2) 저는 이 일에 있어서 당신이 이해해주는 것에 감사드립니다.

in this matter, your understanding, appreciate

I (   ).

(3) 저는 당신이 계속해서 하이볼의 성공에 기여하길 바랍니다.

continue to, will, you, HiVol's success, contribute to,

I hope that (   ).

Exercise Writing

왼쪽의 글을 읽은 후 그를 바탕으로 거절편지의 본문을 영작해 보세요.

우리는 당신의 우리 회사에 대한 관심에 대해 감사합니다. (grateful, interest, company) 우리는 당신의 경력을 주의 깊게 평가했습니다. (background, have evaluated) 하지만 현재로서는 당신을 위한 적절한 자리가 없습니다. (however, at this time, appropriate) 만약 기회가 생기면 우리는 기꺼이 당신에게 연락하겠습니다. (an opportunity, becomes, available, will) 우리는 당신의 구직에 성공을 기원합니다. (success, your, search)	

Exercise You be the editor

다음 감사편지의 내용을 읽고 밑줄친 부분을 올바르게 고치세요.

Thank you for taking the time to send us a letter detailing your accomplishments in our company.

We value your efforts, your good work ethic, and your work experience.

That is why we have been pleased to have you worked with us for the past few years.

While our company sympathizes to all the points that you have mentioned in your letter, we do not believe that a rise is appropriate at this time.

It is our company's practice to review employee benefits and compensation every three years.

So at the end of this year we will take an increase in your salary into consideration, assumed the sales figures for your store are increased.

I appreciate your understanding in this matter and hope you will continue to contribute to our company's success.

Warm up

Summary

1. The format of a letter of rejection

① Return Address

② Date

③ Inside Address

④ Greeting

⑤ Body

⑥ Closing

⑦ Signature

⑧ Name

⑨ Job Title

2. Key expressions for writing a letter of rejection

① We cannot comply with your request at this time.

② We have found that we do not have an appropriate position for you.

③ We will keep you in mind for future opportunities.

④ We do not believe that a raise is appropriate at this time.

Wrap up

Assignment I

오늘 학습한 주요 문형을 활용하여 영어문장을 작성하여 봅시다.

thank A for B	A에게 B에 대해서 감사하다
give + 간목 + 직목	~에게 ~을 주다
find that + 주어 + 동사	~을 알게 되다
while + 주어 + 동사, 주어 + 동사	비록 ~하지만, ~하다
주어 + will + be + pleased + to + 동사	기꺼이 ~하겠다
if + 주어 + 동사, 주어 + will + 동사	만약 ~하면 ~하겠다
wish + 간목 + 직목	~에게 ~을 바라다
that is why + 주어 + 동사	그 이유 때문에 ~하다

Wrap up

Assignment II

오늘 학습한 주요내용과 제시된 조건에 맞게 거절편지를 작성해 봅시다. 영어(한글) 형태로 작성한 후 〔제출하기〕버튼을 클릭하면 〔과제방〉주관식 과제〕에 등록됩니다.

조건	과제
1. 본문만 작성하시오. 2. 각 문장의 한글해석을 괄호에 넣으시오. 3. 최소 5문장 최대 10문장이 되게 하시오. 4. 다음 표현을 반드시 사용하시오. (1) grateful for your interest~ (2) evaluate your background and credentials (3) do not have appropriate position (4) pleased tocontact you	

Answers

Lesson 11. We cannot comply with your request at this time.

Warm up

Check up

1)

Dear Mrs. Lim,

B. The Admissions Committee has carefully reviewed your application to the sophomore class in our school in March 3, 2009.

A. However, we regret to inform you that because of the very intense competition for a limited number of slots, we are unable to offer you admittance.

C. I wish you every success in the future and hope you find a suitable institution to meet your needs.

D. Good luck in your future endeavors.

Sincerely yours,

2) 롯데백화점 신용카드 신청에 대한 거절

3) - 우리는 당신에게 우리가 당신의 요청을 들어 줄 수 없음을 알리게 되어 유감이다.
- 우리는 당신에게 우리가 당신의 요청을 들어 줄 수 없음을 알린 것을 후회한다.

Practice 1 Comprehension Check up

1) ② Informing the applicant that she was not accepted to the company

2) ① A position at Heinz

3) ① Human Resources Manager
4) ④ Daegu
5) ① Because there is no appropriate position for her.

Practice 1 Task 1

1) Thank you for giving us the chance to consider you for employment.
2) We are always looking for quality people such as you.
3) We are really grateful for your interest in Heinz.

Practice 1 Task 2

1) Our team has carefully evaluated your background and credentials.
2) We have found that we do not have an appropriate position for you at this time.
3) While we understand that this is unwelcome news, we would like to keep your application on file for future openings.

Practice 1 Task 3

1) If an opportunity becomes available, we will be pleased to contact you.
2) We appreciate your applying for a position at Heinz and will keep you in mind for future opportunities.
3) We wish you success in your search.

Practice 2 Comprehension Check up

1) ② Informing the employee that his request was not accepted
2) ③ A pay raise
3) ④ Time is not appropriate for a raise
4) ③ District Manager
5) ④ At the end of the year

Practice 2 Task 4

1) Thank you for taking the time to send us a letter detailing your accomplishments at your company.
2) HiVol definitely values your efforts, your ethic, and your sales experience.
3) That is why we have been pleased to have you working with us for the past few months.

Practice 2 Task 5

1) While HiVol sympathizes with all the points that you have mentioned in your letter, we do not believe that a raise is appropriate at this time.
2) It is HiVol's practice to review employee benefits and compensation at the end of each year.

Practice 2 Task 6

1) At that time we will take an increase in your salary into consideration, assuming the sales figures for your store are increased.
2) I appreciate your understanding in this matter.
3) I hope that you will continue to contribute to HiVol's success.

Exercise Writing

We are grateful for your interest in our company. We have carefully evaluated your background. However, we do not have an appropriate position for you at this time. If an opportunity becomes available, we will be pleased to contact you. We wish you success in your search.

Exercise You be the editor

Thank you for taking the time to send us a letter detailing your accomplishments in our company.
We value your efforts, your good work ethic, and your work experience.
That is why we have been pleased to have you working (have + 목적어 + 현재분사: ~하게 되다) with us for the past few years.

While our company sympathizes with (sympathize with: 동감하다) all the points that you have mentioned in your letter, we do not believe that a raise (raise: 급여인상) is appropriate at this time.
It is our company's practice to review employee benefits and compensation every three years.
So at the end of this year we will take an increase in your salary into consideration, assuming (assuming + 주어 + 동사: ~라는 전제 하에) the sales figures for your store are increased.
I appreciate your understanding in this matter and hope you will continue to contribute to our company's success.

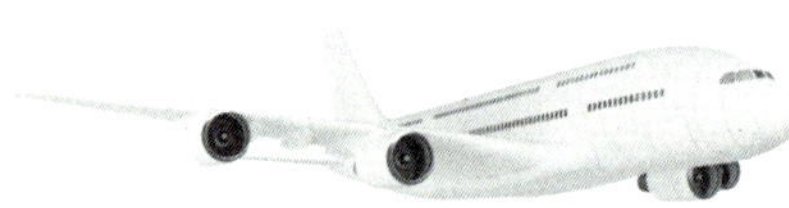

Business
Management
Writing
Basis and Application

Lesson 12

Please accept my apologies for the mistake.

Lesson 12 Please accept my apologies for the mistake.

Introduction

Lesson objectives

1. Writing a letter to express apology

2. Learning key expressions for writing a letter of apology.
   (1) We sincerely apologize for any inconvenience that this may have caused.
   (2) We hope that this has not caused any difficulties or confusion.
   (3) We will make every effort to ensure that such a mistake will not happen again.
   (4) Please remember that we are happy to replace your clothes or refund your money.

Warm up

① Minjean Kim
Guui 3-dong
Gwangjin-gu, Seoul 143-706

② June 30, 2013

③ Bae Jung-Hoon
539-3 Noeun-dong,
Yuseong-gu Daejeon 305-325

④ Dear Mr. Bae:

⑤
We have found that we unintentionally applied your payment of 845,847 won to another account holder's account. We have remedied the error by transferring it to your account, and it will appear on your November statement.

We apologize sincerely for any inconvenience this may have caused. We take these kinds of errors very seriously and will make every effort to ensure such a mistake will not happen again. We hope this has not caused you any difficulties or confusion.

If you have any questions or if we can be of further service, please call a customer service representative at the telephone number listed on your monthly billing statement. You may also contact me by email at the address below.

⑥ Cordially,

⑦ *Mi Jean Kim*

⑧ Mi Jean Kim
mjke@*****.com

⑨ Senior Manager

① 발신인 주소

사과편지를 쓰는 사람의 주소를 기재합니다. 편지를 쓰는 사람의 이름, 번지수 동, 구, 시, 그리고 우편번호를 기재합니다. 동의 명칭과 구의 명칭 사이에 쉼표(,)가 들어갑니다.

② 날짜

사과편지를 쓰는 날짜를 기재합니다. 날짜를 기재할 때는 기수로 기재 할 수 도 있고 서수로 기재 할 수 도 있습니다. 하지만 읽을 때는 거의 언제나 서수로 읽습니다.

③ 수신인 주소

수신인 주소에는 사과편지를 받는 사람의 이름과 주소를 기재합니다. 국내주소인 경우는 번지수 동, 구, 도, 시, 그리고 우편번호를 기재합니다. 국제우편인 경우는 우편번호 뒤에 국가명을 기재합니다.

④ 인사

사과편지의 인사는 격식체 또는 비격식체를 사용합니다. 격식체와 비격식체의 인사는 다음과 같습니다.

수신인	격식체	비격식체
남성	Dear Mr. + 수신인의 성:	Dear Mr. + 수신인의 성,
기혼여성	Dear Mrs. + 수신인의 성:	Dear Mrs. + 수신인의 성,
미혼여성	Dear Miss + 수신인의 성:	Dear Miss + 수신인의 성,
기혼 또는 미혼여성	Dear Ms. + 수신인의 성:	Dear Ms. + 수신인의 성,

⑤ 본문

본문은 사과편지에서 가장 중요한 부분입니다. 사과편지의 본문에는 무엇에 대해서 사과하는지를 명시합니다. 사과편지는 정중하게 쓰는 것이 바람직합니다.

⑥ 끝인사

사과편지의 끝인사는 격식체 또는 비격시체를 사용합니다.

구분	형식
격식체	Sincerely, Sincerely yours, Cordially, Cordially yours,
비격식체	Regards, Best regards, Best wishes, With best wishes,

⑦ 서명

사과편지를 쓰는 사람의 서명을 기재합니다.

⑧ 이름

사과편지를 쓰는 사람의 이름을 기재합니다. 필요에 따라서 이름 밑에 전자우편주소를 기재할 수 있습니다.

⑨ 직책

필요에 따라서 사과편지를 쓰는 사람의 직책을 기재할 수 있습니다.

Warm up

Check up

사과편지의 구조와 내용에 대한 다음 문제를 풀어보겠습니다.

1. 사과편지의 본문에 들어가는 내용을 순서에 맞게 배열하세요.

보기	A. We are sorry that the stereo you purchased from our store has a defect. B. Dear Ms. Anderson, C. We assure you that your stereo will be replaced or refunded as soon as possible. D. Again, we are sorry for the inconvenience this may have caused you. E. Please call my office and let us know which option you prefer. F. Cordially yours

1. ______ → 2.______ → 3.______ → 4.______ → 5.______ → 6.______

2. 다음은 사과편지의 본문을 읽고 무엇에 대한 사과편지인지 기술하세요.

I am sorry for not keeping the appointment with you. I had intended to arrive for our appointment ahead of time, but my daughter suddenly became ill. I immediately called my husband and asked him to take her to the doctor, but he was not able to do so. So I had no choice but to take her to the doctor myself. I am really sorry for what has happened. I would really like to make another appointment with you. Let me know a convenient time for you. Again, I am sorry for the inconvenience.

3. 다음 두 문장의 의미를 한국어로 쓰시오.

① I intended to keep the appointment with you.

② I had intended to keep the appointment with you.

Practice 1 Comprehension Check up

Mijean Kim
224 Guui 3-dong, Gwangjin-gu
Seoul 143-706

October 31, 2013

Jeong-Hoon Bae
33 Nonhyun-dong, Gangnam-gu
Seoul 135-010

Dear Mr. Bae:

We have found that we unintentionally deposited your monthly remuneration of 2,000,000 won into another employee's account. We have remedied the error by transferring the money to your account. Confirm this by updating your account book.

We sincerely apologize for any inconvenience that this may have caused. We take these kinds of errors very seriously and will make every effort to ensure such a mistake will not happen again. We hope that this has not caused you any difficulty or confusion.

If you have any questions, please call us at 447-8857. You may also contact me at the email address below.

Cordially,
Mijean Kim
Mijean Kim
kmj@*****.com
Accountant General

1. What is the letter about?

① Apologizing for the unintentional mistake in depositing the payment
② Informing the employee of an increase in payment
③ Informing the employee how much he will get paid a month
④ Asking the client to open a new account in the bank

2. How much does Mr. Jeong-Hoon Bae get paid a month?

① 200,000 won
② 400,000 won
③ 2,000,000 won
④ 4,000,000 won

3. What can Jeong-Hoon Bae do if he has further questions? (Choose two)

① He can ask questions of his colleagues.
② He can ask questions of his boss.
③ He can call 447-8857.
④ He can write an email to Mijean Kim.

4. What is the job title of the person who wrote this letter?

① District Manager
② Manager of Accounting Department
③ General Manager of Accounting Department
④ Accountant General

5. What is the relation between Mijean Kim and Jeong-Hoon Bae likely to be?

① Employees in the same company
② Business partners
③ Businessman and client
④ Old friends

서울 광진구
구의 3동 224번지 143-706
김미진

2013년 10월 31일

서울 강남구
논현동 33번지 135-010
배정훈

배정훈 님께

우리는 당신의 월 급여 200만 원을 본의 아니게 다른 사람의 계좌에 입금한 것을 알게 되었습니다. 그 돈을 당신의 계좌로 이체함으로써 실수를 해결했습니다. (당신은 그것을) 당신의 은행 통장을 정리해보면 이를 확인할 수 있습니다.

우리는 이 일이 야기하였을 불편에 대해서 진정으로 사과 드립니다. 우리는 이러한 종류의 실수를 매우 심각하게 받아들이며 이러한 실수가 다시 발생하지 않도록 하기 위해 모든 노력을 다할 것입니다. 우리는 이 일이 당신에게 어떤 어려움이나 혼란도 야기하지 않았기를 바랍니다. 혹시 문의사항이 있으면 447-8857로 우리에게 전화주세요. 당신은 또한 밑에 나와있는 전자우편 주소로 저에게 연락할 수 있습니다.

안녕히 계십시오.

김미진
kmj@*****.co.kr
회계부 과장

1. 이 편지는 무엇에 관한 내용입니까?
① 급여를 입금하는 데 있어서 본의 아니게 생긴 실수에 대해 사과하는 내용
② 고용인에게 급여의 인상을 통보하는 내용
③ 고용인에게 받게 될 월 급여에 대해 통보하는 내용
④ 고객에게 은행구좌를 개설하라고 부탁하는 내용

2. 배종훈 씨는 월 급여가 얼마입니까?
① 20만 원
② 40만 원
③ 200만 원
④ 400만 원

3. 배종훈 씨는 문의 할 내용이 더 있으면 어떻게 해야 하나요? (둘을 고르시오)
① 자신의 동료에게 문의한다
② 자신의 상사에게 문의한다
③ 447-8857로 전화한다
④ 김미진님에게 이메일을 쓴다

4. 이 편지를 쓴 사람의 직책은 무엇입니까?
① 지사장
② 회계부 대리
③ 회계부 차장
④ 회계 과장

5. 김미진 씨와 배종훈 씨는 어떤 관계일까요?
① 같은 회사의 직원
② 사업 파트너
③ 비즈니스맨과 고객
④ 오랜 친구

Practice 1 Lecture

01

We have found that we unintentionally deposited your monthly remuneration of 2,000,000 won into another employee's account.
(당신의 월 급여 200만 원을 본의 아니게 다른 직원의 계좌에 입금한 것을 알게 되었습니다.)

어 휘

① find : ~을 알게 되다

예문1) She found that she was mistaken.
(그녀는 자신이 틀렸음을 알게 되었다.)

② unintentionally : 본의 아니게

③ deposit : 입금하다

예문1) She has deposited a lot of money in her account.
(그녀는 자신의 계좌에 많은 돈을 입금했다.)

④ remuneration : 급여

예문1) He received a large remuneration.
(그는 많은 급여를 받는다.)

02

We have remedied the error by transferring the money to your account.
(그 돈을 당신의 계좌로 이체함으로써 실수를 해결했습니다.)

어 휘

① remedy : 교정하다, 시정하다

예문1) He instantly remedied his mistake.
(그는 즉각적으로 자신의 실수를 정정했다.)

② error : 실수

③ transfer : 이체하다

예문1) He transferred 2,000,000 won to her account.
(그는 그녀의 계좌로 2백만 원을 이체했다.)

④ account : 계좌

예문1) When will you open a bank account?
(당신은 언제 은행에서 구좌를 개설할건가요?)

03 You can confirm this by updating your account book.

(당신은 그것을) 당신의 은행통장을 정리해보면 이를 확인할 수 있습니다.

어 휘

① confirm : 사실로 확인하다

예문1) I sent a fax to confirm my order.
(나는 주문 내용을 확인하기 위해서 팩스를 보냈다.)

관용표현

① update one's account book: 자신의 통장을 정리하다

예문1) I need to visit the bank to update my account book.
(나는 통장을 정리하기 위해서 은행에 가야 한다.)

04 We sincerely apologize for any inconvenience that this may have caused.

(우리는 이 일이 야기하였을 불편에 대해서 진정으로 사과 드립니다.)

어 휘

① sincerely : 진정으로

② apologize for : ~에 대해 사과하다

예문1) He apologized to her for stepping on her foot.
(그는 그녀의 발을 밟은 것에 대해 그녀에게 사과했다.)

③ inconvenience : 불편

예문1) It causes a lot of inconvenience when buses don't come.
(버스가 오지 않으면 정말 불편하다.)

05 **We take these kinds of errors very seriously and will make every effort to ensure that such a mistake will not happen again.**
(우리는 이러한 종류의 실수를 매우 심각하게 받아들이며 이러한 실수가 다시 발생하지 않도록 하기 위해 모든 노력을 할 것입니다.)

어 휘

① ensure : ~이 반드시 이루어지도록 하다

예문1) If you want to ensure that you catch the train, take a taxi to the station.
(만약 그 기차를 반드시 타려면 역까지 택시를 타시오.)

구 문

① take + 목적어 + 형용사 : ~을 ~하게 받아들이다

예문1) He always takes things seriously.
(그는 항상 모든 일을 심각하게 받아들인다.)

② make every effort to + 동사 : ~하기 위해 모든 노력을 하다

예문1) She made every effort to pass the exam.
(그녀는 시험에 합격하기 위해 모든 노력을 했다.)

06 **We hope this has not caused you any difficulty or confusion.**
(우리는 이 일이 당신에게 어떤 어려움이나 혼란도 야기하지 않았기를 바랍니다.)

어 휘

① hope : 바라다, 희망하다

예문1) I hope that he will win the election.
(나는 그가 선거에서 당선되길 바란다.)

② cause : 야기시키다

예문1) This car causes me a lot of trouble.
(이 자동차는 나에게 많은 문제를 야기시킨다.)

③ difficulties : 어려움

④ confusion : 혼란

07 If you have any questions, please call us at 447-8857.

(혹시 문의사항이 있으면 447-8857로 우리에게 전화주세요.)

구 문 ① If + 주어 + 동사, 주어 + 동사: ~하면 ~하다

예문1) If we take a taxi, we can catch our flight.
(우리가 택시를 타면 우리는 비행기를 탈 수 있다.)

② call + 목적어 + at + 연락처: ~로 전화하다

예문1) Please feel free to call me at 010-3290-****.
(010-3290-****으로 저에게 자유롭게 전화하세요.)

08 You may also contact me at the email address below.

(당신은 또한 밑에 나와있는 전자우편 주소로 저에게 연락할 수 있습니다.)

어 휘 ① email address: 전자우편 주소

예문1) Let me know your email address.
(당신의 전자우편 주소를 저에게 알려주세요.)

구 문 ① contact + 목적어 + at + 연락처

예문1) I contacted her at miok@*****.net.
(나는 그녀에게 miok@*****.net으로 연락했다.)

Practice 1 Task 1

주어진 단어를 이용하여 문장을 완성하세요. 필요한 경우는 동사의 형태를 변형시키세요.

보기	remedy	deposit	find	transfer	update	confirm

(1) We have (   ) that we unintentionally (   ) your monthly remuneration of 2,000,000 won into another person's account.

(2) We have (   ) the error by (   ) the money to your account.

(3) You can (   ) this by (   ) your account book.

Practice 1 Task 2

빈 칸에 들어갈 적절한 단어를 입력하여 문장을 완성하세요.

(1) 우리는 이 일이 야기하였을 불편에 대해서 진정으로 사과 드립니다.
We sincerely (   )(   ) any inconvenience that this may have caused.

(2) 우리는 이러한 종류의 실수를 매우 심각하게 받아들입니다.
We (   ) these kinds of errors (   )(   ).

(3) 우리는 이러한 실수가 다시 발생하지 않도록 하기 위해 모든 노력을 할 것입니다.
We will (   )(   )(   ) to ensure that such a mistake will not happen again.

Practice 1 Task 3

제시되어 있는 단어를 배열하여 올바른 문장을 만들어 보세요. (문장의 첫 철자는 대문자로 쓰세요.)

(1) 우리는 이 일이 당신에게 어떤 어려움이나 혼란도 야기 하지 않았기를 바랍니다.

this caused has not you any difficulties or confusion that

We hope ( )

(2) 혹시 문의사항이 있으면 447-8857로 우리에게 전화주세요.

call please at us 447-8875

If you have any questions, ( )

(3) 당신은 또한 밑에 나와있는 전자우편주소로 저에게 연락할 수 있습니다.

contact at may the also email me address below you

( )

Coffee break

Personality Test

If you're looking to learn a little more about yourself in a fun and entertaining way, then get out a piece of paper and a pen. Are you ready? Take a deep breath, and draw a pig. (Don't read any further until you have drawn the pig.)
After you draw the pig, examine your artwork. If you drew the pig at the top of the page, you are an optimistic person. If your pig is in the middle of the page, you are realistic. Is your pig at the bottom of the page? If so, you are probably have a negative attitude.
Which direction is your pig facing? If it's facing right, you are innovative, but you might not be close to your family. If your pig is facing left, you are traditional and friendly, and you are good at remembering dates. If your pig is looking straight at you, you are direct and not afraid of intense discussions. If you drew a pig with many details, you are analytical and unlikely to trust people. If you drew only a few details, you are emotional.
How many legs can you see? If four legs are visible, you are secure and possibly even stubborn. If fewer than four legs are showing, you may be insecure. If your pig has big ears, this means you are a good listener. If your pig has small ears or even no ears at all, you should try to improve your listening skills. Did you surprise yourself? Then why not have some more fun and do this test on a friend! You might find out something very interesting.

성격 테스트

만약 자신에 대해서 재미있고 유쾌한 방법으로 조금 더 알고 싶다면 종이 한 장과 펜을 꺼내세요. 준비 되었나요? 숨을 깊게 쉬고 돼지를 그리세요.
(돼지를 다 그리기 전까지는 더 이상 읽지 마세요.)
돼지를 그린 후에 당신 그림을 살펴보세요. 돼지를 종이 위쪽에 그렸다면 당신은 긍정적인 사람입니다. 만약 돼지를 종이 중간에 그렸다면 현실적인 사람입니다. 당신의 돼지는 종이 아래쪽에 있나요? 그렇다면 당신은 아마도 부정적인 태도가 있을 것입니다.
돼지가 어느 쪽을 향하나요? 만약 오른쪽을 향한다면 당신은 혁신적이지만 가족과는 가깝지 않을 것입니다. 돼지가 왼쪽을 향한다면 당신은 전통적이고 친근하고 날짜를 잘 기억할 것입니다. 돼지가 당신을 곧바로 쳐다본다면 당신은 직접적이고 심도 있는 토론을 두려워하지 않습니다.. 상세하게 돼지를 그렸다면 당신은 분석적이고 사람들을 잘 믿지 못합니다. 만약 세부적으로 그리지 않았다면 당신은 감성적입니다.
몇 개의 다리가 보이나요? 다리 네 개가 보인다면 당신은 안정적이고 아마도 고집이 있을 것입니다. 다리가 네 개보다 적게 보인다면 당신은 불안정할 것이다. 돼지의 귀가 크다면 당신은 좋은 청취자라는 뜻입니다. 만약 돼지의 귀가 작거나 없다면 당신은 듣는 능력을 향상 시켜야 할 것입니다. 자기 자신에게 놀랐나요? 그렇다면 더 재미있게 친구에게 테스트 해보세요. 아주 흥미로운 사실을 찾아낼 거예요.

Practice 2 Comprehension Check up

다음 사과편지를 읽고 질문에 답을 선택한 후 [확인] 버튼을 클릭하세요.

Ji Hye Yang
61-3, Choongmu-Ro 2-ka
Chung-Ku, Seoul 100-012

July 31, 2013

Margaret Cho
Hanmaeum Apt. 3-505
Songkang-dong, Yuseong-gu
Daejeon 305-503

Dear Ms. Cho:

We at Bang Bang Corporation confirm that the clothes you returned have indeed shrunk in the dryer. The clothes were not washable even though many clothes today are. Our sales clerk should have explained the proper laundering instructions to you. Sometimes, however, an employee may be inadvertently forgetful.

Whether this was the case or not, we are sorry for the inconvenience. We value you as a customer and hope that you will continue shopping at our store. Your satisfaction with our apparel is of great importance to us.

Please remember that we are happy to replace your clothes or refund your money. Let us know which option you prefer.

Sincerely,
Ji Hye Yang
Ji Hye Yang
Store Manager

1. What is the letter about?

① Apologizing for not giving exact change.

② Apologizing for not giving laundering instructions about the clothes.

③ Informing the client that the store will offer a discount.

④ Informing the client that the store is open on weekdays.

2. What kind of clothes did Ms. Margaret Cho buy from the Bang Bang branch store?

① Washable clothes

② Unwashable clothes

③ Nonrefundable clothes

④ Clothes on sale

3. What remedies did Ji Hye Yang suggest to Ms. Magaret Cho? (Choose two)

① Replacing the clothes

② Refunding the money

③ Giving a discount for the clothes

④ Offering other clothes free of charge

4. What compensation did Ms. Margaret Cho choose for her clothes?

① Replacing the clothes

② Getting a refund

③ Getting other clothes free of charge

④ Not determined yet

5. What is the job title of Ji Hye Yang?

① Store Manager

② District Manager

③ Assistant Manager

④ General Manager

서울시 중구
충무로 2가 61-3 번지 100-012
양지혜

2013년 7월 31일

대전시 유성구
송강동 한마음 아파트 3동 505호 305-503
조마가렛

조마가렛님께

우리 뱅뱅 회사에서는 당신이 반납한 옷이 탈수기에서 실제로 줄어들었다는 것을 사실로 확인합니다. 비록 요즘 많은 옷들이 세탁 가능하지만 그 옷은 세탁 가능하지 않습니다. 우리의 판매원이 당신에게 적절한 세탁 지침을 설명해야 했었습니다. 하지만 가끔 고용인이 무심코 잊을 수 있습니다.

사정이 이랬든 아니든 불편을 끼쳐드려 미안합니다. 우리는 당신을 고객으로서 소중하게 생각하며 당신이 계속해서 우리 가게에서 쇼핑하길 바랍니다. 우리 옷에 대한 당신의 만족은 우리에게 중요합니다.

우리는 기꺼이 당신의 옷을 교환해주거나 당신의 돈을 환불해주려고 한다는 점을 기억하기 바랍니다. 당신이 어느 선택 사항을 선호하는지 우리에게 알려주세요.

안녕히 계십시오.

양지혜
지점 관리자

1. 편지는 무엇에 관한 내용입니까?
   ① 거스름 돈을 정확하게 주지 않은 것에 대한 사과
   ② 옷에 대해서 세탁 지침을 주지 않은 것에 대한 사과
   ③ 고객에게 가게에서 할인판매를 하는지를 통보
   ④ 고객에게 주중에 가게가 언제 문을 여는지 통보

2. 조마가렛 씨는 뱅뱅 지점에서 어떤 종류의 옷을 샀나요?
① 세탁 가능한 옷
② 세탁 불가능한 옷
③ 환불 불가능한 옷
④ 세일 중인 옷

3. 양지혜 님은 조마가렛 씨에게 어떠한 구제책을 제시했나요? (답안 2개 선택)
① 옷을 교환해주기
② 돈을 환불해주기
③ 옷에 대해서 할인을 제공하기
④ 무상으로 옷을 한 벌 제공하기

4. 조마가렛 씨는 자신의 옷에 대해 어떠한 보상책을 선택했나요?
① 옷을 교환하기
② 돈을 환불 받기
③ 무상으로 다른 옷을 한 벌 얻기
④ 아직 결정 되지 않음

5. 양지혜의 직책은 무엇입니까?
① 가게 지배인
② 지사장
③ 대리
④ 부장

Practice 2 Lecture

01

We, at Bang Bang Corporation, confirm that the clothes you returned have indeed shrunk in the dryer.

(우리 뱅뱅 회사에서는 당신이 반납한 옷이 탈수기에서 실제로 줄어들었다는 것을 사실로 확인합니다.)

어 휘

① corporation : 회사, 주식회사

예문1) She works for a chemical corporation.
(그녀는 화학회사에서 근무한다.)

② confirm : 사실임을 확인하다

예문1) His statement confirmed what we already believed.
(그의 진술은 우리가 이미 믿고 있었던 것이 사실이라는 것을 확인해주었다.)

③ return : 반환하다

예문1) Don't forget to return my keys to me.
(나의 열쇠를 나에게 꼭 돌려주세요.)

④ shrink : 오그라들다

예문1) Clothes made of wool easily shrink in water.
(울로 만든 옷은 물세탁하면 쉽게 줄어든다.)

⑤ dryer : 탈수기

02

The clothes were not washable even though many clothes today are.

(비록 요즘 많은 옷들이 세탁 가능하지만 그 옷은 세탁 가능하지 않습니다.)

어 휘

① clothes : 옷

예문1) He spends a lot of money on clothes.
(그는 옷에 많은 돈을 쓴다.)

② washable : 세탁 가능한

예문1) Dress suits are usually not washable.
(정장은 대개 세탁 가능하지 않다.)

구 문 ① even though + 주어 +동사 : 비록 ~일지라도 ~하다

예문1) Even though it's difficult work, I enjoy it.
(비록 그 일이 어려운 일이지만 나는 그 일을 즐긴다.)

03 Our sales clerk should have explained the proper laundering instructions to you.

(우리의 판매원이 당신에게 적절한 세탁 지침을 설명해야 했었습니다.)

어 휘 ① sales clerk : 판매원

② explain : 설명하다

예문1) I don't understand this. Please explain it to me.
(나는 이 일을 이해하지 못하겠어요. 저에게 설명해주세요.)

③ proper : 적절한

④ laundering instructions : 세탁 지침

예문1) We should check laundering instructions before washing clothes.
(세탁을 하기 전 세탁 지침을 확인해야 한다.)

구 문 ① should have + 완료형 과거분사 : ~해야 했었는데 하지 못했다

예문1) She should have finished the work by the deadline.
(그녀는 그 일을 마감시간까지 끝내야만 했었는데.)

04 Sometimes, however, an employee may be inadvertently forgetful.

(하지만 가끔 종업원이 무심코 잊을 수 있습니다.)

어 휘 ① employee : 고용인, 종업원

예문1) There are five employees in that overseas branch.
(그 해외 지점에는 5명의 고용인이 있다.)

② inadvertently : 고의 아니게, 우연히, 무심코

예문1) She inadvertently knocked over her cup of coffee.
(그녀는 무심코 자신의 커피잔을 엎질렀다.)

③ be forgetful : 잊다

예문1) One should not be forgetful of one's duties.
(사람은 자신의 의무를 잊어서는 안된다.)

05 Whether this was the case or not, we are sorry for the inconvenience.

(사정이 이랬든 아니든 불편을 끼쳐드려 미안합니다.)

어 휘

① inconvenience : 불편, 불편한 일

예문1) Waiting for a bus is a great inconvenience to me.
(버스를 기다리는 일은 나에게 매우 불편한 일이다.)

관용표현

① this is the case : 사정이 이러하다, 사실이다

예문1) If this is the case, I will not do the work.
(사정이 이러하다면 나는 그 일을 하지 않겠다.)

구 문

① whether + 주어 + 동사 + or not : ~이든 아니든

예문1) Whether you like it or not, I will do it.
(당신이 그 일을 좋아하든 좋아하지 않든 나는 그 일을 하겠다.)

06 We value you as a customer and hope that you will continue shopping at our store.

(우리는 당신을 고객으로서 소중하게 생각하며 당신이 계속해서 우리 가게에서 쇼핑하길 바랍니다.)

어 휘

① value : 소중하게 생각하다

예문1) I have always valued our friendship very highly.
(나는 항상 우리의 우정을 매우 소중하게 생각해왔다.)

② customer : 고객

예문1) The store has many female customers.
(그 가게는 많은 여성 고객이 있다.)

③ continue : 계속 ~하다

예문1) Will you continue working after dinner?
(당신은 저녁식사 후에도 계속 일을 할건가요?)

④ shopping : 쇼핑

예문1) She went out to do some shopping.
(그녀는 쇼핑을 하러 나갔다.)

07 **Your satisfaction with our apparel is of great importance to us.**
(우리 옷에 대한 당신의 만족은 우리에게 중요합니다.)

어 휘

① satisfaction : 만족

예문1) I get a feeling of satisfaction from doing good things.
(나는 좋은 일을 함으로써 만족감을 얻는다.)

② apparel : 옷, 의류

예문1) Ladies' ready-to-wear apparel is not very expensive.
(여성들의 기성복은 매우 비싸지 않다.)

구 문

① be of importance : 중요하다

예문1) Whether we should go or not is of great importance.
(우리가 가야 되는 지 여부는 매우 중요하다.)

08 **Please remember that we are happy to replace your clothes or refund your money.**
(우리는 기꺼이 당신의 옷을 교환해주거나 당신의 돈을 환불해주려고 한다는 점을 기억하기 바랍니다.)

어 휘

① remember : 기억하다

예문1) I can't remember where he lives.
(나는 그가 어디 사는지 기억나지 않는다.)

② replace : 교체하다, 교체하다

예문1) We have replaced an old computer with a new one.
(우리는 오래된 컴퓨터를 새 컴퓨터로 교체했다.)

③ refund : 환불하다

예문1) They refunded my money.
(그들은 나의 돈을 환불해주었다.)

구 문 ① be happy + to-부정사 : 기꺼이 ~해주다, 기쁘게 ~하다

예문1) I am happy to do the work for you.
(내가 기꺼이 너를 위해 그 일을 해줄게.)

09 Let us know which option you prefer.

(당신이 어느 선택 사항을 선호하는지 우리에게 알려주세요.)

어 휘 ① option : 선택사항

예문1) The government has two options: either to reduce spending or increase taxes.
(정부는 지출을 줄이거나 세금을 늘리는 두 가지 선택사항이 있다.)

② prefer : 선호하다

예문1) Do you prefer that I come on Tuesday instead of Wednesday?
(당신은 내가 수요일 대신 화요일에 오는 것을 더 원하나요?)

구 문 ① let + 목적어 + know : ~에게 알려주세요

예문1) Let me know when you will come back.
(당신이 언제 돌아올지 저에게 알려주세요.)

Practice 2 Task 4

보기에 있는 단어를 이용하여 문장을 완성히세요. 필요한 경우는 단어의 형태를 변형시키세요.

보기	shrink confirm wash explain have forget

(1) We at Bang Bang Corporation (   ) that the clothes you returned have indeed (   ) in the dryer.

(2) The clothes were not (   ) even though many clothes today are.

(3) Our sales clerk should (   ) (   ) the proper laundering instructions to you.

(4) Sometimes, however, an employee may be inadvertently (   ).

Practice 2 Task 5

빈 칸에 들어갈 적절한 단어를 입력하여 문장을 완성하세요.

(1) 사정이 이랬든 아니든 불편을 끼쳐드려 미안합니다.
Whether this was the (   ) (   ) (   ), we are sorry for the inconvenience.

(2) 우리는 당신을 고객으로서 소중하게 생각하며 당신이 계속해서 우리가게에서 쇼핑하길 바랍니다.
We (   ) you as a customer and (   ) that you will continue shopping at our store.

(3) 우리 옷에 대한 당신의 만족은 우리에게 매우 중요합니다.

Your satisfaction with our apparel (   ) (   ) (   ) (   ) to us.

Practice 2 Task 6

제시되어 있는 단어를 배열하여 올바른 문장을 만들어 보세요. 문장의 첫 철자는 대문자로 쓰세요.

(1) 우리는 기꺼이 당신의 옷을 교환해주거나 당신의 돈을 환불해주려고 한다는 점을 기억하기 바랍니다.

please   remember   happy   replace   clothes   refund

(   )

(2) 당신이 어느 선택 사항을 선호하는지 우리에게 알려주세요

know   option   prefer   let

(   )

Exercise Writing

왼쪽의 글을 읽은 후 그를 바탕으로 사과편지의 본문을 영작해 보세요.

우리는 당신의 반환한 옷이 탈수기에서 줄어들었다는 것을 사실로 확인합니다. 그 옷은 세탁 가능하지 않습니다. 우리 판매원이 당신에게 적절한 세탁지침을 설명해야만 했습니다. 우리는 기꺼이 당신의 돈을 환불해주겠습니다. 우리는 불편을 끼쳐드려 미안합니다.	

Exercise You be the editor

다음 사과편지의 내용을 읽고 밑줄친 부분을 올바르게 고치세요.

I have found that I deposited your monthly payment of 3,000,000 won <u>at</u> another person's account. I have remedied the error by <u>transferred</u> the money to your account. You can check it on your bankbook.

I sincerely <u>apology</u> for any inconvenience this may have caused. I take these kinds of errors seriously and will make every effort to ensure such a mistake will not happen again. I hope this has not caused you any difficulties.
If you have any questions, please call me <u>into</u> 010-3800-****. Again, I am sorry for the inconvenience.

Wrap up

Summary

1. The format of a letter of an apology

① Return Address
② Date
③ Inside Address
④ Greeting
⑤ Body
⑥ Closing
⑦ Signature
⑧ Name
⑨ Job Title

2. Key expressions for writing a letters of apology.

(1) We apologize for any inconvenience that this may have caused.
(2) We hope that this has not caused you any difficulty or confusion.
(3) We will make every effort to ensure that such a mistake will not happen again.
(4) Please remember that we are happy to replace your clothes or refund your money.
(5) Let us know which option you prefer.

Wrap up

Assignment I

오늘 학습한 주요 문형을 활용하여 영어문장을 작성하여 봅시다.

take + 목적어 + 형용사	~을 ~하게 받아들이다
make every effort to + 동사	~하기 위해 모든 노력을 하다
If + 주어 + 동사, 주어 + 동사	~하면 ~하다
call + 목적어 + at + 연락처	~로 전화하다
contact + 목적어 + at + 연락처	~에게 ~로 연락하다
should have + 완료형과거분사	~했어야 했는데 하지 못했다
whether or not + 주어 + 동사	~이든 아니든
be of importance	중요하다

Answers

Lesson 12. I Please accept my apologies for the mistake.

Warm up

Check up

1)

B. Dear Ms. Anderson,

A. We are sorry that the stereo you purchased from our store has a defect.

C. We assure you that your stereo will be replaced or refunded as soon as possible.

E. Please call my office and let us know which option you prefer.

D. Again, we are sorry for the inconvenience this may have caused.

F. Cordially yours,

2) 약속을 지키지 못한 것에 대한 사과

3) - 나는 너와의 약속을 지키려고 했다.
(약속을 지킬 수도 있고 지키지 못할 수도 있음)
- 나는 너와의 약속을 지키려고 했었다. (약속을 지키지 못함)

Practice 1 Comprehension Check up

1) ① Apologizing for the unintentional mistake in depositing the payment
2) ③ 2,000,000 won
3) ③ He can call 447-8857, ④ He can write an email to Mijean Kim.
4) ④ Accountant General
5) ① Employees in the same company

Practice 1 Task 1

1) We have found that we unintentionally deposited your monthly remuneration of 2,000,000 won into another person's account.
2) We have remedied the error by transferring the money to your account.
3) You can confirm this by updating your account book.

Practice 1 Task 2

1) We sincerely apologize for any inconvenience that this may have caused.
2) We take these kinds of errors very seriously.
3) We will make every effort to ensure such a mistake will not happen again.

Practice 1 Task 3

1) We hope that this has not caused you any difficulties or confusion.
2) If you have any questions, please call us at 447-8857.
3) You may also contact me at the email address below.

Practice 2 Comprehension Check up

1) ② Apologizing for not giving laundering instructions about the clothes
2) ② Unwashable clothes
3) ① Replacing the clothes ② Refunding the money
4) ④ Not determined yet
5) ① Store manager

Practice 2 Task 4

1) We at Bang Bang Corporation confirm that the clothes you returned have indeed shrunk in the dryer.
2) The clothes were not washable even though many clothes today are.
3) Our sales clerk should have explained the proper laundering instructions to you.
4) Sometimes, however, an employee may be inadvertently forgetful.

Practice 2 Task 5

1) Whether this was the case or not, we are sorry for the inconvenience.
2) We value you as a customer and hope that you will continue shopping at our store.
3) Your satisfaction with our apparel is of great importance to us.

Practice 2 Task 6

1) Please remember that we are happy to replace your clothes or refund your money.
2) Let us know which option you prefer.

Exercise Writing

We admit that your clothes shrank in the dryer.
The clothes were not washable.
Our sales clerk should have explained the proper laundering instructions to you.
We are happy to refund your money.
We are sorry for the inconvenience.

Exercise You be the editor

I have found that I deposited your monthly payment of 3,000,000 won into (deposit money into account: 돈을 계좌에 입금하다) another person's account. I have remedied the error by transferring (by + 동명사: ~함으로써) the money to your account. You can check it on your bankbook.

I sincerely apologize (apologize for: ~에 대해서 사과하다) for any inconvenience this may have caused. I take these kinds of errors seriously and will make every effort to ensure such a mistake will not happen again. I hope this has not caused you any difficulties.

If you have any questions, please call me at (call + 목적어 + at + 연락처: ~에게 ~로 연락하다) 010-3800-****. Again, I am sorry for the inconvenience.

Business
Management
Writing
Basis and Application

Lesson 13

Review

Lesson 13

Review

Lesson 01

Writing an email

1. email의 Greeting(인사)과 잘 어울리는 Closing(끝인사)을 보기에서 찾아 입력해 보세요.

보기	Sincerely yours, Warmly, Best regards,

(1) Dear Mr. Jackson: ______________________________

(2) Dear Lina, ______________________________

(3) Hi Freddy, ______________________________

2. email에서 @는 무엇을 나타내는지 선택 보기에서 찾아 적어 보세요.

보기	from with at for

____

Lesson 02 Writing a diary

1. 아래 제시된 항목을 순서대로 나열하세요.

2013 Cloudy March 15 Sunday

( )

2. 아래 제시된 날씨에 대한 표현을 보기에서 찾아 써 넣어 보세요.

보기	chilly windy snowy rainy fair cloudy

(1) 맑은 날씨 ____________

(2) 흐린 날씨 ____________

(3) 비 오는 날씨 ____________

(4) 눈 오는 날씨 ____________

(5) 추운 날씨 ____________

(6) 바람 부는 날씨 ____________

Lesson 03 Writing a resume

1. 이력서의 경력을 작성하는 부분입니다. 각 위치에 알맞은 항목을 넣으세요.

| 보기 |

Period Location Job description Department Job Title Company

| Work experience |

2. 이력서의 학력을 작성하는 부분입니다. 각 위치에 알맞은 항목을 넣으세요.

| 보기 |

School Minor Major Period Location

| Education |

3. 다음은 이력서의 특기사항입니다. 빈칸에 적절한 전치사를 입력하세요.

| Special Skills |

Foreign Language	Fluent (①) English
	Score 990 (②) the TOEIC
Computer	Proficient (③) MS Word

Lesson 04 Writing a letter of self-introduction

1. 다음 영문 자기소개서의 내용을 잘 읽고 각 내용에 해당하는 소제목을 넣으세요.

보기	Personal History School Days Strengths and Weaknesses Career Objectives

(1)

[   ]

My family includes my parents, my younger brother, my younger sister, and me. I am the eldest son in my family. I was home-educated to be a responsible person.

(2)

[   ]

In high school biology and chemistry were my favorite subjects. I was more interested in biology than in chemistry. Because of the interest in biology I majored in biology at university. After graduating from university I entered graduate school and majored in microbiology.

(3)

[   ]

I try to have a good character. I always try to help people around me. On the other hand, I depend on others for making decisions. Also I am trying to be an independent person.

(4)

I will improve my English and Japanese until I become a fluent speaker of English and Japanese. I will work hard to develop more competitive products for the company.

Lesson 05 Writing a job application letter

1. 영문 지원서의 포맷을 보고 빈 칸에 들어갈 항목이 무엇인지 보기에서 골라 보세요.

보기	Inside address	Return address	Closing	Greeting	Enclosure

(1) ____________________

June 22, 2013

(2) ____________________

(3) ____________________

I am interested in the secretary position in your company, and I would like to apply for that position. I am currently employed by New World Agency, but now I am seeking a new position. I believe that my experience and qualifications make me perfect for this job.

I would like to discuss this position with you, so please feel free to contact me at any time.

(4) ____________________

Soyoung Kim

Soyoung Kim

(5) ____________________

Lesson 06 Writing a fax

1. 영문 팩스의 포맷을 보고 빈 칸에 들어갈 항목이 무엇인지 보기에서 골라 보세요.

보기	Delivery of wrong products Purchase order 03-5345-9 This page only

FAX

Date: June 1, 2013

To: Keechol Park
Mirae Eelectronics

From: Minyoung Kim
World Tour

Subject: (1) ____________________

Reference: (2) ____________________

Number of pages: (3) ____________________

Message The wrong products were mailed. We are returning them. Please send new products as soon as possible. I look forward to your prompt action.

Lesson 07 Writing an invitation card

1. 영문초대장의 포맷에 대한 문제를 풀어 보세요.

보기	Directions General Information RSVP

A Beautiful Moment in Time

We are delighted to invite you and your family to the wedding anniversary of the lovely Mr. and Mrs. Kim.

Event

As you may be aware, the Kims are celebrating 40 beautiful years of marriage.

Host

The party will be hosted by the loving children of the honored couple.

Date and Place

The affair will be on the evening of March 23, 2008 at the home of Billy Kim. The night will begin at 5 pm.

(1) ____________

The party is casual and there will be food and drinks. We hope that you can share this special and fun evening with our family.

(2) ____________________

Please RSVP to Billy Kim at Billykim@*****.com

(3) ____________________

Directions will be sent through email after RSVP.

Lesson 08 Writing a letter of recommendation

영문추천서에 본문에 대한 문제를 풀어 보세요.

보기	A. It is with great pleasure that I recommend Sally Forth for the history teacher position at Seoul International High school. B. Her primary responsibilities were teaching social studies and general history C. She taught at Mirae High school from March 4, 2007 to February 25, 2012, during which time I was principal. D. I strongly recommend her and am sure that you will be more than satisfied with her performance in the classroom.

1. 보기에 주어진 영문추천서의 본문을 가장 잘 배열한 것을 고르시오.

① A, B, C, D　　② A, C, B, D

③ A, B, D, C　　④ A, D, C, B

Lesson 09

Writing a thank you letter

Ben Faller
337 Wilson Boulevard
San Francisco, CA 19237

June 23, 2013

Martin Fisher
259 Sixth Avenue
Honolulu, Hawaii 90073

Dear Mr. Fisher:

A. I am looking forward to hearing from you and wish to thank you again for your courtesy.
B. Thank you for the time and consideration you extended to me during my interview with you yesterday.
C. I appreciate having had the opportunity to speak with you about my experience in related fields and my future goals.

Sincerely,
Ben Faller
Ben Faller

1. 위 영문감사편지의 순서를 가장 잘 배열한 것을 고르시오.

① A, B, C
② A, C, B
③ B, A, C
④ B, C, A

Lesson 10 Writing a letter of congratulations

Leslie Rocker
3992 San Antonio Blvd.
Santa Barbra, California 15702

January 4, 2013

Jin Lee
Rose Apt. 3-323
Seongbuk-dong, Seongbuk-gu
Seoul 136-020
South Korea

Dear Mr. Lee,

A. Please accept our best wishes for your success in your college life.
B. Congratulations on your acceptance to the University of California, Los Angeles.
C. We know how hard you have worked to prepare for the exam.

Sincerely,
Leslie Rocker
Leslie Rocker
Admissions Counselor

1. 축하편지의 본문에 들어가는 내용을 순서에 맞게 배열하세요.

① A, B, C　② A, C, B
③ B, A, C　④ B, C, A

Lesson 11 Writing a letter of refusal

Mijin Kim
349-1 Guui-dong, Gwangjin-gu
Seoul 834-939

June 15, 2013

③ Jung In Seong
367 Gajeong-dong
Daejeon 994-348

④ Dear Mr. Jung,

A. We are not able to increase your credit line, as we have discovered that the amounts you presently owe are sufficient, taking into consideration your income.

B. Thank you for your recent request for a credit line increase on your Mastercard account.
Regrettably, we cannot comply with your request at this time.

C. It is our pleasure to serve you.

D. In the event that you experience a change in your financial situation and you wish to be reconsidered for a credit line increase, please contact us again.

⑥ Sincerely,

⑦ *Mijin Kim*

⑧ Mijin Kim

⑨ Senior Manager

1. 영문거절편지의 본문에 들어가는 내용을 순서에 맞게 배열하세요.

① A, B, C, D　　② B, A, D, C

③ A, C, B, D　　④ B, C, A, D

Lesson 12 Writing a letter of apology

① Minjean Kim
Guui 3-dong
Gwangjin-gu, Seoul 143-706

② June 22, 2013

③ Bae Jung-Hoon
539-3 Noeun-dong
Yuseong-gu, Daejeon 305-325

④ Dear Mr. Bae:

⑤

A. We assure you that your stereo will be replaced or refunded as soon as possible.
B. We are sorry that the stereo you purchased from our store has a defect.
C. Again, we are sorry for the inconvenience this may have caused.
D. Please call my office and let us know which option you want.

⑥ Cordially yours,
⑦ *Mi Jean Kim*
⑧ Mi Jean Kim
⑨ Senior Manager

1. 영문 사과편지의 본문에 들어가는 내용을 순서에 맞게 배열한 것을 골라보세요.

① A, B, C, D
② A, D, C, B
③ B, A, D, C
④ B, C, D, A

Answers

Lesson 13. Review

Lesson 01 The format of email

1. email의 Greeting(인사)과 잘 어울리는 Closing(끝인사)을 보기에서 찾아 입력해 보세요.

(1) Dear Mr. Jackson	Sincerely yours,
(2) Dear Lina	Best regards,
(3) Hi Freddy	Warmly,

2. email에서 @는 무엇을 나타내는지 선택 보기에서 찾아 적어 보세요.

at

Lesson 02 Writing a diary

1. 아래 제시된 항목을 순서대로 나열하세요.

Cloudy, Sunday, March 15, 2013

2. 아래 제시된 날씨에 대한 표현을 보기에서 찾아 써 넣어 보세요.

(1) 맑은 날씨	fair
(2) 흐린 날씨	cloudy
(3) 비 오는 날씨	rainy
(4) 눈 오는 날씨	snowy
(5) 추운 날씨	chilly
(6) 바람 부는 날씨	windy

Lesson 03 Writing a resume

1. 이력서의 경력을 작성하는 부분입니다. 각 위치에 알맞은 항목을 넣으세요.

Period	company	Location
	Job Title	Department
	Job Description	

2. 이력서의 학력을 작성하는 부분입니다. 각 위치에 알맞은 항목을 넣으세요.

Period	School	Location
	Major:	Minor:

3. 다음은 이력서의 특기사항입니다. 빈칸에 적절한 전치사를 입력하세요.

① in
② on
③ in

Lesson 04 Writing a letter of self-introduction

1. 다음 영문 자기소개서의 내용을 잘 읽고 각 내용에 해당하는 소제목을 넣으세요.

(1) Personal History
(2) School Days
(3) Strengths and Weaknesses
(4) Career Objectives

Lesson 05 Writing a job application letter

1. 영문 지원서의 포맷에 대한 다음 문제를 풀어 보세요.

(1) Return address
(2) Inside address
(3) Greeting
(4) Closing
(5) Enclosure

Lesson 06 Writing a fax

1. 영문 팩스의 포맷에 대한 다음 문제를 풀어 보세요.

(1) Delivery of wrong products
(2) Purchase order 03-5345-9
(3) This page only

Lesson 07 Writing an invitation card

1. 영문초대장의 포맷에 대한 문제를 풀어 보세요.

(1) General Information
(2) RSVP
(3) Directions

Lesson 08 Writing a letter of recommendation

1. 보기에 주어진 영문추천서의 본문을 가장 잘 배열한 것을 고르시오.

② A, C, B, D

Lesson 09 Writing a thank you letter

1. 위 영문감사편지의 순서를 가장 잘 배열한 것을 고르시오.

④ B, C, A

Lesson 10 Writing a letter of congratulations

1. 축하편지의 본문에 들어가는 내용을 순서에 맞게 배열하세요.

④ B, C, A

Lesson 11 Writing a letter of refusal

② B, A, D, C

Lesson 12 Writing a letter of apology

③ B, A, D, C

Review Exercises

비즈니스영어작문 총정리 연습문제 (Lesson 9~14)

비즈니스 영어작문 총정리 연습문제 (Lesson 8~12)

Part 1. 다음 영문 e-mail을 잘 살펴보고 물음에 답하시오.

1-27 Myongryoon-dong
Chongno-gu, Seoul 110-521

March 21, 2013

Mr. Minseok Park
Principal
Incheon Foreign Language High School
434 Kaja-dong, Seo-gu
Incheon 404-250

Dear Mr. Park:

It is with great pleasure that I recommend Mr. Michael Kim for the position of music teacher at Incheon Foreign Language High School.

Mr. Michael Kim taught at Seoul International High School from March 2, 2006 to February 28, 2013. His primary responsibilities were teaching musical composition, performance and appreciation. He was one of the best teachers that we have had at our school. We were deeply saddened when he and his family moved to Incheon. I can assure you that you will be more than satisfied with his performance in the classroom.

He is dedicated, reliable, and efficient. I strongly recommend him for the position of music teacher at your school.

Sincerely,
Dongmin Yang
Dongmin Yang
Principal

1. What is the job title of the person who wrote the recommendation letter?

① English teacher
② Principal
③ Vice Principal
④ Coordinator

2. Who is the recommendation letter addressed to?

① Mr. Minseok Park
② Mr. Dongmin Yang
③ Mr. Michael Kim
④ Mr. Michael Kim's colleague

3. What did Mr. Michael Kim teach at Seoul International High School? (Choose two)

① Music appreciation
② Music history
③ Music performance
④ Music discussion

4. Why did Mr. Michael Kim have to quit his job at Seoul International High School?

① Because he wanted a different job.
② Because he wanted to make more money.
③ Because he moved to Incheon.
④ Because he left Korea.

5. How did Mr. Dongmin Yang describe Mr. Kim? (Choose two)

① Dedicated
② Independent
③ Creative
④ Ambitious
⑤ Dependable

Part 2. 다음 영문 e-mail을 잘 살펴보고 물음에 답하시오.

Jacob Vest
7346 Longhorn Blvd.
Boston, MA 77345

May 9, 2013

Geoffrey T. Cartwright
594 West Avenue
Scranton, Pennsylvania 77378

Dear Mr. Cartwright,

Thank you very much for having taken the time to interview with me. I was most favorably impressed with you. It is my hope that you will consider my skills and personal experience when deciding how to fill the open position.

If you are still interested in my references, please feel free to call any of the numbers listed in the attached file.

I look forward to hearing from you. Again, thank you for your interest in my application and for having taken the time to talk with me.

Best wishes,
Jacob Vest
Jacob Vest

6. Where does the recipient of the letter live?

① Scranton ② Boston ③ New York ④ Manhattan

7. What is this letter about?

① Expressing gratitude for taking the time for the interview
② Expressing gratitude for purchasing the product
③ Expressing gratitude for taking the time to view the sales presentation
④ Expressing gratitude for visiting the company from overseas

8. What is the purpose of Mr. Vest's meeting with Mr. Cartwright?

① To recruit people
② To go sightseeing
③ To have a job interview
④ To arrange a convenient time for the next meeting

9. If Mr. Cartwright is interested in contacting Jacob's references, what should he do?

① Visit Mr. Vest
② Call the phone numbers listed in the attachment
③ Write a letter to Mr. Vest
④ Meet more members of the recruiting committee

10. What is Mr. Cartwright's job title likely to be?

① Director of the Accounting Department
② Human Resources Manager
③ Manager of the Planning Department
④ Manager of Research and Development

Part 3. 다음 영문 e-mail을 잘 살펴보고 물음에 답하시오.

Mary Stephens
1992 San Antonio Blvd.
Austin, TX 77925

March 4, 2013

Jinsoo Kim
Samsung Apt. 5-224, Gyesan-dong
Seo-gu, Incheon 407-050
South Korea

Dear Mr. Kim,

Congratulations on your successful application for the position of sales manager of our company. You may now be challenged with making the very important decision of selecting which company you will work for. We know that this can often be an extremely difficult decision for young professionals about to enter the workforce.

At our company we recognize the importance of your decision. This decision may well have an impact on the quality of your life.

My best wishes to you for your success with your new job. And I sincerely hope that you will be joining our company in the fall.

Sincerely,
Mary Stephens
Mary Stephens

11. What is the letter about?

① Offering employment to the applicant
② Confirming the reservation that the client has made
③ Scheduling the flight for the client
④ Rescheduling the flight for the client

12. What position has the applicant applied for?

① Human Resources Manager
② Administrative Assistant
③ Chairperson of the Department
④ Sales Manager

13. Where does Mary Stephens live?

① Seoul
② Incheon
③ Austin
④ California

14. What decision does the applicant have to make?

① Which job to select
② Which college to select
③ Which adviser to select
④ Which city to live in

15. When does the new job begin at the company?

① In the spring
② In the summer
③ In the fall
④ In the winter

Part 4. 다음 영문 e-mail을 잘 살펴보고 물음에 답하시오.

June Kang
HiVol Sound Systems
234 Guui 5-dong, Gwangjin-gu
Seoul 399-956

March 8, 2013

Minwoo Hyun
Samik Apt. 3-224
Jisan-dong, Seo-gu
Seoul 305-390

Dear Mr. Hyun:

Thank you for taking the time to send us a letter detailing your accomplishments at our company. HiVol definitely values your efforts, your work ethic, and your sales experience. That is why we have been pleased to have you working with us for the past few months.

While HiVol sympathizes with all the points that you have mentioned in your letter, we do not believe that an increase in your paid vacation time is appropriate at this time. It is HiVol's practice to review employee benefits and compensation at the end of each year.

At that time we will take an increase in your paid vacation time into consideration, assuming the sales figures for your store are increased. I appreciate your understanding in this matter and hope that you will continue to contribute to HiVol's success.

Sincerely,
June Kang
June Kang
District Manager

16. What is the letter about?

① Informing the employee that his request was accepted
② Informing the employee that his request was not accepted
③ Informing the job applicant that he was accepted to the company
④ Informing the job applicant that he was not accepted to the company

17. What did Mr. Hyun request?

① To open a new bank account
② To get a credit card
③ An increase in paid vacation
④ A loan from the bank

18. Why was Mr. Hyun's request not granted?

① He is heavily in debt.
② He has too many credit cards associated with his store.
③ His financial status is not stable enough.
④ It is not the right time yet.

19. What is the job title of Mr. June Kang?

① President
② Human Resources Manager
③ District Manager
④ Admissions Counselor

20. When will Mr. Hyun's request be considered again?

① At the beginning of April
② At the beginning of May
③ At the end of August
④ At the end of December

Part 5. 다음 영문 e-mail을 잘 살펴보고 물음에 답하시오.

Mijean Kim
224 Guui 3-dong, Gwangjin-gu
Seoul 143-706

October 31, 2013

Jeong-Hoon Bae
33 Nonhyun-dong, Gangnam-gu
Seoul 135-010

Dear Mr. Bae:

We have found that we unintentionally overcharged your account for your recent purchase by 50,000 won. We have remedied the error by transferring the appropriate funds to your account.

You can confirm this by ((1)   ) your account book.

We sincerely apologize for any inconvenience that this may have caused. We take these kinds of errors very seriously and will make every effort to ensure that such a mistake will not happen again. We hope that this has not caused you any difficulty or confusion.

If you have any questions, please call us at 447-8857. You may also contact me at the email address below.

Cordially,
Mijean Kim
Mijean Kim
kmj@*****.com
Accounts Manager

21. What is the letter about?

① Apologizing for the unintentional mistake in collecting payment
② Informing the employee of an increase in payment
③ Informing the employee how much he will get paid a month
④ Asking the client to open a new account in the bank

22. How much money did the company return?

① 20,000 won ② 40,000 won
③ 50,000 won ④ 70,000 won

23. What can Jeong-Hoon Bae do if he has further questions? (Choose two)

① He can ask questions of his colleagues.
② He can ask questions of his boss.
③ He can call 447-8857.
④ He can write an email to the Accounts Manager.

24. What is the best word for blank (1)?

① confirming ② updating
③ upgrading ④ opening

25. What is the relation between Mijean Kim and Jeong-Hoon Bae likely to be?

① Employees in the same company ② Business partners
③ Businessman and client ④ Employer and employee

Part 6. 다음 영문 e-mail을 잘 살펴보고 물음에 답하시오.

Ji Hye Yang
61-3, Choongmu-Ro 2-ka
Chung-Ku, Seoul 100-012

July 31, 2013

Margaret Cho
Hanmaeum Apt. 3-505
Songkang-dong, Yuseong-gu
Daejeon 305-503

Dear Ms. Cho:

We at Bang Bang Corporation confirm that the clothes you returned have indeed shrunk in the dryer. The clothes were not washable even though many clothes today are. ((1) 우리의 판매원이 당신에게 적절한 세탁 지침을 설명해야 했었습니다.) Sometimes, however, an employee may be inadvertently forgetful. ((2) 이게 사실이든 아니든), we are sorry for the inconvenience. We value you as a customer and hope that you will continue shopping at our store. ((3) 우리 옷에 대한 당신의 만족은 우리에게 중요합니다.)

Please remember that we are happy to replace your clothes or refund your money. ((4)당신이 어느 선택 사항을 선호하는지 우리에게 알려주세요.)

Sincerely,
Ji Hye Yang
Ji Hye Yang
((5) 지점 관리자)

26. 위 영문 e-mail의 (1)에 들어갈 적절한 문장을 영어로 완성하시오.

27. 위 영문 e-mail의 (2)에 들어갈 적절한 문장을 영어로 완성하시오.

28. 위 영문 e-mail의 (3)에 들어갈 적절한 문장을 영어로 완성하시오. (apparel, of importance를 사용하시오)

29. 위 영문 e-mail의 (4)에 들어갈 적절한 문장을 영어로 완성하시오.

30. 위 영문 e-mail의 (5)에 들어갈 적절한 표현을 영어로 완성하시오.

Answers

비즈니스 영어작문 총정리 연습문제 (Lesson 8~12)

Part 1.

1. (2)
2. (1)
3. (1), (3)
4. (3)
5. (1), (5)

Part 2.

6. (1)
7. (1)
8. (3)
9. (2)
10. (2)

Part 3.

11. (1)
12. (4)
13. (3)
14. (1)
15. (3)

Part 4.

16. (2)
17. (3)
18. (4)
19. (3)
20. (4)

Part 5.

21. (1)
22. (3)
23. (3), (4)
24. (2)
25. (3)

Part 6.

26. Our sales clerk should have explained the proper laundering instructions to you.
27. Whether this was the case or not
28. Your satisfaction with our apparel is of importance to us.
29. Let us know which option you prefer.
30. (1) Store Manager

비지니스영어작문 기초와 실전

초판 1쇄 발행 2014년 4월 21일
초판 2쇄 발행 2015년 9월 1일

엮 은 이 조기석
발 행 인 김인철
발 행 처 한국외국어대학교 지식출판원
02450 서울시 동대문구 이문로 107
전화 (02)2173-2493~7
팩스 (02)2173-3363
홈페이지 http://press.hufs.ac.kr
전자우편 press@hufs.ac.kr
출판등록 제6-6호(1969. 4. 30)
디자인·편집 디자인퍼브 02)2254-4308
인쇄·제본 성전기획 031)955-8826

ISBN 978-89-7464-918-0 13740 정가 20,000원

* 잘못된 책은 교환하여 드립니다.

HU:NE 은 한국외국어대학교 지식출판원의 어학도서, 사회과학도서, 지역학 도서 Sub Brand이다. 한국외대의 영문명인 HUFS, 현명한 국제전문가 양성(International+Intelligent)의 의미를 담고 있으며, 휴인(携引)의 뜻인 '이끌다, 끌고 나가다'라는 의미처럼 출판계를 이끄는 리더로서, 혁신의 이미지를 담고 있다.